W9-ASV-447

UNTIL WE RECKON

UNTIL WE RECKON

VIOLENCE, MASS INCARCERATION, AND A ROAD TO REPAIR

DANIELLE SERED

NEW YORK
LONDON

© 2019 by Danielle Sered
All rights reserved.
No part of this book may be reproduced, in any form, without written permission from
the publisher.

Requests for permission to reproduce selections from this book should be mailed to:
Permissions Department, The New Press, 120 Wall Street, 31st floor, New York, NY
10005.

Published in the United States by The New Press, New York, 2019
Distributed by Two Rivers Distribution

ISBN 978-1-62097-479-7 (hc)
ISBN 978-1-62097-480-3 (ebook)
CIP data is available

The New Press publishes books that promote and enrich public discussion and
understanding of the issues vital to our democracy and to a more equitable world. These
books are made possible by the enthusiasm of our readers; the support of a committed
group of donors, large and small; the collaboration of our many partners in the
independent media and the not-for-profit sector; booksellers, who often hand-sell New
Press books; librarians; and above all by our authors.

www.thenewpress.com

Funding generously provided by the Art for Justice Fund, a sponsored project of
Rockefeller Philanthropy Advisors.

Book design and composition by Bookbright Media
This book was set in Bembo and Centaur

Printed in the United States of America

10 9 8 7 6 5 4 3 2 1

And the walls became the world all around.

—*Maurice Sendak*

We can make America what America must become.

—*James Baldwin*

Contents

UNTIL WE RECKON

Introduction

As a teenager, sleeping on a friend's couch, I woke up one night to the sound of the bullets stopping. There was a time once when I would have awakened to them starting, but that was long before—before the level of violence in Chicago went through the roof, before the "crack epidemic," before mass incarceration. And of course, in a way I didn't fully understand yet, it was also after. After slavery, after Jim Crow, after Martin and Malcolm were shot, after redlining, after Nixon, after the founding of our country on the bones of the people who lived here before, after years and years and years of talking about anything other than what came before.

By the time I came of age in Chicago in the 1980s and early 1990s, America had long become a country where violence was normal. That normalization was not a blip in our history, however hard a period that was for urban centers in particular. Rather, it was an expression of our values and history—and of what those values and that history had produced. It was tempting to think of the pain and loss in that time and place as an exception, but it wasn't one. It was the rule.

It is an American habit to try to solve problems apart from their context. We like baseball and apple pie and the flag and not talking about the past. We praise optimism and ingenuity and self-reliance and we repeat our history over and over again. We talk about liberty and equality and the pursuit of happiness and we cannot or will not break down the barriers to equal access for all. We are often beautiful and usually stubborn and sometimes brave and our homes and our neighborhoods and our country are racked with violence that we do not deserve and that is entirely ours.

Sometimes I think of America not as a place or a nation, but a promise. It is the only way I can continue to love this country. The notions of equality and liberty that are meant to define us and bind us can only truly be ours if we understand them as a destination to which we are relentlessly headed, not a station we have already reached. I think James Baldwin was right (as he usually was) when he wrote, "American history is longer, larger, more various, more beautiful, and more terrible than anything anyone has ever said about it."[1] This may be particularly true of the history of our national relationship to violence. But despite the persistence of violence as a defining feature of our culture, I continue to believe we can become a country that makes violence our shared enemy and begins the work of eradicating it. I continue to believe in our chances of finding and choosing the road from the America we are to the America we still have a chance of becoming. I believe our chances of doing so will depend on our ability to look squarely and honestly at what we have done and what we are doing and to choose to do something different instead. This book aims to be an imperfect, useful tool in our shared work to do just that.

One thing is certain about the problem of violence: we will never solve it through incarceration. That is in part because incarceration is an inadequate and often counterproductive tool to transform those who have committed violence or protect those who have been harmed. It is neither the most effective way to change people nor the most effective way to keep people safe. Its standing in society is based largely on its role in protecting people from violence and those who commit it, but as a violence intervention strategy, it fails to deliver the outcomes everyone deserves—at great human and financial cost. Increasingly, this message is being sounded not only by justice reformers, but by crime survivors as well.

Incarceration is also limited as a tool because it treats violence as a problem of "dangerous" individuals and not as a problem of social context and history. Most violence is not just a matter of individual pathology—it is created. Poverty drives violence.[2] Inequity drives violence.[3] Lack of opportunity drives violence.[4] Shame and isolation drive violence.[5] And like so many conditions known all too well to public health professionals, violence itself drives violence.[6]

In the United States, many policies have in fact nurtured violence, by exacerbating the very things that foster it, including poverty, instability, substandard education, and inadequate housing.[7] We see this in long-standing policies and practices that perpetuate these drivers of violence in communities across the country—where people disproportionately live below the poverty line, including parents working multiple jobs whose employment still does not guarantee them a living wage. We see it in massive, growing investments in law enforcement at a time when public education and health care systems are struggling to meet basic needs.[8] We see it in union busting, food deserts, and predatory lending.[9] These problems are compounded by limited and broken ideas of "manhood" that equate strength with wealth and violence in places where wealth is almost completely unattainable but violence is an option at every turn.[10]

Not only does incarceration fail to interrupt these drivers, it intensifies them—interrupting people's education, rendering many homeless upon return from jail or prison, limiting their prospects for employment and a living wage, and disrupting the social fabric that is the strongest protection against harm, even in the face of poverty.[11] On the individual level, violence is driven by shame, isolation, exposure to violence, and an inability to meet one's economic needs—factors that are also the core features of

imprisonment. This means that the core national violence prevention strategy relies on a tool that has as its basis the central
drivers of violence.

Nearly all poor communities bear the brunt of policy choices
that have nurtured violence. In communities of color, the detrimental impact of these policies is amplified by historical and
present injustices. These harms trace back to colonization, continued with slavery and its more proximate counterpart, convict
leasing, morphed into Jim Crow, and persist in countless forms,
including the more recent phenomenon of redlining—the practice of refusing loans or insurance to people because they live
in areas deemed to be "poor financial risks"—a practice applied
almost exclusively in communities of color.[12] Those institutions
and policies were supported by widespread violence that rarely
met with punishment and often met with the tacit or active sanction of police and other government actors, including lynching,
the burning of churches, and mob attacks.[13] Exacerbating the
divestment from, harm to, and under-protection of communities of color is a concurrent investment in unevenly applied law
enforcement—practices rife with disparities from stop-and-frisk
all the way through sentencing and parole, which means that at
strikingly disproportionate rates, communities of color bear the
brunt of our justice systems' failures.[14]

Mass incarceration also fails to solve the problem of violence
because it is a response that treats violence as a matter of "good
vs. evil." The reality is far more complicated. Nearly everyone
who commits violence has also survived it, and few have gotten
formal support to heal.[15] Although people's history of victimization never excuses the harm they cause, it does implicate our
society for not having addressed their pain earlier. And just as
people who commit violence are not exempt from victimization, many survivors of violence have complex lives, imperfect
histories, and even criminal convictions.[16] But just as it would be
wrong to excuse people's actions simply because they were previ-

ously victimized, it is also wrong to ignore someone's victimization because the person previously broke a law or committed harm. Such a response to violence reinforces the notion that some people deserve to be hurt: the exact thinking about violence that we have to uproot if we are to end it.

Just as we cannot incarcerate our way out of violence, we cannot reform our way out of mass incarceration without taking on the question of violence.

The United States sits at the crest of two rising tides. Trump's presidential administration and many states' governing bodies have brought a resurgence of "law and order" rhetoric and policy, as well as calls for harsher punishment. But at the same time (and in some cases, even in the same places), a consensus and growing momentum have emerged to end the nation's globally unique overreliance on incarceration. This momentum is in response to the stories and evidence demonstrating the devastating effects of jail and prison on people and communities. It is the product of decades of advocacy and organizing efforts—particularly on the part of those most impacted by the criminal justice system—which have commanded new allies and energetic support in recent years. Some states made major strides in criminal justice reform, including victories like Proposition 57 in California and State Questions 780 and 781 in Oklahoma, changes that stand to dramatically reduce their state prison populations.[17] Voters elected progressive candidates as local prosecutors and sheriffs in Illinois, Florida, Texas, Arizona, New York, Pennsylvania, and beyond—outcomes that would have been unthinkable even five years ago.[18] Although federal policy is influential in setting both law and tone, criminal justice remains largely a state-based and local issue—and often a bipartisan one. We have reason to be hopeful.

But there is a problem. As consensus and momentum to end mass incarceration have grown, the current reform narrative, though compelling, has been based on a fallacy: that the United States can achieve large-scale transformative change (that is, reductions of 50 percent or more) by changing responses to nonviolent offenses. That is impossible in a nation where 54 percent of people incarcerated in state prisons were convicted of violent crimes.[19] In New York State, for instance, where some of the country's most substantial reductions in incarceration for drug offenses have already occurred, reducing by half either the number of people incarcerated for drug crimes or the time they serve would decrease the prison population by only 1 percent by 2021.[20] Although these types of reforms are essential, the country will not get anywhere close to reducing the number of people incarcerated by 50 percent—or better, to 1970s levels—without taking on the issue that most of these campaigns avoid: violence. It is not just a matter of morality and strategy, though it is both of those things. It is a matter of numbers.[21]

The issues of violence and mass incarceration are inextricably intertwined, but they are not the same. Some strategies that reduce violence will not impact incarceration rates: a substantial portion of violence happens out of reach of the criminal justice system, so its reduction does not translate inherently or cleanly to a parallel reduction in arrests or imprisonment. And of course, many strategies to reduce incarceration will not touch the issue of violence. This book is situated at the messy and sometimes slippery place where these questions overlap and aims to point a way forward that accounts for the reality that these issues cannot be equated with each other and the fact that that we will not see our way out of either without tackling both.

When efforts to reduce the nation's use of incarceration move beyond a focus on nonviolent crime, we face a wide range of deep-seated and well-known challenges, both political and practical. Such efforts come up against the continued salience of "tough on crime" and "law and order" rhetoric; the limited power of data as a tool to shape public opinion; deep misconceptions about who crime survivors are and what they want; the persistent tentativeness of even forward-thinking elected officials to enter this terrain; and the need to develop capacity to foster and demonstrate solutions that can displace incarceration.

But crossing the line and dealing with violence also opens up a range of possibilities not otherwise available—possibilities that will be even more necessary in the current political landscape. It allows us to think holistically about the communities profoundly affected by violence and incarceration and not just about small segments of those neighborhoods. It allows us to center the needs of crime survivors in their vision—not tiptoe around them or engage them in a limited opportunistic fashion. And it allows us to envision a justice system that is not just smaller, but is truly transformed into the vehicle for accountability, safety, and justice that everyone deserves.

If incarceration worked to secure safety, we would be the safest nation in all of human history.

We would not be a nation where, by the most conservative estimates available, every year nearly three thousand young men of color are murdered before their twenty-fifth birthday; more than 57,000 children survive sexual violence; nearly half a million women are beaten in their relationships; nearly three million men are robbed or assaulted; countless transgender people are killed for who they are; where every year, we bury our own children, gunned down in our own streets.[22] If incarceration worked to stop violence, we would have eradicated it by now—because no nation has used incarceration more.

In all the world and all recorded time, no country has locked up their own people at the rate we do.[23] The United States has nearly 5 percent of the world's population and nearly 25 percent of its incarcerated people.[24] More than 2.3 million people are behind bars on any given day—and the number of black people incarcerated or under correctional control exceeds the total number of adults enslaved nationwide in 1861.[25] A black boy born today has a one-in-three chance of going to prison in his lifetime.[26] Incarceration is not just a dimension of how we punish crime in our country. It exists at such a scale that it is a defining feature of our culture. It is who we are, who we have become.

And it comes at great cost. In addition to the deprivation of their freedom, people who are incarcerated are unconscionably likely to endure violence, including sexual violence.[27] Incarcerated people are likely to experience enormous mental distress and endure serious and lasting trauma, and are all too likely to take their own lives.[28] When they return home from prison, they face enormous barriers to securing safe housing, obtaining and retaining employment that pays a living wage, accessing medical care, voting and serving on juries, obtaining an education, reconnecting with their families, and meeting their basic needs.[29] Because they relate directly to the core drivers of violence, each of these barriers makes a person more likely to commit and to experience harm.

The families of incarcerated people also pay a price—both while they are incarcerated and when they come home. For instance, more than 60 percent of incarcerated women have children, and more than 40 percent were primary caregivers for their children before being incarcerated.[30] Although many incarcerated parents remain central and engaged figures in their children's lives, they are nonetheless unable to be present for the day-to-day care-taking, guidance, and protection that free parents can provide. Children of incarcerated parents spend holidays and birthdays apart from their mothers and fathers, endure stigma and may feel shame, and struggle with feelings of abandonment, even as they and their parents fight to maintain deep connections across the boundaries of concrete and barbed wire. Their young lives are often deeply unsettled by their parents' absence. Children whose parents are incarcerated are more likely to experience depression and poverty, and while many find ways to thrive despite the substantial obstacles and losses they endure, they remain more likely to be incarcerated over time.[31]

Alongside the human cost, some of the cost of incarceration is financial—incarceration is extraordinarily expensive.[32] Over the past three decades, state and local government expenditures on jails and prisons have increased roughly three times as fast as spending on elementary and secondary education. As a nation, we spend more than $80 billion a year on incarceration.[33] One of the only things we spend more on than prisons is war.[34]

We know enough to know that incarceration generates devastating and often lasting negative repercussions and that it has an intergenerational effect. That said, no one in human history knows what we will soon learn as a country: what happens to a generation that grows up in a place where incarceration is a primary feature of its culture. We do not know what becomes of neighborhoods that have so many of their members taken from them, subjected to the harms of prison, and then returned. We do not know what happens to generations of children who grow up with the experience of their caregivers and protectors behind bars. We do not know how a community or a people absorb that much pain and trauma, and what happens if that pain and trauma go unhealed. We do not know what happens to the psyche and character of a nation that surpasses all others in its use of confinement. Add to that the reality that incarceration not only fails to produce safety—it can, in fact, generate violence—and we have a recipe for a difficult awakening. As these lessons bear down on us, it is hard to believe that they will affirm the policy choices of these past several decades. Rather, it is far more likely that we will have to face the profound impact of what we have done and the searing reality that we should have known better.

Meaningful change will require understanding how we got where we are. Most concretely, we got here through a series of cumulative policy decisions made at the municipal, county, state, and federal levels that drove law enforcement practice toward greater and greater punitiveness. But however critical those policy choices, the story of the rise of mass incarceration is not the story of 1,000 bills, 20 in each of the 50 states, that produced this landscape. It is the story of the tide those bills rode in on.

As the lawyer and scholar Michelle Alexander has argued decisively in her now canonical text *The New Jim Crow*, the precipitous rise of mass incarceration in this country, couched as "the war on drugs," was part of a continuous history of racial inequity that extends back through history to Jim Crow and convict leasing and slavery before it.[35] In this latest iteration, leaders ranging from Presidents Nixon, Reagan, Bush I and II, and Clinton, together with local and state legislators, enacted a strategy that blocked or reversed many of the gains secured for people of color through the civil rights movement. Under Nixon, the newly weaponized category of "felon" replaced a racialized designation in the public discourse with one that was about criminality (the f-word took the place of the n-word, as a formerly incarcerated leader once explained).[36] This framework was mobilized to keep in place various forms of disenfranchisement and inequity previously secured by Jim Crow laws but poised to be disrupted by the mounting gains of civil rights advancements. Later, the American public devoured stories about Willie Horton, a man who, while on a weekend furlough program while serving a life sentence for murder, absconded and was later convicted of assault, armed robbery, and rape.[37] And we were warned of "superpredators," a new generation of children (yes, children) who were supposedly so vicious and monstrous and so unlike any other kids we had ever known that they were impervious to guidance or even typical deterrence, incapable of empathy, and built only to devour and destroy.[38]

Neither the motivation for nor the impact of the war on drugs had much to do with drugs. Nor did the narrative that secured the rise of mass incarceration. That narrative was largely about violence. As a nation, we say (and often believe) that we put people in prison to keep the rest of us safe. That story retained its power even as the great ballooning of mass incarceration included locking up a great number of people for drug-related and other nonviolent offenses. It is crucial not to mistake the numbers for the narrative: while the war on drugs dramatically increased penalties for drug-related and other offenses, the line of argument that buttressed it remained steady and familiar, and it was centrally one about danger.

At the heart of that narrative is the story of an imagined monstrous other—a monster who is not quite human like the rest of us, who is capable of extraordinary harm and incapable of empathy, who inflicts great pain but does not feel it as we do, a monster we and our children have to be protected from at any price. This is not a new story. It is as old as our nation. And it is not a race-neutral story. To the contrary: it has long been a story white people have told about black people, and at times, including these times we are in now, about immigrants. It is a deadly, dishonest story, one with blood on its hands. It is a story that divides us, that impairs our ability to act rationally, and that underpins our culture's response to violence. When we make policy changes that leave this story in place, the resulting gains are limited and temporary. We secure the release of some people convicted of nonviolent offenses, for instance, and find ourselves increasing mandatory minimum sentences for violent crime in the next legislative session (if not in the very same one). We trim the edges of the tree while we inadvertently water its roots. It appears smaller for a moment, but it grows back quickly and stronger. Any substantial and lasting change will require that we not dance around this, but rather that we take on the story at its roots and topple it once and for all. Doing so is not only a prerequisite for ending mass incarceration. It is also a prerequisite for ending violence, because we cannot solve a problem we do not accurately understand.

———

Displacing our current approach to violence will require that we foster new ways to support those who are harmed by violence; develop and implement new strategies to address those who commit it; and change our story about who survives violence, who commits it, and what it will take to end it so that we can make room for new solutions.

Doing so will require—in addition to bravery and stamina—more nuance than we have brought to the challenge thus far as a society. All too often violence is discussed as a monolithic problem without an appreciation for the context in which it takes place, the people responsible for it, the needs of those harmed by it, the opportunities for intervention, and the long-term impacts of responsive strategies. A domestic-violence homicide in a small rural town and a shooting related to an open-air drug market in a large city are not the same—nor are they the same as a robbery and mugging committed by a group of teenagers, a sexual assault committed by someone known to the survivor, or a stabbing that results from a long-standing dispute between former friends. The context in which violence happens matters, as do the identities and experiences of those involved. Some acts of violence are committed by people who suffer from serious mental illness.[39] Other violent behavior arises out of addiction.[40] Those underlying causes are important because they influence the range of effective interventions.

Regardless of the type of violence in question, U.S. justice systems typically rely on incarceration as the single blunt instrument in their toolbox—all without any data-driven indications that it is the tool most likely to secure the short- and long-term safety of the survivors and others who have a stake in the outcome. Rising to the challenge of addressing and reducing violence will require a new basis of understanding about who is committing harm, the people they are hurting, what the circumstances and context are, and what consequences arise from the harm.

This work—and this book—begins with the needs of survivors. It is in survivors' names that we have built mass incarceration, and it is survivors who carry some of the heaviest burdens when incarceration fails to produce the safety it promises. We might ask of ourselves as it relates to our responsibility to these survivors: *Who do we answer to and how?* Who is being hurt? Whose lives are at stake? What do they need to heal and be safe? Have we asked them what they want? What do they say when we do? When we ask these questions, we find not only fundamental challenges to our current thinking about who survivors are and what they want; we also find the seeds of a way forward to sustainable and lasting safety.

Securing that safety will require transforming how we respond to people who commit harm. It will require that we make accountability a central facet of our response to violence in ways it has never been, and that we develop solutions to violence that are built to address the causes of violence. We do, in fact, know a good deal about what produces violence, but our near-exclusive dependence on punishment has left little room for either meaningful accountability or solutions that are poised to actually change behavior. If we are serious as a nation about addressing violence and its consequences, we have to acknowledge that relying only on incarceration (or any single tool, for that matter) is not an adequate response, either morally or practically. To secure the safety of survivors and communities, we will need to implement interventions that can transform the behavior of people who have caused harm. Doing so will require an honest grappling with the limitations of our current approaches and an openness to solutions that can produce better results. And it will require prioritizing pragmatism over emotion and safety over politics in a way that runs contrary to business as usual for our country but is decidedly possible to accomplish.

For the past decade, I have directed Common Justice, an organization that seeks to address violence without relying on incarceration. The framework used at Common Justice and explored in this book suggests that any responses to violence should adhere to four core principles. Our responses should be survivor-centered, accountability-based, safety-driven, and racially equitable.[41] Developing solutions aligned with those principles will require a fundamental realignment in our values and practice. It will require that we demand and build a country where fewer people are harmed by violence and fewer people are incarcerated; place regard for human dignity at the center of policies and practices; and prioritize survivors' needs for healing, safety, and justice. It will require that we draw on the leadership, expertise, and authority of people most impacted—including crime survivors, those who are or have been incarcerated, and the loved ones of both—and that we nurture community-led strategies that prevent and address trauma and violence, create healthy communities, and help foster protection for everyone. It will require that we make a commitment to accountability for violence in a way that is more meaningful and more effective than incarceration; engage in an honest reckoning with the current and historic role race has played in the use of punishment in the United States; and change the socioeconomic and structural conditions that make violence likely in the first place.

The biggest barrier to significantly reducing both violence and incarceration is not the resistance of survivors to new solutions, nor is it the absence of such solutions. Rather, it is the story we tell about violence that precludes the development and expansion of new strategies. We will not work our way out of violence if we continue to believe that solving violence is about managing monsters. Nor will we do it if we continue to believe that punishment is an adequate substitute for healing. Displacing our old stories will require allowing new ones—full stories, messy ones, ones that include wounds and rage and loss and sorrow and ambivalence and—sometimes, though not always—hope; stories that include the context in which violence takes place not as an excuse, but as a piece of the puzzle of ending it; stories that hold everyone accountable for harm, both the individuals who commit it and the societies that allow it; stories with both a before and an after.

We will change these stories only if we trace them to their roots and address them there. This will mean contending not only with interpersonal violence, but also with the longer view of the country's racialized history of violence and the larger context of the ways that history persists. It will mean facing the long-standing normalization of violence against people of color in America from slavery to the present. It will mean uprooting old, deadening stories about whose pain is and is not of importance and why. It will mean owning our nation's violent past wholly and honestly. The work of grappling with that violence will not differ substantially from the way we will have to grapple with the violence between individuals: it will require acknowledgment and it will require repair. It will mean finally engaging in that repair.

It is commonly understood that one of the effects of grief is that it can foreclose our ability to imagine. It is as though each of us can look only as far into the future as we can into the past. Healing, therefore, as a process of dealing with what has happened, is at its heart a labor of forming a life-affirming relationship with what is to come. We wrest the future from the grip of the past. We look back so we can look ahead. We grieve so we can imagine. In that sense, this book is an invitation to grief; it is also an invitation to imagination. What is possible and what we deserve will almost surely require both.

1

Across the River of Fire

"I sometimes think of myself as a scar." It was years after his face was slashed open that Elijah would describe himself that way. In part, it was because his scar had transformed his appearance and, he believed, how people saw him. But it was also because the violence he sustained had become so great a part of him as to obscure the rest. Other facets of his identity—as a son, a brother, a nerd (his own words)—all paled in comparison to his experience as a survivor. It was not just that violence had added something awful to his life. It was that it had displaced so much else. I have always thought the phrase "all-consuming" was a particularly good description of the experience of some stages of trauma: not all-hurting or all-enraging or all-terrifying—all-*consuming*. It is as though trauma is not simply an additional set of emotions and experiences. It is as though it devours all others. "It is not the unending presence of pain that hurts," a mother who lost her son once said to me, "it is the unending absence of joy."

Becoming a country that can end violence will have to begin with facing the pain that violence causes. There is no pathway to safety, healing, or justice that does not begin with a deep regard for what has been done and what has been lost. We cannot solve a problem we cannot look at squarely. Envisioning responses to violence therefore requires that we contend honestly and unflinchingly with the lasting impacts of harm, take seriously

those consequences and the people who experience them, regard
the transformation of the pain violence causes as our collective
responsibility, and commit to understanding that pain more fully
so that we may help ease it.

We are not practiced in that attention. However prevalent violence may be in our culture and media, its aftermath is largely rendered invisible. Plotlines for action movies rarely include the hero's
flashbacks, night tremors, or arduous physical therapy. We watch
violence compulsively, and we just as compulsively turn from it the
moment it occurs. Righting our national course to respond effectively to violence will require turning back and facing it head-on.

The consequences of violence that may be the easiest to see
and understand are physical injuries, particularly ones that impair
how people live or cause them chronic pain. The limitations and
pain can themselves be sources of substantial loss and suffering for
survivors—people who can no longer walk, no longer speak, no
longer use their dominant hand, no longer digest their own food,
no longer hold their children, no longer go more than an hour
without pain; survivors whose lives are shaped by surgeries and
doctors' appointments and medication regimens and the constant
specter of pain.

But this pain has another layer to it: it is a reminder of what
was done to us. Each new X-ray, each new specialist, each new
sick day from work can remind survivors of the day we were
harmed and can make it nearly impossible for us to go for long
stretches that aren't shaped or haunted by that memory. The feelings of powerlessness, rage, self-blame, terror, and sadness associated with the violence we survived can be woven into our daily
rituals of taking a given medication, hoisting ourselves into our
wheelchairs, taking the bus to physical therapy, or practicing the
breathing exercises we learned to manage our chronic pain. These
physical repercussions extend beyond the immediate effects of
violence: the lasting effects of trauma and post-traumatic stress

include a wide range of challenges, including cardiovascular and endocrine disease.[1]

Then there are the scars. For some survivors, our bodies may function as they once did but still bear the marks of what happened. These scars tell stories survivors often want to keep private—or at least want to choose when they tell and to whom. Scars have no regard for that legitimate desire. They tell the stories constantly and to everyone. They expose private loss to anyone who can see. They invite speculation and intrusiveness and pity and judgment, virtually none of which are helpful to any survivor. Scars resist evolution and healing; they insist on the permanence and persistence of the past. They drive a wedge into the present where the pain can always slip in.

Physical scars are not the only way the past steals into the present. Trauma can include the reliving of our pain and terror. When survivors experience flashbacks, it is not simply that we are reminded of a terrible event. Many experience a flashback as though that event is happening *now*. Unlike other experiences, which we successfully organize into memory, traumatic experiences can stay endlessly current. As one Common Justice community member put it, "I don't remember it happening. It *is* happening." When we suffer from flashbacks, we experience many of the symptoms that accompanied the original experience—panic, escalated heart rate, fight or flight, difficulty controlling our bowels, cold sweats, abject terror. Our community member continued: "Healing doesn't mean I get to forget it. Healing means I get to remember it. Right now I don't remember it. I relive it."

Trauma transforms us. As survivors, we can feel rage so intensely that we become unrecognizable to ourselves. We can feel loss so deeply that we want to wring out the marrow of our bones just to be free from it for one moment. We can experience earthshaking fear in our own homes, in our own beds, in the arms of the people we love and trust most in the world. For some of us, our symptoms meet the diagnostic criteria for post-traumatic stress disorder (PTSD).[2] For others, it may feel more like a haunting.

We wrestle with the force of this distress in a wide variety of ways. We blame ourselves, we rage, we overwork, we drink and self-medicate with legal and illegal drugs, we withdraw, we trust no one, we attach too intensely, we feel everything, we feel nothing, we become intensely cautious, we take unreasonable risks, we bury our dead, we bury our hearts, we dig everything up, we sleep for days, we can never sleep, we make ourselves invisible, we expose ourselves completely, we cannot feel our bodies, we can only feel our bodies, we eat, we starve, we weep, we cannot even weep, we forget things, we remember everything, and we heal. We heal. We rise, we wrestle, and we heal. And we bring others along with us when we do.

Transforming our national response to violence will require placing the people who survive it at the center of any response to it. This is not what we currently do—though we pretend that it is. Legislators have enacted draconian criminal justice laws in the names of survivors.[3] Others have drawn on crime victims' stories to motivate sympathy, horror, and outrage. But the one thing rarely done is to ask the full range of survivors what they want.

We are used to two main tropes about victims and what they want. The first, and overwhelmingly dominant one, is the victim who wants the greatest possible penalty for the person who hurt them. This includes victims who call for the death penalty, who insist on the maximum allowable sentences for the people who hurt them or their loved ones, and who oppose parole when the person who caused them harm is eligible. These stories make it into the news, into the halls of legislatures, and into legislation itself. One might think of it as grieving by punishment. It is appropriate to have deep compassion for those who do it, even as we know it causes great harm and almost never delivers them from their own pain in the way they deserve. These voices are certainly part of the picture and deserve to be heard. But they reflect a far smaller portion of victims than we are led to believe, and their power is dangerously outsized as compared with other victims.

The other stories that are told—often offered as counterpoints to the dominant narrative about revenge—are stories of what we might call extreme mercy. This is the story of Charleston, where in 2015 the twenty-one-year-old white man Dylann Roof entered a church, prayed with its congregants, and then opened fire and murdered nine people and injured others. As early as Roof's bond hearing, some of the survivors of the dead offered him their forgiveness.[4] It is the story of Kate and Andy Grosmaire, whose daughter Ann was murdered by her boyfriend, Conor. The Grosmaires forgave their daughter's killer and participated in a restorative dialogue with him that reduced the prison sentence he faced for the murder.[5] It is the story of Mary Johnson, whose only son, Laramiun, was killed by four gunshots during a gang-related altercation in 1993. Mary forgave Oshea Israel, the young man who murdered her son, and even arranged his coming-home party in 2010 when he was released from prison.[6]

Sometimes we pathologize the angriest victims, but equally, we pathologize the forgiving ones. The angry ones scare us, but they also affirm our system as it is. They reassure us that the system we have built in their names is the right one, that it embodies the right values and takes the right actions in response to harm. Forgiving victims complicate matters. They suggest that winning justice and securing the maximum possible penalty might not be equivalent. They suggest that the tools we have available to respond to harm might not be the right ones. They make clear that however much we set policy in victims' names, we do not respond to their wishes in its application. After all, even after many of the victims' families in Charleston forgave Dylann Roof, the U.S. Department of Justice still declared its intention to seek the death penalty in that case.[7]

We need these stories of extraordinary forgiveness and the complication they introduce. They are critical testaments to the human capacity for compassion. They, like the pained stories of hungry revenge, deserve their place in our public consciousness. But like those other stories, they are not fully representative of most survivors. Most of us lie in the vast space between complete hatred and full forgiveness. And far less than is true of extreme mercy, that messy middle is almost nowhere in our public understanding of violence, justice, and healing.

For many survivors, anger is a central part of their response to the harm they survive. When we reduce survivors' responses to that anger, though, we miss the other emotions that exist alongside it. If you were to ask most survivors if they could choose only one emotion to describe their feelings, many would indeed choose anger. But if you allowed them, as in multiple-choice tests, to select all of the responses that apply, they would choose more. They would choose anger. But they would also select compassion, grief, loss, fury, and confusion. They would select love, despair, resentment, terror, and hope. They would choose them all, and none would cancel the others out.

Our criminal justice system does not know how to hold all of these things at once. The only space to hear information about a defendant's own experience of pain is for the purpose of mitigating their sentence—though of course, the defendant's pain doesn't in any way lessen the survivor's. Most often the only place for a survivor's pain is in a victim impact statement typically meant to enhance the defendant's sentence, regardless of what the victim finds healing. In our zero-sum system, complexity is a liability, and survivors are nothing if not complex.

The system protects its purported simplicity in part by excluding the voices that belie it. In that way, when the image of an innocent white woman is invoked as the prototypical victim, it not only supplants and displaces the lived experience of the vast majority of victims who do not belong to that demographic. It is also meant to conjure up a story about what justice looks like—justice in which the victim is pure and innocent, in which the person who caused harm is heartless and monstrous, in which the protector is righteous and vengeful, and in which the system as we know it contains them all in a proper and rightful order.

Resisting this formulation does not require excluding even a single furious and pained voice, denying the validity of a single call for revenge, or pretending merciful people are better than angry ones. What it requires is allowing it all in—all the mess, all the seeming contradictions, all the survivors—and committing to building a system that can hold them all. We have to resist the urge to cancel things out and instead allow them to build, to accumulate, and in their aggregate, to become something different, more honest, and more just than anything we have envisioned thus far. We will stand a chance at doing that only if we take seriously the pain of every survivor, every time.

For the vast range of experiences and responses survivors embody, when we do ask them, their responses are notably consistent—and notably consistent with what the trauma recovery field has identified as critical components of healing and recovery. That is to say, for all their variability, on the whole survivors crave precisely the things that have been demonstrated to alleviate their pain and support their well-being. These things, it turns out, are also consistent with the interests of justice and safety.

To begin the conversation about appropriate responses to violence, survivors first want validation that what happened to them is wrong. They want their pain taken seriously, and they do not want to be blamed or judged for what happened to them. They deserve this validation no matter who they are, what they did, or where they were when they were hurt. They need it no matter what our societal biases are about "people like them," no matter what their criminal record may be, no matter whether they reported the crime to the police or didn't. This validation matters in part because it reaffirms exactly what has been compromised when someone has been hurt: the belief that they live in a world that rejects violence and in which they should be able to be safe. It is easier to come through a terrible aberrant experience and be held in a society that recognizes its impact than to experience violence as an expression of the society's norms, values, and expectations. In clearly, directly, and repeatedly affirming that what a survivor sustained is wrong, we stake a claim for a world in which what people endured should not have happened in the first place, and we walk with them in the process of re-creating and returning to (or creating for the first time) that world.

Once we have established our recognition that what happened to them is wrong, survivors want answers. Information contributes substantially to what people in the trauma recovery field describe as the formation of a "coherent narrative"—a story about what happened and why that the survivor can believe, make sense of, find some meaning in, and live with. So, for example, for survivors who before the crime believed that bad things do not happen to good people, there are two primary ways within that narrative for them to tell the story of what happened: either (a) that they are actually a bad person and therefore less deserving of safety, of good things, even of love; or (b) that their goodness, the way they live, their righteous behavior, their attempts to be consistently caring and ethical and kind do not matter and will not keep them safe. Both of those stories are far worse than the one they believed before the crime. In coming through the traumatic experience, the survivor who is telling this story will have to grieve the worldview they once held—one that made them feel whole and made it possible to expect at least some real measure of safety—and will have to form a new worldview that is workable and includes the reality of what has happened to them. That new narrative may be as simple (and as profound) as "Even terrible things are survivable with love," or "I am more resilient than I ever knew," or "Hurt people hurt people," or countless other ways survivors make sense of and integrate their pain. These stories also help survivors accomplish a core feat of trauma healing: to arrange the story into their memory so they no longer experience it as eternal and ongoing.

But these new narratives are hard to build on the basis of mystery and doubt, so the more information a survivor has about what happened and why, the more thoroughly and quickly they are positioned to heal.[8] There is almost never anyone who knows more about what happened to a survivor and why than the person who caused them harm. Survivors who want answers to their questions therefore need and deserve to be able to ask these questions and get those answers: *Why did you do it? Why did you choose me? What, if anything, could I have done to stop you? Did you think I did something to you? Did you think I was someone else? Was that a real gun? Were you really prepared to shoot me? Did you feel bad at the time? Do you feel bad now? What would you have done if I had fought back? What happened to you? Did you think you could get away with this?* People are built to heal, and when we have information, we are profoundly capable of putting it into the service of our healing. The problem is that survivors rarely have access to such information because every response our systems have created to manage their relationship with the person who hurt them is designed to keep them separate rather than to help them come together productively.

Survivors do not only want to ask questions. They want to speak and they want their voices heard.[9] In that way, forming a coherent narrative is not just about listening. It is also about talking. Survivors want to be able to say, "How dare you?" They want to be able to say, "My brother was killed the year before you stabbed me. Can you imagine how it felt to my mother to get the call from the hospital that I was unconscious in the ER and had been stabbed?" Or: "I was going to spend that money you stole on a present for my daughter's birthday the next day. It was all I had. And so you left me with a terrible choice: make it look like I had forgotten her birthday or tell my five-year-old

baby girl that she lives in a world where someone can hurt her
daddy like that." Survivors want to say, "You had no right."
They want to say, "If it had been five years earlier, I would have
killed you for what you did to me, but I've grown, and you're
lucky." They want to say, "The fact that I am okay now does
not let you off the hook for the impact you had on me then."
They want to say, "I did not deserve what you did to me" or "I
have not slept one solid night since you robbed me" or "Every
time I see my scar in the mirror, I think of you" or "I wished
you were dead" or (and I really should say "and/or") "I forgive
you." Survivors are right to want to speak. Speaking about their
experience helps in the formation of their story and can contribute substantially to the abatement of their symptoms and to
their healing.[10] When we think about the association of trauma
with cardiovascular disease, the phrase "I got it off my chest"
becomes perfectly salient and clear.

Survivors want what they say to have an impact, and more
broadly, they want what they want and what they do to have
an impact, too. They want a sense of control relative to what
happened to them. Trauma is fundamentally an experience of
powerlessness.[11] Experiences that counterbalance that powerlessness with some degree of power—including over the story and
the response to the harm involved—can contribute substantially
to a survivor's healing process.[12] For some, this sense of control
can arise from shaping the outcome of their case if it proceeds
through the criminal justice system.[13] It can arise, if we are honest, through retaliatory violence.[14] It can arise in meaningful
accountability processes in which survivors get to shape the outcome.[15] And it can also arise by developing an enhanced ability
to make choices that keep them safe (such as by having the economic means to move, change jobs, or buy a car so they do not
have to walk to the bus) and by fostering their inherent ability
to heal.[16] For some survivors, working to change the conditions
that made them unsafe in the first place can give them a sense

of greater power and connection. We see countless survivors in movements to end violence, and their presence is not only generous, it can also be life-saving for them.[17]

In that spirit, survivors want access to the resources they need to heal and be safe—and they want them available even if they choose not to involve the police. Trauma can disrupt all parts of a survivor's life. For survivors who are students, common responses to traumatic experiences—including flashbacks triggered by sounds or smells, trouble sleeping, a sense of danger even in safe spaces, and panic attacks—can interrupt their education, contribute to disciplinary concerns, and diminish the chance of academic achievement.[18] Similarly, exposure to trauma can affect people's ability to function effectively, do their best at work, or obtain and keep a job.[19] And some people who are harmed and do not get well are more likely to commit violence themselves.[20] Each of these factors carries a financial cost in addition to a human one, and can have an impact on social service systems like law enforcement, hospitals, and public aid.[21]

Still, despite the moral and financial benefits of helping victims heal, the services and support to help them come through their pain are often scarce—and frequently leave out a significant portion of survivors.[22] A truly survivor-centered response to violence would include the broad availability of mental health treatment, counseling, trauma-informed care, and culturally rooted healing practices, and would emphasize the removal of barriers to these supports. This holds true not only for community-based services, but also for public victim-compensation resources, which reimburse survivors for costs such as hospital bills associated with a crime. Despite widespread recognition that many survivors do not believe that engaging police will make them safer, federal law nonetheless requires that victims "cooperate" with law enforcement to receive this help.[23] When that cooperation feels neither safe nor just to victims, they are barred from getting this key support to meet their basic needs.

Survivors do not want their healing resources tied to the person who hurt them, but they often do want things from that person. In addition to answers, many survivors want the person who harmed them to repair the harm as best they can.[24] It is a basic human desire to want what is broken to be fixed, and to want those who broke it to take responsibility for that repair however possible. Survivors who experience that repair can be greatly aided in their healing processes. For many survivors, repair can be most meaningful when it comes from the person who caused the harm. At Common Justice, for instance, a number of the survivors we have served have expressed a desire to see the person who harmed them apologize, contribute positively to their community, or pay restitution. The desire for restitution is not only about the money itself. It is about who should bear the burden for the responsible party's choices and what it means when the person who does wrong actively acknowledges their impact and bears that burden—and sometimes the suffering and other costs—of repair.

With or without that repair, survivors want to be safe.[25] They want to be protected from the person who hurt them in the short term. They want legitimate reason to believe they will be safe from that person in the long term. They want other people to be safe from that person. They do not want other people to hurt them in similar ways.[26] And they want the conditions that put them at risk of violence to change.[27] Sometimes (though not always, as discussed below) that means they want the person who hurt them incapacitated. It almost always means they want that person to stop hurting people. But sometimes it means they want the ability to relocate to another neighborhood; they want economic mobility; they want self-defense classes and new locks on their doors; they want support addressing the trauma symptoms that they know not only make them feel less safe but put them at greater risk of repeat victimization; they want support in breaking cycles of addiction, poverty, violence, and pain; they want help for their children and families; they want a transformation of the conditions in their neighborhoods so that fewer people are desperate, furious, and hurt, because desperation, fury, and pain put everyone at risk.[28]

Survivors' need for safety—their own and others'—should not be equated with an appetite for incarceration. Even though incarceration provides some people with a temporary sense of safety from the person who harmed them or satisfies a desire to see someone punished for wrongdoing—or both—many victims find that the person's incarceration makes them feel less safe.[29] For some, this is because they fear others in the community who may be angry with them for their role in securing the responsible person's punishment. For others, it is because they know that person will eventually come home, and they do not believe that he or she will be better for having spent time in prison; to the contrary, they often believe that incarceration will make the person worse. Many victims who live in communities where incarceration is common are dissatisfied with its results.[30] And even victims who *do* want the incarceration of those who hurt them are often disappointed by what it delivers in practice.[31] Many survivors seek incarceration only to find later that it did not make them safe and did not heal them in the way they had hoped.[32]

Survivors' own safety is not always their most essential desire. We have talked with hundreds of survivors at Common Justice, and there is only one thing that has been important to all of them. Some want retribution and revenge; some do not. Some want restitution; for some it is unimportant. Some want apologies; some find them meaningless. Some want to look the person who harmed them in the eyes; some never want to see that person again. Some want to be heard publicly; some want privacy. Some want a space to talk about what happened; some want to be given space to forget. Some care about the transformation of the person who harmed them; some could not care less. And though almost all survivors talk about their own safety, for some that has not been a core concern or priority. But every single survivor we have spoken to has wanted one thing: *to know that the person who hurt them would not hurt anyone else.*

It is, in fact, an extraordinary commonality, one that speaks to a degree of compassion and altruism in the human spirit. But it also makes pragmatic sense and is in the self-interest of the survivors themselves. Our experience of being harmed is often one that isolates us. One way we reconnect to the community from which the violence separated us is by caring about and seeking the safety of others like us. Survivors know the harm done to them may be partially repaired, but it will never be fully undone, so many seek meaning, power, and peace in the notion that the violence they survived could somehow be leveraged to help protect others from the same pain. That impulse to make meaning is also supported in the literature about trauma recovery as a basic element of coming through harm.[33]

These needs are widely recognized, legitimate, and imminently possible to meet—when it is our priority to meet them. We know what survivors need to heal and be safe. The problem is that our criminal justice system delivers almost none of these things to the vast majority of victims. Most victims do not report crime, a significant portion of reported crimes do not result in arrest, many arrests do not result in convictions, and the results of convictions—including incarceration—often do not meet victims' needs.[34] Victims' voices are almost never heard during this process. Although trial may offer an opportunity for some victims to speak, 94 to 97 percent of convictions nationwide are the result of plea bargains, not trials, so exceedingly few victims see a day in court.[35] Their questions are unanswered, their voices excluded, their input legally not required (with the exception of victim impact statements, which have not been shown to significantly affect sentencing outcomes), and their preferences frequently disregarded.[36] Many victims describe their experience of the justice system as re-traumatizing; many report being treated with suspicion or hostility; and many report experiencing bias based on their identity.[37]

People concerned about crime survivors must grapple with two things when thinking about criminal trials: (1) It is important to understand how trials affect victims in practice, not just theory; and (2) What happens at a criminal trial has very little to do with almost any victims' experiences.

A number of studies document the negative impact of trials on crime victims.[38] The experience can be overwhelming and even harmful, due to the stress of the process, the lack of clarity about the timeline of the proceedings, the difficulty of facing the person who harmed them or their loved ones, the desire and/or pressure to testify, the experience of being doubted or invalidated by defense counsel (whose job it is to doubt and invalidate testimony that will result in their client's conviction), the difficulty of dealing with gaps or contradictions in memory (a common feature of trauma and a problem on the stand), the experience of reliving the crime through hearing testimony (including often heart-wrenching testimony like a coroner's report on an autopsy of a loved one or a doctor's report about a surviving victim's own body), the sense that their voices are not nearly as central or consequential in the process as they had imagined and/or been led to believe, the strains of taking days or weeks off of work, of getting back and forth to court, of coordinating child care during the trial, and of managing expectations—their own and others'.

Each of these experiences can be painful; taken together, they can be damaging and re-traumatizing. During and after a trial, many victims experience a recurrence of symptoms that had abated or an amplification of symptoms that have persisted.[39] The result of a trial can provoke in a significant portion of victims feelings ranging from disappointment to outrage.[40] Even victims who are satisfied with the result report that they found the process extraordinarily difficult and even harmful.[41] And for victims who are ambivalent about the extreme punishment of the person who hurt them, even a "victory" can feel at best hollow and at worst like another addition to their pain.

However difficult and even detrimental trials can be, they remain the only formal forum in which victims get to have their voices heard and sometimes get answers to their questions—a forum that the prevalence of plea bargains has all but eliminated. In most jurisdictions, more trials probably air on reruns of *Law and Order* in a given month than take place in court. As mass incarceration has grown, so have the systems that feed it— including court processing and policing. The work required of all parties to go to trial creates a shared disincentive to do so. But the prevalence of plea bargaining is also the product of practices in which prosecutors pursue charges that are in excess of what defendants actually did (or what can be proved). The higher penalties associated with these magnified charges present defendants with a hard choice: they can admit their guilt and be offered a shorter sentence (say, one to three years in prison) or they can run the risk of going to trial—and if they are found guilty of the top charge against them, they could face a much longer sentence and even life in prison. Many defendants do not have confidence that they will get a fair hearing at trial, so the risk becomes too much and they accept the lesser offer, even when they would have had a strong chance of being found not guilty at trial.

This practice also distorts victims' experience of the process. Someone who committed an assault, for instance, might be charged with attempted murder but may ultimately accept a deal to plead guilty to a lesser charge of attempted assault. For the defendant, the specter of the attempted murder charge, artificially inflated though it may be, compels him to take a plea without exercising his right to a trial. For the victim, the conviction for the lesser charge of attempted assault can feel profoundly disrespectful of his experience. As one survivor once said to me, "What about the assault on me was 'attempted'? He didn't attempt it. He did it. And I still have the scar to show for it." We are left with a result that is not satisfying to either party, does not reflect the reality of what occurred, and has not been subject to the rigors promised by the Constitution to defendants accused of crimes in our courts.

It is crucial in this context to note that a survivor-centered system is not a survivor-ruled one. Valuing people does not mean giving them sole and unmitigated control. The criminal justice system maintains a responsibility to safety, justice, and human dignity that it should uphold even when those interests run contrary to survivors' desires. So if a survivor wants someone free and that person poses a present and demonstrable threat to others, the survivor's opinion should not inherently outweigh the safety of others. Similarly, when a survivor wants a level of retribution that runs contrary to the values of justice and fairness, the system does not have an obligation to satisfy the person's desire for punishment. The system's actors do, however, have an obligation to listen to the survivor, be transparent and honest with the person about the decisions they make, and connect the survivor with healing supports. And when it is possible for these actors to fulfill their obligations to safety and fairness while also meeting the needs of the survivor, they should do so, even if that means seeking a less punitive response than they might otherwise have sought.

That said, even a plea bargain is far more than most victims will ever see from the justice system. Fewer than half of reported violent crimes result in an arrest and fewer than half of those arrests end in convictions.[42] But what's more is the fact that only a fraction of violence gets reported to the police in the first place.

In considering survivors' experience of the criminal justice system, we must begin far earlier than the revictimization that often happens during the court process: we have to begin with a survivor's decision whether to engage with the system at all.

In recent years, a full 52 percent of violent victimizations in the United States went unreported.[43] Even in cases of the most serious violence, reporting rates were strikingly low: a full 56 percent of cases in which victims were injured went unreported, as did 42 percent of cases involving a weapon.[44] Even 29 percent of cases involving a serious injury went unreported to police (for example, when the victim was knocked unconscious or sustained a broken bone, a gunshot or stab wound, or internal injuries).[45] More than half of the people who survive serious violence prefer *nothing* to everything available to them through law enforcement.

The reasons victims give for not reporting to law enforcement include a belief that police could not or would not do anything to help; a belief that the crime—even a violent one—was not important enough to report; or, most commonly, a decision to handle the victimization another way, such as reporting it to someone else or addressing it privately.[46]

Even though people's experience of victimization varies based on their identity and where they live, these reporting patterns hold across demographic groups.[47] What's more, these estimates are widely regarded as understating the issue, as they reflect the participation of only those people reached by (and who decided to participate in) the National Crime Victimization Survey. Those who do not interact with or have access to systems of contact and care—or whose victimization is so minimized that they do not even identify it as such—are not represented in these already strikingly high numbers. When one considers the short- and long-term consequences of unaddressed violence—ranging from physical and emotional pain for people harmed to cycles of violence that result when harm is unhealed—these rates point to a practical and moral crisis in tending to the needs of crime survivors as well as a formidable challenge to securing public safety.

Survivors make practical decisions about whether to engage law enforcement, based in part on whether they believe that doing so will meet their needs for safety and justice. It has been widely debated and documented that these beliefs often stem from survivors' views of the police.[48] But another factor is likely underestimated: survivors' views of jail and prison. What if the barriers to survivors reporting crime involve a disbelief that the end result of the justice system's involvement—the incarceration of the person responsible—is right or will work? Thus far, debate about the causes of underreporting has focused almost exclusively on whether victims believe police involvement will make a difference. The discussion has rarely examined the degree to which survivors consider incarceration an effective means of securing justice and safety. If survivors believe that a police investigation is likely to result in the incarceration of the people who hurt them, and if they do not believe that incarceration will result in greater safety or justice, why would they pick up the phone in the first place?

When people are deciding whether or not to call the police, they are likely to ask two questions: *Will it advance my sense of safety?* and *Will it advance my sense of justice?* If the answer to both is *yes*, we call. If it is *no*, we do not. And if we answer *yes* to one question and *no* to the other, we make a judgment about which of those things is more important to us. In a criminal justice system that produced safety and justice, crime survivors could consistently answer *yes* to both of those questions. But that is not what they do in this country. Rather, in the richest nation in the world with arguably the largest and most expensive criminal justice system in human history, the majority of people who survive violence prefer *nothing* to everything we have to offer. It is an extraordinary fact to absorb, and one that points to a moral crisis that is ours to answer to.

For years, we have been told a story that crime victims in this country want and need incarceration. We have been told that it is their overwhelming preference for what happens to the people who hurt them and that it delivers them healing.

In the 1990s, I had the fortune to learn from a mentor who

helped me see more clearly through this myth than I had before. Annie was an elder I knew and loved living in East Point, Atlanta, and she was brutally robbed and assaulted one night by a young man roughly the age of her teenage son. Everything in the criminal justice system's response went as well as it could have. The police came quickly and treated her with respect. The person who hurt her was identified and arrested. The assistant district attorney showed Annie care and compassion and worked hard on the case. The case went to trial (one of the few that would not be resolved by plea bargain that year in that county), and the jury convicted the person who assaulted her of the most serious charge against him. The judge sentenced him to the maximum allowable prison sentence—a long one by any measure. The system worked as seamlessly as it possibly could.

Several years later, when I came to know Annie well, one day I asked: *Ms. Annie, with all my respect, may I ask, when that man who assaulted you was sentenced to that long prison term, were you relieved?* And she answered: *Oh yes, honey, of course I was.* And I asked: *Can I ask how long that relief lasted?* And she said: *Oh, baby, at least three or four hours.*

And then I took the bus home, she said, *and I was still afraid. And I got to my apartment, and I was still poor. And when I crawled into bed that night, I still couldn't sleep, and when exhaustion finally took me and I fell asleep, I still had those same nightmares. And when I woke up that next morning, the only difference was that I could not shake the image of that boy's mother's face in court when those guards took her baby from her for good. Because that is my face.*

For all my formative experience that taught me otherwise, I had still held on to a desire to believe that prison—at least sometimes—provided victims what they deserve. I did that partly because the thought of it failing to do so was crushingly hard to bear—because of what it meant for both survivors and those incarcerated. But I also continued to search for proof of that outcome because I, too, had been so deeply socialized to believe it was there to be found.

To be clear, I am not saying that no victims want incarceration. They do. Nor am I saying that the incarceration of someone who causes harm never contributes to a victim's sense of safety or justice. It undoubtedly can. But it accomplishes those things far less frequently than we are led to believe, and even when it does, it invariably falls short of contributing to healing in the way that victims deserve.

Years ago, I began to pay attention to a particular phrase that I kept hearing in news reporting about crime: "sigh of relief." It was an odd phrase to hear so often, because it does not seem to meet the journalistic standards for precision; it is hard to distinguish between different types of sighs, so it seems unlikely that reporters could consistently identify a sigh of relief when they heard it. But still, it was everywhere. "The victim breathed a sigh of relief tonight, knowing the person who robbed her had been apprehended." Or "The shaken victim breathed a sigh of relief, knowing she will sleep soundly tonight now that the burglar who invaded her home and held her hostage is finally in police custody." The truth is, that's not how trauma works. The night after your home has been invaded and you have been held hostage is not a night you are likely to sleep, no matter who is in police custody. The apprehension of the person who harmed you can surely help, but in itself will not deliver you peace. In all likelihood, you will be up for days, and when you finally collapse from sheer exhaustion, you are likely to experience night terrors, which will carry into the day in the form of flashbacks in which you relive the experience as though it is currently happening again—even though the person who did it is in custody. Trauma is profound; it is a persistent creature that burrows its way into our minds and bodies, and shifts and evades us when we try to rid ourselves of it. It is possible, though not easy, to heal through trauma. But for all the long-standing and emerging treatments that show great promise, an arrest is not one of them.

The story we tell about the role arrests play in healing is a dangerous one for survivors. First, I think of the victim from the news story that next morning, after she has been up all night, after she slept for just thirty minutes at dawn and was awakened by a nightmare so intense, it took her ten minutes to stop shaking. When she hears that report, it suggests that the arrest should have been enough—and therefore that something is wrong with her, that she is not like other victims whose symptoms stop when the person is caught—that she is different, broken, weak. Given how common it is for victims to blame themselves for what happened and for the symptoms they experience as a result, perpetuating a narrative that fortifies this belief is not only inaccurate, it is harmful.

But it is not only harmful to the victims whose experiences make the nightly news. The same story is one that many of us internalize. If I do come to believe the story, then when I am harmed, I want the person arrested and sentenced because I believe it will bring me relief—as I have been told it has done for so many others. We hear few other examples in our public discourse about what will bring such relief—other than, perhaps, retaliatory violence. Nothing really about healing, nothing about taking sanctuary in the people I love, in therapy, in faith, in physical exercise, in meditation. And rarely about restorative justice or accountability other than prison. So I seek the one thing I have been told might ease my pain—because my pain is enormous, my pain is nearly unbearable—and I call the police and I participate in the process, and, if I am like most victims, at the end of doing so, I am still unhealed, I still feel unsafe, and my appetite for justice is still unsatisfied. But now, unlike before I sought that remedy, I am heartbroken, because the thing in which I invested my hope, my time, my energy, and my sense of a possibility other than unending pain has failed, and I am not better, and I think something is wrong with me because what I was told worked for others did not work for me, and I have been offered nothing else, and for a while at least, the only things left to me are rage and despair.

We hear a common narrative when news outlets, police, prosecutors, and other elected officials talk about an arrest or a prison sentence. They suggest that the consequence imposed on the person responsible for harm is adequate to meet the needs of the person harmed—that the survivor is safe now, relieved, resolved, even healed. This narrative is familiar, but it is not based in fact. There is no evidence whatsoever, for instance, that connects the length of a defendant's sentence to the well-being of a victim of crime. None.[49]

The evidence there *is* includes the following: victims want to be heard: they want to provide statements in court and are often more satisfied when given the opportunity to do so.[50] They want to provide input into sentencing and are often more satisfied when they feel their input is heeded.[51] They want the option to participate—or *not* participate—to the degree they choose.[52] They want information about the status of the case, the timing of its resolution, the sentencing outcome, and the whereabouts of the person who hurt them (including when they are going to be released from incarceration).[53] Some victims report greater satisfaction at longer sentences, but that satisfaction has never been demonstrated to have any correlation with improvements in mental health, reduction in trauma symptoms, or overall well-being, nor is there evidence that their satisfaction remains greater over time—and of course these studies represent a small and typically nonrepresentative sample of victims.[54]

But none of what we know about what victims prefer amounts to evidence that the long sentences we seek in victims' names increase their well-being or alleviate their trauma in any way. One of the places we see this most clearly—though it is never held up as evidence of this point—is in victims' letters to parole boards. It is important to acknowledge that these letters represent only a small subset of victims' views. Most parole boards operate in secret, meaning that there is no way to know how many victims provide letters to parole boards, or what they say or request when given the opportunity.[55] We do know that victims who want to oppose parole are more likely to participate in the parole process than those who favor it or are neutral; many believe this is in part because of the more positive relationship these victims have maintained with the prosecution or correctional system (as compared with victims who are not opposed to parole).[56] So we have even less information from those letters about the experience and thinking of victims who do not oppose parole.

That said, these letters reflect trends that are telling. And the most basic one is this: time after time, victims tell the parole board that they still feel exactly the way they did the day the crime occurred. Ten, fifteen, twenty years later—they feel the same. We also hear this in victims' testimonials beyond the context of parole. Their stories of ongoing, ceaseless pain implicate us all. How heartless do we have to be to fail to develop other ways to support healing in the face of the unwavering evidence that what we are doing for victims is not working? If someone's pain does not subside over time, it means the tools we are using to transform it are at worst wrong and at best inadequate. If prison worked, survivors would feel better as a result of the incarceration of the person who hurt them. And yet so many survivors do not. Their pain continues unabated because they are relying on an intervention—incarceration—that is not equipped and was never even designed to help them heal. And yet, when they testify at parole boards that even ten years of a defendant's incarceration has made no dent in their pain, many people assume the problem is simply that the person has not been incarcerated long enough, as though one day (after fifteen years? thirty?) we will reach the juncture where incarceration will finally help the victim, despite no indication that it has contributed to their well-being thus far.

Imagine someone suffering from terrible, debilitating migraines. He goes to the doctor and reports his unbearable pain and the doctor prescribes a medication. He returns the next year and tells the doctor that his pain has not diminished at all; the doctor says to just keep taking the same medication. A full decade letter, still racked with pain, he goes back, and the doctor tells him to stay on the medication a little longer. There is no way we would regard that as good medicine or as ethical care. And there is no way it is what a person in pain deserves. When we hear victims attest to the unremitting intensity of their pain, we should not hear it as a straightforward justification of more incarceration—we should hear it at least in part as an indictment of our reliance on incarceration to help them heal.

But despite a profound lack of evidence demonstrating incarceration benefits victims' well-being—and despite evidence to the contrary—we continually lengthen sentences in victims' names. Elected officials do so through legislation; judges and prosecutors do so through the sentences they impose; and parole boards do so in their denials of applications for parole. As a culture, we repeatedly tell victims that these longer sentences will bring them relief, and we do this without evidence (or any basis in the psychological literature) to suggest that it would be true. Trauma is not resolved by the infliction of pain on another person. How much simpler things would be if it were.

Our society's continual retelling of this story is, quite simply, unethical. As a culture, we are selling survivors something that we claim will deliver them from pain, even though we have no legitimate basis to believe it will. We are talking to people who have survived serious violence, in their moments of most profound suffering, and, knowingly or not, we are lying to them over and over again. That is not what a society that cares about survivors does.

Compounding the fact that prison is almost always inadequate in securing victims' healing (in part because that is just not its function) is the reality that prison all too often fails to deliver on its most explicit purpose: providing safety to crime victims. Chapter 2 discusses the limitations of incarceration as a public safety strategy in far more detail, but it is important to note here that the problem with our reliance on incarceration is not just about failing to meet survivors' emotional needs—it is also about failing to meet their most basic need to be safe.

Across the country, people are working to develop responses to harm that meet survivors' needs. It is in the presence of these options that survivors' wishes become far clearer. For instance, at Common Justice, the vast majority of victims who have been given the choice of seeing the person who harmed them incarcerated or seeing them take part in an alternate restorative justice process *have chosen* the alternate process.[57] All of these survivors are people who participated in the criminal justice system. They are among the less than half of victims who called the police and are part of the even smaller subgroup who continued their engagement through the grand jury process. They are people who initially chose a path that could lead to prison. They are people who have suffered serious violence—knives to their bodies, guns to their heads, lacerations to their livers, punctured lungs—and have engaged the criminal justice system in a way likely to result in the incarceration of the person who hurt them. Even among these victims, when another option is offered, *90 percent* choose something other than that very incarceration they were initially pursuing.

Ninety percent is a stunning number in context of the story we have been told about what victims want. And the reality it points to may not be as obvious as it appears. Some certainly choose an alternative process for the reasons we think of first—compassion, forgiveness, the belief that people can change, an experience having caused harm themselves or having loved someone who did, a desire to be part of transformation. But most are simply more practical. Most choose it because they believe something other than incarceration stands a better chance of meeting their short- and long-term needs for safety and justice and for ensuring that others won't experience the same suffering that they did.

As a country, we have failed to provide victims of violence with real options other than incarceration to hold the person who harmed them accountable. The decisions of survivors given other options points to an essential way of anticipating survivors' needs: what survivors choose when they have only one option does not predict what they will want when multiple options are present. Absent other options, when we ask victims, "Do you want incarceration?" we are essentially asking: "Do you want something or nothing?" And we know that when any of us are hurt, we want—we need—*something*. But if instead of asking, "Do you want something or nothing?" we ask, "Do you want this intervention or that prison?" many victims want the intervention. And the least we can do is offer them the option.

It is essential to note that the overwhelming support among victims for a restorative justice process is not just about the promise of those processes—it is more specifically and more broadly about the failure of incarceration to meet victims' needs—including their need for safety.[58] As one victim of a violent crime said to me, "Two things in these [robbery] cases are always true. One is they [the people who did it] come back. The other is that their friends don't go with them. Tell me, what am I supposed to do with that?" This victim's question is a fair one, and one our criminal justice system has abdicated responsibility for answering. If we are going to rise to the challenge of reducing violence, we will have to pay attention to the impact that incarceration has on victims, listen to the full range of people who survive harm, and become honest as a nation about the profound limitations of prisons as a method of delivering safety or healing. When we do that, we will understand that accountability to survivors requires that we break our dependence on incarceration to address the pain they endure.

Choosing alternatives to prison in no way requires survivors to be forgiving or to be invested in the well-being of the person who hurt them. Early in Common Justice, a case was referred to us in which a boy—just fourteen years old—was badly beaten and robbed. The young man who did it was facing three years in prison. I went to speak with the survivor's mother, to see whether she and her son wanted the young man who committed the crime to be given the opportunity to participate in Common Justice.

She said to me: *When I first found out about this, I wanted that young man to drown to death. And then I wanted him to burn to death. And then I realized as a mother that I don't want either of those things. I want him to drown in a river of fire.*

But three years from now, when my nine-year-old son is twelve, he is going to be coming to and from his aunt's house, to and from school, to and from the corner school alone. And one day he's going to walk by that young man. And I have to ask myself: when that day comes, do I want that young man to have been upstate or do I want him to have been with y'all?

And the truth is, while if that young man were before me today and I had my machete, I would chop him to bits, bury him under the house, and sleep soundly for the first night since he dared hurt my child, the truth is I'd rather him be with y'all.

This mother did something I have since seen countless survivors do over and over again: she put aside an individual desire for revenge in the interest of what would secure the safety of her child and children like him.

During a conversation a few months later with another survivor also faced with the choice between incarceration and Common Justice for the person who robbed him, he began drawing a series of boxes on the piece of paper in front of him. Then he began drawing x's through some of the boxes. I asked him what he was doing. He said, *The boxes are everyone I know who has returned home from prison. The x's are everyone who went back. What did you say your success rate was?* I told him that fewer than 10 percent of people in the program had been terminated for new crimes (by 2018 that figure was only 6 percent). And he nodded and said, *Let's do it.* Another man who had been robbed at gunpoint asked me, *Can he get life without parole for this?* I told him the statute in New York did not allow for it. And he said, *Well, then, let's do Common Justice.* So his first preference was that the person die in prison; his second was that he get access to an alternative to incarceration in which he would serve no prison time; and his third and by far least favorite was that the person serve any amount of time other than a life sentence. As he put it, *If he can't be gone forever, then I'd rather he be changed.* For some, that may seem incoherent—wouldn't a long sentence be better than nothing? But for someone who has seen the limitations of incarceration in producing safety and who is considering his own safety and the safety of others as his primary decision-making criteria, it makes perfect sense: if not forever, then none at all.

These survivors' decisions align with national findings. In 2016, the Alliance for Safety and Justice conducted the first national poll of crime survivors that explores their preferences regarding criminal justice policy. The poll found overwhelming support—even higher than among the general public—for rehabilitative programming, alternatives to incarceration, and shorter sentences, as well as greater investments in education, mental health treatment, jobs programs, and drug treatment. Roughly 52 percent of crime victims answered that they "believe that time in prison makes people more likely to commit another crime rather than less likely."[59] Perhaps for that reason, 69 percent of victims preferred holding people accountable through options beyond prison, such as rehabilitation, mental health treatment, substance use treatment, community supervision (mostly probation and parole), or community service.[60] The findings are not surprising to people who work closely with crime survivors, but they are directly contrary to the public and law enforcement narrative about what victims want.[61]

Even in the context of what could fairly be described as a four-decade media and public education campaign promoting incarceration, the portion of victims who see it as an effective remedy is far smaller than public discourse reflects.[62] When it comes to punishment, survivors consistently express a desire for options other than incarceration and an interest in them when they are available. Yet the criminal justice system rarely offers alternatives to prison as responses to violence. According to the Downstate Coalition for Crime Victims in New York, "Survivors/victims want the people who harm them to be held meaningfully accountable. Many survivors/victims find the criminal justice system, including incarceration, to be inadequate and/or counterproductive to that end."[63] What this means in practice is that when the country relies almost exclusively on incarceration to address serious crime, many survivors lose out.

Survivors' preferences about criminal justice policy are only one part of their larger set of needs and desires, including real hunger for solutions that have nothing to do with punishing the person who hurt them. These priorities include safety, housing, trauma-informed care, fair treatment, prevention, and having a real voice in potential solutions.[64] Opening these avenues of support is therefore as essential to developing survivor-centered responses as any reform of the criminal justice system will ever be.

Imagine there is a hamburger stand in the middle of the desert that sells really bad burgers. There is nothing for two hundred miles in any direction. You pull up to it and you see an extremely long line. If you concluded, based on that line, that you had just come across the most delicious burgers in America, you would be missing something.

In this country we have offered survivors nothing but that bad hamburger stand in the middle of nowhere. We have offered only two choices: something or nothing, bad burgers or nothing for miles. And when some survivors have chosen *something*, we have used it to promote the hamburger stand, we have claimed they loved what we gave them, that they wanted more. We have done that never having asked them why they chose it, never having asked them how they felt later, and never having asked them what they would have liked instead. It is not hard to understand why so many people are in that line for burgers. We have all done it. When we have been hungry enough, whether because of need or circumstance, we have eaten food that we know will not nourish us, food we do not want or like, food that would make us feel sick later, food we had sworn we would not eat anymore, food we would never choose if there were other options—because we are too hungry to eat nothing at all. The fact that we ate it should not be used as evidence that it was good food.

I believe we owe it to victims to offer them something better than a nasty burger. I believe that if there were a chicken spot and a veggie spot and a pizza spot and a taco spot alongside that burger stand, the line for burgers would be dramatically shorter and more people would be well fed. I believe that what people choose when they have only one option is no predictor of what they will choose when they have others.

There is another thing you would see, standing in that long line at the hamburger stand, if you looked off to your left. You would see a long line of people driving by—people who knew there was nothing else for two hundred miles, people who were as dizzy with hunger as you were, people whose mouths were watering but who could not bear the thought of eating that food because they knew how bad it would be for them and that in the end it would be worse than nothing. Those people are the majority of victims who do not even call the police in the first place, and we owe them exactly as much as we owe the people in line for those awful burgers.

The former Brooklyn district attorney Charles Hynes used to tell a story about a bumper sticker his colleague, another DA, had. It said, "Victims say: Catch & release is for fish—not felons."[65] The first few times I heard the story, my only reaction was to be horrified by the dehumanizing comparison it drew, and by the levity with which it did so. But after a while, something else struck me about the story—the line "victims say." Here was the top-ranking law enforcement official in his jurisdiction, and his bumper sticker didn't say "*I say* catch & release is for fish—not felons." It said, "*Victims* say." And the more I thought about the bumper sticker, the more I realized it revealed something about criminal justice policy in the United States: that regardless of whether our policy is motivated by a concern for victims, whether it produces the outcomes they seek and deserve, and whether their input is gathered to inform our practice, we still do what we do in their names. Their experience—their pain—is the well from which decision makers draw their moral authority, and the stories we tell always start with their names.

I have become persuaded that if we made a record of what victims really say—if we listened deeply and well and asked open-ended questions—we would end up with a criminal justice system that would look surprisingly like the one we would develop if we listened to what defendants say. It would be characterized by accountability, by safety, by justice, and by healing. And it would look very little like what we have today.

This is not mostly about mercy. When survivors advocate for shorter prison sentences, parole, or the reallocation of funding from the criminal justice system to the social service infrastructure that prevents and heals violence, they are often presumed to be forgiving. It is assumed that their policy preferences are motivated by mercy and grace. For some, they surely are. But for most, they are displaying what I would argue is one of the most common and vastly underestimated qualities of crime survivors: survivors are pragmatic. Saying survivors are pragmatic does not mean that they are not emotional. It means that their emotionality does not prevent them from making highly rational decisions, even in the face of their pain and fear and rage. Survivors' safety, well-being, and sometimes even survival depend on the efficacy of responses to violence, and jails and prisons are largely ineffective responses. Incarcerating the person responsible for harm is inadequate even in the limited number of cases in which it produces some concrete benefit—and it is often devastating to survivors when its impact is directly contrary to the aims of safety, healing, and justice that their lives depend on. Survivors know this better than anyone. They have paid the price for prison's failure with their pain.

Survivors therefore need something from those of us committed to them. If it is true that survivors are a far wider-ranging group of people than we know, if it is true that incarceration does not consistently deliver safety and almost never delivers healing, if it is true that basic things like validation, control, and a coherent narrative are necessary elements for coming through trauma, if it is true that survivors who are given options almost always choose anything other than prison, if it is true that millions of survivors tell us again and again every time they do not call the police that what the criminal justice system has to offer does not work for them, then it does seem to follow that survivors absolutely, urgently need all of us to end mass incarceration. It may be the only practical thing we can do in their names.

2

Prison's Broken Promise

America has long had a love affair with punishment. With a few critical exceptions, at virtually every decision point in the criminal justice system, we choose the more punitive option over any available alternative. As a publication by the John Jay College of Criminal Justice describes it, "This has become manifest in all aspects of the criminal justice system—at the front end through more aggressive policing practices, in the court system with fewer diversion programs or alternatives to prosecution, during the period of confinement as the nation's jails and prisons have become more crowded and the experience of incarceration more punitive, and at the back end of the system where the conditions of supervision have become more oriented toward surveillance and monitoring and less oriented toward supportive services and reintegration."[1] We mete out long, harsh prison sentences that contribute to a rate of incarceration that is historically unprecedented and internationally unique. We suspend children from school beginning as early as preschool.[2] We arrest people for low-level offenses that other countries regard (and we in the United States have previously regarded) as either nuisances or prompts for help and support. We punish addiction and "incapacitate" mental illness. We control each other, punish each other, and throw each other away. In the criminology field, this tendency even has its own term: people call it "American penal exceptionalism."

Some of the clearest and most devastating examples of this punitiveness in recent history lie in mandatory minimum sentencing laws (which specify a minimum prison term to which a judge must sentence someone found guilty of a certain offense). These laws functionally remove judges' discretion to act with mercy, to factor in complex circumstances or causes, to take into account a victim's view when the person doesn't favor a lengthy term of imprisonment, or to consider the impact on public safety (both the degree to which incarceration is necessary to secure it and the point at which it might become counterproductive) in the decisions they make. We as a nation are so punitive that we do not even trust U.S. judges—who have sentenced millions of people to prison terms that would be unfathomable anywhere else in the western world—to be punishing enough. In setting these minimums, we etch a belief system into stone, formalizing our disinterest in the details of a particular case or the humanity of the people involved, our misplaced and outdated assumptions about what helps victims heal and be safe, our disregard for the context of a crime as a relevant factor in determining an appropriate consequence, our failure to understand prison as a tool with limitations that should be treated as such, and our assumption that all people who cause certain harm are fundamentally the same as one another and essentially monstrous. We remove our ability not only to empathize, but to think, to act rationally, and to make decisions that prioritize healing, safety, and justice.

As a nation, we have chosen to constrain ourselves as a way of assuring that any options other than extreme punishment—mercy, reason, practicality, fairness—will not overwhelm us in the face of an opportunity to punish. In so doing, we not only lose our ability to apply fair, strategic, proportionate consequences, we also insulate ourselves from responsibility for the decisions we are making because, from a legal perspective, we have taken all other decisions off the table. Former U.S. district judge Nancy Gertner observed that "over a 17-year judicial career, I sent hundreds of defendants to jail—and about 80 percent of them received a sentence that was disproportionate, unfair, and discriminatory."[3]

In part because of the way in which these decisions run contrary to our nation's core pronounced commitment to life, liberty, and the pursuit of happiness, we also see political and communications strategies that both normalize and Americanize a level of punishment citizens of other countries would find unimaginable. Perhaps the most obvious of these are the variety of "three strikes" laws that mandate courts to impose harsher sentences—often mandatory sentences of twenty-five years to life—on people who commit a third felony crime (in some states, these enhancements apply at just the second strike).[4] Just over half of states have "three strikes" laws, and though most require that at least one of the three felony crimes that trigger the consequence is a violent crime, in many states, the other two can be nonviolent felonies.[5] In a particularly egregious (but all too common) example, a man named Curtis Wilkerson, who had participated in a robbery when he was a teenager, stole a pair of socks nearly fifteen years later. The theft constituted his third strike, and he was sentenced to a life term in prison for the crime.[6]

Although it is a common and relatively long-standing practice in the United States to impose longer sentences for people who were previously convicted of crimes, it was not until the 1990s that this became mandatory, stifling judges' ability to use their discretion when they thought it was appropriate to set a less extreme sentence. While Washington State's Initiative 593 in 1993 was arguably the first "three strikes" legislation, it was Proposition 184 in California the following year that would take the "three strikes and you're out" message to the voters and would be credited broadly for starting the trend that resulted in twenty-six states and the federal government having "three strikes" laws on the books just a decade later.[7] These laws were part of a wave of policy shifts that contributed to the rise of mass incarceration nationwide, and they have come under fire in recent years as not only draconian, but ineffective. (The 2012 Proposition 36 in California, for instance, went a distance to limiting the reach of the three strikes law there, though it did not eliminate it.)[8]

If initial harsh sentencing is one extreme of punishment, another is the elimination of the possibility of parole and other forms of early release. When people are paroled, they are released after completing the required sentence a judge imposed, but before completing the allowable maximum penalty above and beyond that requirement. Parole is designed to recognize, reward, and motivate good behavior in prison, and it acknowledges the fact that people's consequential thinking, remorse, maturity, and risk to public safety change over time—and reflects a belief that sentences should reflect those changes. As mass incarceration has increased in this country, we have seen more people going into prisons, but have also seen far fewer coming out, as the portion of those who are eligible for parole and released declines, mirroring the increase in sentences.[9]

From "truth in sentencing" laws (which require people to serve a certain portion of their sentence regardless of good behavior or rehabilitation) to the functional elimination of parole in states that rarely grant it, the decision to keep people in prison no matter what happens while they are there enforces a disbelief in the human capacity for change and even transformation. Enshrining this belief system in law didn't come easily. It took work to normalize these laws and policies and make them feel "American," particularly in a nation where so many people hold religious beliefs rooted in doctrines of redemption.

This normalizing and Americanizing of punishment didn't begin or end in the 1990s, and it was almost always interwoven with another American narrative: the long story of race and racism. Although punishment is by no means an exclusively white-on-black phenomenon (white people punish one another, people of color punish one another, white people punish people of color who aren't black, and, much less frequently, people of color punish white people), its evolution in the United States is inextricably intertwined with the history of slavery and its aftermath. The history of slavery exemplifies the mutually reinforcing link between racialized dehumanization and extreme punishment. Whole generations of people do not give up their freedom willingly, and the level of violence required to keep slavery in place was extraordinary. Black people were subjected to horrific acts of violence, and their race was used as a justification not only for their enslavement, but for the violence that kept them enslaved. That racialization and all its attendant myths regarding the biological and moral inferiority of black people was necessary for white slave owners to become people who could commit that level of harm against other human beings.

It is hard for anyone to inflict extreme pain on people we see as fully human and whose experience we see as reflective of our own. Our capacity for empathy is powerful, and when it is present, it interferes with our ability to hurt others. The act of empathizing is one of linkage—we draw on our own experience to imagine the experience of another person. So to imagine how extreme punishment would feel (lashings, beatings, burnings, and more), we would have to imagine how it would feel to survive it ourselves. But if we can persuade ourselves that there is something about the person we seek to punish that is fundamentally different from us, less than us, we become more capable of disabling our empathy, of telling ourselves that the pain they feel will not be like ours because they are not like us. In that way, racism is a profound enabler of cruelty by white people, because it provides a way to bypass the otherwise natural and often overpowering capacity for empathy. In so doing, it augments white people's capacity to engage in punishment that exceeds what a person would otherwise regard as appropriate or allowable within shared human community.

Countless white people have told ourselves for centuries—
beginning at an extreme, all-consuming level in the context of
forced labor and punishment—that black people do not feel pain
the way we do. The legacy of this thinking is tenacious. Even
when white people begin to see the unquestionable reality of
black people's humanity, the notion of black people's imperviousness to pain can persist and can shape white people's responses to
black people as victims and as people responsible for harm. When
black people are victims, white people too easily ignore their
pain. And if white people are using pain in an instrumental way,
as punishment, it is too easy to infer that black people will need
to feel more pain for it to register at the same level as it would for
their white counterparts. (If we had to concretize that difference,
one might argue perhaps even a 100:1 ratio would be reflective
of white people's ethos, that is, if the disparate sentencing for
powder vs. crack cocaine were used as a guide.)[10]

Arguably the most pervasive justifier of dominance and control,
white supremacy (and here I do not just mean the KKK and its
equivalents, but the far broader, more prevalent, and often less overt
set of views and behaviors that state or imply the superiority of white
people and justify their use of power to maintain inequity) is the
ultimate normalizer of violence. To persist, the violence that white
dominance depends on has to become so ingrained in the culture
that it is regarded not as an immoral aberration, but as part of the
natural order of things. White supremacy had to make the enslavement and torture of human beings normal; it has to make police violence against people of color normal; it has to make sexual violence
against women and trans people of color normal; it has to make putting people in cages and beating them as "rehabilitation" normal.
The Harvard historian Khalil Gibran Muhammad describes these
kinds of normalizing efforts as the "condemnation of blackness."[11]
This normalization allows for the continued violence against people
of color and secures white people's impunity for this kind of harm.
After all, we punish people for breaking our culture's norms, not
for upholding them.

As punishers, white people can further protect ourselves from the pain our empathy would cause us and free ourselves from the constraints it would place on our behavior if we add to dehumanization another familiar American ingredient: paternalism. If we go a step beyond telling ourselves that the person we are punishing will not feel pain in the same way we would and also tell ourselves that the pain we inflict will make them better in some way—"teach them a lesson"—then we may even feel ethical as we do harm that would otherwise be unthinkable.

As slavery ended, white people substituted punishment for the other forms of control they had exerted when they had legally reduced human beings to property. As historian Douglas Blackmon documented so powerfully in his book *Slavery by Another Name*, the same people who had just been enslaved were often arrested for petty crimes and made to work—often in the same fields from which they had just been set free—as part of the nation's "convict leasing" program.[12] This practice was insulated from constitutional challenge because the Thirteenth Amendment outlawing slavery retained a caveat that has continued to shape our culture to this day: it says that "Neither slavery nor involuntary servitude, *except as a punishment for crime whereof the party shall have been duly convicted,* shall exist within the United States."[13]

This was not the last time America would substitute explicit race-based control with control based on one's status as a convicted criminal. Michelle Alexander's *The New Jim Crow* traces this history with unrelenting clarity, meticulously drawing a damning continuity between slavery, convict leasing, Jim Crow, and mass incarceration.[14] "Like Jim Crow (and slavery)," Alexander argues, "mass incarceration operates as a tightly networked system of laws, policies, customs, and institutions that operate collectively to ensure the subordinate status of a group defined largely by race."[15] Or as she puts it more explicitly: "Today's lynching is a felony charge. Today's lynching is incarceration. Today's lynch mobs are professionals. They have a badge; they have a law degree. A felony is a modern way of saying, 'I'm going to hang you up and burn you.' Once you get that F, you're on fire."[16]

People of color are not immune from acting as agents in the expansion of incarceration. That said, their participation in its expansion in no way disproves the fact that systems have structural racism at their core, nor does it indicate that black people's relationship to the punishment of their communities is the same as white people's. As legal scholar James Forman Jr. traces in his book *Locking Up Our Own*, black people—as constituents and elected officials, and as practitioners in the criminal justice system—have long been a part of the rise of mass incarceration. For some, this was rooted in a particular demand for morality and a belief that a small portion of the community was compromising the integrity of the rest and should be separated from it for the well-being of the whole. For others, it arose out of a desperate need to secure the safety of their families and loved ones in a context in which structural factors made violence nearly inevitable and punishment seemed the only near-term solution available. And for some, it stemmed from—only somewhat ironically—a distrust of white people: of their permissiveness about drugs that were poisoning a generation of young black people; and of their restrictiveness about guns, which black people had not been allowed to own for generations because white people feared the power they could wield collectively if they were armed.[17] None of these responses required dehumanizing black people, but to the contrary, were often rooted in a deep regard for their fellow black people's humanity. But all of the responses involved grappling with the impact that structural racism was having on black communities and the inaccessibility of more transformative solutions, such as policy shifts that would bring about improved economic stability, education, or health care.[18]

Alongside the country's exceptional punitiveness runs a concurrent trend of extreme impunity. A society can abide this level of punishment only if some people are promised protection from it. We see that protection throughout our culture. Wealthy people are far less likely to be imprisoned for crimes, whether violent offenses or white-collar crimes.[19] Men are highly unlikely to be convicted of and sentenced to incarceration for crimes like rape and domestic violence.[20] White people are far less likely than their black counterparts to be arrested, charged, convicted, sentenced, or given the maximum sentence for any crimes, including drug, property, and violent offenses.[21] And strikingly, although black people who kill white people account for a disproportionate number of those sentenced to death, virtually no one receives this ultimate sanction for killing a black person.[22]

Educating white people about these disparities will not be enough to end them. In fact, evidence shows that the opposite may be true: the disparities are not just a product of policy; they drive it. A heart-wrenching Stanford University study found that when white people were asked about the appropriate level of punishment for a crime, they showed some moderation in their responses.[23] When a matched group of white people was first told about racial disparities, that group supported a higher level of punishment than their counterparts who had not been given that information. That means that when white people understood that the law had a disproportionately negative impact on people of color, they became more supportive of that law, not less. That reflects two interconnected realities: (1) deep-seated anti-black racism continues to thrive among white people, whether conscious or not, and (2) white people expect insulation from punishment (and overall are not as afraid of draconian laws we think will not ever be applied to us or our white loved ones).

The problem is that punishment and impunity are both incompatible with the response to crime that can transform behavior and heal harm: accountability. The following chapter will explore why accountability works so well. But first it will be useful to explore why punishment does not.

———

Some of America's attachment to prison comes from overestimating the efficacy of punishment as an agent of change. Social psychologists have long noted the ways in which punishment is limited as a method to affect behavior positively. Research shows limited returns from punishment overall, and diminishing returns on both the individual and societal level as penalties are used more frequently.[24] Similarly, research has shown that many people experience other types of sanctions imposed against them as comparable to or even more difficult than incarceration.[25] Punishment is often presumed, particularly in public discourse, to be effective, with little rigor applied to that presumption—whether intellectual rigor or careful examination of the results that punishment produces. An exception to that trend, a 2014 National Academy of Sciences report on the causes and consequences of incarceration, maintains that "any punishment that is more severe than is required to achieve valid and applicable purposes is . . . morally unjustifiable."[26] The moral integrity of our criminal justice policy depends on our accurately understanding the roles punishment can—and cannot—effectively serve.

There is a vast theoretical literature about punishment written by scholars trying to make some sense of what we do as a people.[27] Most of these theories converge around four key purposes of punishment: deterrence, rehabilitation, incapacitation, and retribution.[28] It is useful to explore each purpose as it relates to the reduction of violence—and to scrutinize why punishment has not delivered safety to the degree that much of this foundational theory suggests it could and should.

Deterrence

Individual deterrence is the belief that punishment will keep someone who has committed a crime from doing so again—or that the threat of punishment will prevent someone from committing a crime in the first place. General deterrence suggests that punishing one person for a given crime will deter others from committing the same crime (and possibly even other crimes). As a theory, deterrence is compelling enough, but in reality it is crushed by a combination of pervasive arbitrariness, a lack of civic education, extreme racial disparities, and profound despair in the communities most impacted by crime.

Deterrence theory assumes the existence of a set of circumstances that do not exist. To begin with, it assumes a level of civic knowledge and awareness—that everybody knows what the consequences are for a given crime. Increasing the length of sentences does not work to motivate change if no one knows that those sentences have changed. As a culture, we simply do not possess that level of knowledge or awareness. Nor do people typically learn about their peers' and neighbors' sentences with enough context to anticipate the consequences of their own actions.

In a program I directed more than a decade ago, I asked the young people I worked with—all of whom had been incarcerated—what penalty they thought might accompany the crime they were committing at the time they committed it. Some of them (about a third) admitted honestly that they gave no thought whatsoever to the penalty. Others (roughly another third) said they thought the penalty would be substantially less than it turned out to be. People in the third segment of the group said they had anticipated a far greater penalty than what was in fact allowable but were indifferent to that consequence at the time. Because one might argue that incarcerated young people are precisely the group for whom deterrence did not work and that maybe everyone else got the message, I asked a group of high school students in a poetry class I was teaching what they thought the penalties were for a range of common crimes. The answers were all over the place—extremely low and extremely high—and almost none of them accurate. Some of this is because of the lack of civic education in our society, and some of it is because the sanctions are applied so arbitrarily or in such a biased manner (many people get a slap on the wrist for the same crimes that result in enormous consequences for others) that drawing any correlation between actions and consequences is almost impossible.

The problem with arbitrariness and bias is that deterrence theory also assumes a consistency of sanctions. Deterrence works only if the same action typically results in the same consequence—and the reality of the U.S. justice system could not be further from that. Sanctions are inconsistently applied by different decision makers (and often even by the same ones), shaped irrefutably by race and class (and perceptions about both), and distorted to a degree that would make it difficult for people to predict a likely response to their own behavior.[29]

But perhaps more crucially, deterrence also assumes—and arguably even requires—that people have hope. It assumes that you have reason to believe that if you do not engage in certain negative actions, you will not suffer the same consequences as people who do. That means not only that you will not go to jail if you do not break the law, but that you will be able to get a good education, get a job, raise your family, live in peace, and not be hurt. One of the most underdeveloped dimensions of deterrence—and a significant part of why it fails so profoundly in this country—is that people are not guaranteed the benefits of full healthy participation in our society when they abide by the law. The United States does not deliver on the promise of the social contract. People do not get the benefits of doing their part. And absent that, the whole deal falls apart.

Punishment—and deterrence in particular—is rooted in an assumption that people lack an adequate level of fear, and that if they were more afraid (in this case, of the consequences of their actions), they would behave differently. The trouble is, anyone who has lived and loved people in the communities where violence is most present knows that fear is everywhere. Fear is omnipresent. It is overwhelming. Fear of violence. Fear of prison. Fear of loss. It is based not just on the anticipation that something bad might happen, but in the lived experience of that very thing happening over and over again—of surviving violence, of surviving incarceration, of watching loved ones terribly hurt, of losing loved ones to the grave, of losing them to prison. What appears as adolescent hubris is often in fact its opposite: a heightened sense of vulnerability.[30]

Research has shown that many adolescents anticipate and even overestimate their imminent mortality.[31] They believe their deaths are inevitable, and the feeling that manifests as "risky behavior" is often not a sense of invincibility, but rather a sense of despair. In neighborhoods where people hear gunshots through the night and walk around chalk outlines and police CAUTION tape in the morning, virtually the only people who are not afraid are those who have felt so much fear that they have crossed through it into numbness. And in neighborhoods where, statistically speaking, one in three boys born today are likely to be incarcerated in their lifetime, the only young men who do not fear prison are young men who have accepted its inevitability or have exceeded their maximum capacity for fear so much as to have become inured to it. The problem is that numbness is not indifference, nor is it a feeling of omnipotence. Numbness, like despair, is what experts call "a trauma response" to an unmanageable excess of fear and terror. For the purposes of deterrence, the trouble with trauma responses is that you cannot scare them away. To the contrary: increasing fear only further entrenches such responses and the harm that arises from them.

Research bears this out. Studies show only a limited and disputed link between the length of sentences and an increased deterrent effect—on either the individual or community level.[32] What, then, of the research suggesting that deterrence has some positive effect? It is increasingly clear that while overwhelming evidence demonstrates that the severity of a sanction does not affect behavior, the swiftness and certainty of it might.[33] This means that we do not get to safety through excessive punishment, but rather through consistency. These findings have been used to justify a great deal of interventions focused on certainty and swiftness (with decidedly mixed outcomes) but have not always been put to what is arguably their most profound use: allowing us as a culture to detach from severe sentences with an evidence-based confidence that such detachment will not diminish our safety. That notion is borne out in the data, including recent studies that show the vast reduction of incarceration in California and New York has not contributed in any measurable way to a rise in crime.[34]

The upshot is that a community where people who commit harm are consistently apprehended and meaningful consequences are consistently and quickly imposed does not need those responses to be severe, brutal, or lengthy. In fact, the opposite stands to be true, as we know that the lasting impacts of incarceration on communities include great damage to the very social fabric that holds community well-being in place.[35] What is required, then, is not to ignore the wrongdoing or impose greater and greater sentences, but rather to foster meaningful responses to harm that can displace the current pattern of arbitrariness and the toxic mixture of extreme punitiveness and impervious impunity.

Rehabilitation

The brutalities of prison have been widely documented, from the psychological torture of solitary confinement to the prevalence of sexual and other violence. Prisons suffer from overcrowding, are poorly equipped to handle the significant portion of incarcerated people who have mental illness, and have sustained massive cuts to the very programming—such as substance use treatment and college education—shown to reduce violence in prison and recidivism after release.[36] It would be hard to conceive of a less rehabilitative environment than a U.S. prison.

People often talk about someone being sent to prison to "teach them a lesson." It seems that rehabilitation would consist largely of learning that lesson. But we are never particularly clear about what that lesson is meant to be, nor how it is taught or whether it is ever learned. In theory, the lesson would be whatever the incarcerated person needs to learn to ensure that he or she would not commit further crime. But of course multiple learnings contribute to that transformation. To live a life without crime or violence or both, one needs to understand the impact of one's actions on others, take responsibility for those actions, and make things as right as possible. People need to develop the skill set to make good decisions—both to exercise sound consequential thinking and develop the capacity to control their impulses and wrangle their anger safely and productively. They need to connect their actions to the consequences that follow, and to do so, people need a context in which responses are clear, swift, proportionate, consistent, and fair. People need to be able to make ends meet legally, so they need the skills to get and retain a job that can generate a living wage. They need to heal through old wounds that drive cycles of violence—to uproot the pain, heal what can be healed, and develop strategies to cope with what remains. They need to disrupt any unhealthy relationships to alcohol and other drugs, and to learn strategies to address the underlying drivers of any harmful use. And they need to build healthy, strong, interdependent relationships that can protect the durability of these lessons in the face of change, loss, and other stressors.

These things are hard to do in any context. Prisons make the work of rehabilitation strikingly difficult—though to the great credit of so many people who are incarcerated, never totally impossible. Large portions of incarcerated people live in conditions where there are far more people in each housing unit than intended, as is the case in prisons across the United States.[37] This overcrowding at its worst contributes to substantial and pervasive violence, but even at its best results in constant, piercing clamor, chaos, and sleeplessness.[38] This is not a place conducive to reflection.

What's more, prison does not merely fail to rehabilitate the people it confines: it contributes to the likelihood that they will commit greater harm in the future. Recent research has established prison's criminogenic impact—meaning that it is a measurable, statistically significant *driver* of crime and violence.[39] As scholars Cullen, Jonson, and Nagin summarize, prisons are no likelier than noncustodial sanctions to reduce recidivism—and what is worse, "the use of custodial sanctions may have the unanticipated consequence of making society less safe."[40] Many studies that claim to demonstrate that prison has some efficacy do so by comparing incarceration to nothing at all—rather than comparing it to other strategies or interventions. This distorts the reality of what happens in practice, and conceals the harmful effects of prison that become particularly clear when prisons are appropriately and realistically compared with sanctions like community-based interventions that serve as alternatives to incarceration, treatment programs, and probation (the other likeliest responses to cases that move through the criminal justice system).[41] Cullen et al. describe the criminogenic impact of incarceration as follows: "For a lengthy period of time, they [incarcerated people] associate with other offenders, endure the pains of imprisonment, risk physical victimization, are cut off from family and prosocial contacts on the outside, and face stigmatization as 'cons.' Imprisonment is thus not simply a cost to be weighed in future offending but, more important, a social influence that shapes inmates' attitudes toward crime and violence, peer networks, ties to the conventional order, and identity."

They conclude accordingly that "most criminologists would predict that, on balance, offenders become more, rather than less, criminally oriented due to their prison experience."[42] This is consistent with the findings of a wide variety of related research. In examining the effect of labeling people (in this case with terms such as "convicts" and "felons") on their future behavior, one study of 95,919 people found that those who received a formal label were more likely to recidivate than those who did not.[43] A 1993 study found that prison had strong direct criminogenic effects, and a more recent 2002 study showed no evidence that incarceration reduced recidivism, and in fact found that it was associated with an *increase* in recidivism, particularly when compared with other sanctions like probation.[44] A number of rigorous and highly regarded meta-analyses, which integrate the findings of a range of studies to discern an overall trend or conclusion, have found that incarceration is associated with increases in recidivism ranging from 7 percent to 14 percent.[45]

When we understand what drives violence, the fact that prison contributes to it should not surprise us. Decades of research about the individual-level causes of violence (as opposed to community conditions like poverty and disenfranchisement) has demonstrated four key drivers: shame, isolation, exposure to violence, and a diminished ability to meet one's economic needs. At the same time, prison is characterized by four key features: shame, isolation, exposure to violence, and a diminished ability to meet one's economic needs. As a nation, we have developed a response to violence that is characterized by precisely what we know to be the main drivers of violence. We should not be surprised, then, when the system produces exactly the results we would expect. It is worthwhile to look at these four drivers in more depth.

First, shame. Shame is widely regarded as a producer of violence. Chapter 3 explores this connection in greater depth, but it is essential here to lift up Dr. James Gilligan's influential work developed over decades of practice, which identifies shame as the central driver of people's choices to commit violence.[46] Gilligan distills the desire to commit violence as an attempt to quell arising feelings of shame—which include weakness, inadequacy, worthlessness, and failure—by eradicating or punishing the person perceived as the source of that feeling and displacing shame with a feeling of pride through the exercise of power and control.

This may mean a man beats his girlfriend who has borne witness to his limitations. It may mean that someone who is ashamed of having been unable to protect his loved ones from harm in turn causes harm to someone else, even someone other than the person who hurt his family. It may mean that someone who was disrespected in front of his peers visibly reasserts his power through violence. Shame is a tremendously uncomfortable feeling, and few people can abide it for long without seeking a pathway out. When the most available way out appears to be violence, people often choose it just to quiet the intolerable sense of shame that otherwise agitates and haunts them. Dr. John Rich has talked about this dynamic in the context of street violence, and distills the "code of the street" to being largely a matter of demonstrating and securing respect and managing disrespect.[47] This respect is not just about ego. Rather, respect is widely understood as a safeguard against injury and death—as it is only people who are respected who can expect to be protected from otherwise inevitable and widespread violence. Together with Gilligan's analysis, this means experiences that diminish, degrade, or emasculate people—particularly when that happens visibly and publicly—are a recipe for violence.

Imagine, then, the levels of shame in prison. Begin with the fact that many people are ashamed of the decisions they made that resulted in their incarceration and the great losses they and their loved ones have suffered and will continue to suffer as a result. Add to that the way in which prison is defined in part by an utter lack of privacy and a total exposure over which people have no power: people are showering in front of others, using the bathroom in front of others, dressing and undressing in front of others, being sick when they are sick and broken when they are grieving and visible in every moment and emotion and physical condition they endure. Then add the reality of violence—sexual violence, physical assault, and the constant threat of both. Add the ways in which people are visibly forced into conceding a seat in the dining hall, a turn in the gym, an item obtained from commissary, a place in line, a shower, a meal, a bed.

Add to that the ways that corrections officers frequently diminish the humanity of incarcerated people—not just in the form of violence, but in behavior that is secured by the threat of violence and the enormous power differential: times when correctional officers call incarcerated people names and dare them to respond, push them, insult them, insult their families, tear their bibles and step on their prayer rugs, throw their food away in front of them, subject them to searches of their cells and their bodies, force them to strip, make fun of their bodies, make fun of their conditions, make fun of their lack of freedom, taunt them, threaten them, toy with them, and deny them basic dignities.

Add all the times when people are beaten in plain sight, witnessed as they lie prone, bleeding, unconscious, racked with pain; and when their scars, as well as the process of healing through their injuries, are fully visible to everyone around them. Remember, too, that most of these people are survivors—of violence, of abuse, of harm done to them as children—and so the shame of that unhealed pain underlies every instance of degradation and fear. Together, even when an individual does not directly experience serious violence (and those cases are rare), these factors are a powder keg of shame that not only characterizes the period of a person's incarceration, but often accompanies them home, even as they secure their physical freedom.

Second, isolation. Strong, durable connections to others—particularly those who have our short- and long-term interest at heart—reduce the likelihood that we will commit violence.[48] This makes sense. So much of violence relates to unprocessed pain and loss, and relationships that can witness and help transform those experiences can help people identify outlets other than violence for responding to their hurt. For the parts of violence that relate to a feeling of vulnerability and exposure and an associated powerlessness, supportive relationships can help people feel connected and protected in a way that softens the need to assert their power unilaterally. When violence is about poverty and an inability to meet one's basic needs, having people who will make introductions to potential employers, offer temporary housing, make loans, share or pool resources, and help strategize about pathways to stability can diminish a person's perceived need to acquire resources through violence. Connection is also associated with a greater sense of self-efficacy, including one's ability to make changes to the circumstances that create limitations or pain.

Finally, being witnessed by people we respect can fortify our commitment to be our best selves: for many people, one of the strongest protectors against harmful behavior is our estimation of how those we respect will react to our choices. Isolation is the enemy of all of these protections. It is an ally of trauma, as silence fortifies traumatic stress and can perpetuate cycles of pain. Similarly, isolation stimulates and exacerbates shame, as our separation from people only serves to reinforce our notions of our unworthiness and our distance from human community. Isolation disengages the anchor we have placed in relationship and sets us to sea unmoored from the love, values, and obligations that otherwise guide and constrain our behavior.

Prison is made of isolation. Its fundamental nature is to separate people from their communities. Not only are people physically separated, but phone calls to people on the outside are restricted to particular times and durations and are typically extraordinarily costly (often as much as $13 per call, frequently with additional service and connection fees).[49] Visits are often limited by a wide range of ever-evolving restrictions and, particularly when people are incarcerated in prisons far from where they lived when they were free, can place unsustainable burdens on the loved ones visiting, especially during long sentences. Access to information and news can be limited, many books and periodicals are banned or unaffordable, and mail is restricted and almost always read by prison officials before being delivered to ensure that the content is allowable. (Even when the content is deemed acceptable, the fact that people know their writing will be read by authorities diminishes the honesty and intimacy of what they share.) Although people can form strong bonds with others within a prison, the prevalence of violence and abuse fosters an atmosphere of distrust that impedes the formation and durability of intimate friendships—and even when people build close relationships despite those barriers, friends are often transferred to other units and separated from each other for the duration of their sentences. Prison systematically separates people from those who love them most, who live lives that reflect the best of their shared values, who hold them most accountable, and who would otherwise contribute most to their development, healing, responsibility, and rehabilitation.

Isolation also happens in the extreme within prisons. Many prisons assert their power and control through the use of solitary confinement. Sometimes solitary confinement is used as a punishment for serious and violent infractions. Often is it used for far lesser offenses.[50] And it is too often used as retaliation for reporting harm, for raising concerns, for expressing unpopular views or worshipping the "wrong" God, and for organizing among incarcerated people.[51] Whatever the impetus for someone's relocation to a single cell, often no more than six by nine feet and with no window to the outside world, the experience of solitary confinement stretches the bounds of what human beings can survive with their sanity intact. The United Nations has classified periods of solitary confinement longer than fourteen days as torture.[52] Countless studies have demonstrated the short- and long-term debilitating impact of solitary confinement on people's mental health—consequences that can far outlast the time people spend enduring such intense punitive isolation.[53] As justice reformer Johnny Perez, who served three years (of thirteen years incarcerated) in solitary confinement in New York State, described it in an interview with the nonprofit group Solitary Watch:

> [There is] no interaction whatsoever with other humans. The officer comes by every hour, and even then there's no contact, no talking, no communicating, not even any eye contact in extreme cases. The last meal is at four-thirty in the afternoon with the next meal being at six o'clock in the morning. If you're not standing wide awake, by your door, when the officer walks by, you don't get a tray.
>
> [Solitary confinement] affected me in a number of ways at different times. As a youth—because I did some solitary time as a teenager—it affects your self-esteem, it affects your self-confidence and the way that you see yourself. It makes you aggressive, it makes you angry, it makes you impulsive, it makes you an introvert. . . . There were times when I contemplated thoughts of suicide, though I never voiced it out loud. I tended to internalize a lot of the oppression. . . . Sometimes, officers tell you, "Hey, you ain't shit! This is you, this is your life, you're nothing but a criminal." Hearing that once or twice is nothing, but hearing that day in and day out for months at a time, you start to say, "Damn, you know what, maybe I ain't. Maybe I'm *not* good enough. Maybe I am what they say that I am."
>
> As an adult . . . my behavior was more reactionary towards others. . . . I remember hating all authority figures, no matter who it was. Supervisors, officers, judges, lawyers, just hating the entire world, you know? So a lot of that was more outward, versus when I was a teenager, it was more self-directed. . . .

> I learned that with solitary—or even prison, but more like solitary—it's a second-by-second attack on your soul, where every second is spent thinking about the next second, and that just makes the day so long. You try to sleep it off, but sometimes too much sleeping drives you to be awake for long periods of time. . . . You don't do solitary time, you *survive* solitary time. And I know this to be true because some of my peers did not survive solitary time. They've either left psychologically different than when they came in, or committed suicide.[54]

It is hard to imagine a practice more contrary or detrimental to the aim of rehabilitation, and hard to imagine someone affirmatively transforming in such a tortured context. It is as impractical as it is immoral.

The third driver of violence is exposure to violence. Research and experience show decisively that there may be no experience more likely to predict committing future violence than surviving it.[55] These cycles and the interplay among individual and structural factors is explored further in chapter 6. And it is important to note here, in this context, the way in which violence itself normalizes violence. The prevalence of any experience can make that experience increasingly "normal" to the people who live it. Rather than widespread violence contributing to an increasing sense of its importance and urgency, it can—especially when unaddressed or unhealed—have the opposite effect: it can render that experience normal. When people are continually exposed to violence, it becomes the rule rather than the exception, as though the world arranges itself around violence rather than being disrupted by it. Exposure to violence also increases the likelihood of someone committing harm by modeling power through violence. When young people in particular see others acquire power—respect, positional authority, material wealth, or status—as a result of violence, it suggests a viable pathway to achieving it. Absent other accessible and visible routes to power, those who survive or witness violence may choose violence as the road to their own elevation. Trauma resulting from surviving or witnessing violence only increases the likelihood of these pathways. In addition to rage and numbness and difficulty regulating emotions, the hypervigilance that often results from trauma increases people's sense of danger, even in situations of relative safety, and can broaden the range of situations in which they perceive violence as necessary to securing their safety.

At its most basic, violence creates a context in which people experience a failure of systems or strategies for protection, and so seek out new or enhanced ones to make sure they will not be hurt or be hurt again. When violence itself appears to be such a strategy, people will often deploy it out of real or perceived necessity. And when people cannot secure that protection alone, they will seek connections that help them do so. This may include an individual, a loosely formed peer group, or a more formally organized "gang"—people who have committed or will join them in committing the violence they believe is necessary to ensure their survival. Exposure to violence requires and animates the rapid development of new safety strategies, and when the healthiest and least harmful strategies are unavailable or have failed, people turn to other ways to secure their respect, belongings, and lives. All too often and in far too many contexts, violence seems to be the one remaining strategy available for doing so.

The rates of violence experienced by incarcerated people are extraordinary. It is estimated that roughly half of incarcerated women experienced serious physical or sexual abuse as children, 86 percent experienced sexual violence in their lifetime, more than two-thirds experienced intimate partner violence, and nearly all experienced some form of violence prior to their incarceration.[56] That violence continues in new forms in jails and prison.[57] As author and advocate Donna Hylton, who served twenty-seven years in prison, wrote:

> For many women, imprisonment began long before the day they registered in prison. Years . . . decades . . . lives of abuse and neglect spurred many women to make one desperate decision that finally, ultimately led them to prison. Too often, by the time a woman commits a crime, her only goal has been survival.
>
> The prison system on the inside is the same as law enforcement on the outside, in my eyes and experience. They could do whatever they wanted to you no matter what you told them and no matter what the truth was. Unless you had a good ally in a powerful position to speak up for you, you were at their mercy and whim.
>
> For example, when a woman complains about an officer blackmailing her for sex or raping her, she is promptly thrown into "The Box" for months, even years. Why does the inmate, a woman, get punished for that kind of accusation? It is piling abuse on top of abuse.
>
> Forms of sexual abuse aren't about sex or gratification: they're about power and control. Domination of any kind hurts and manipulates the mind more than anything. Predators target the most vulnerable, and incarcerated women who have been subjected to violence are the most vulnerable of the vulnerable.
>
> In prison, everything is stripped from you, especially your self-pride. The link between domestic abuse and a prison full of wounded, broken, silenced,

crying women is undeniable. I realize that the physical, emotional, and mental abuse inflicted on women by men was universal and felt by most women to some degree—no matter her skin color, education level, or location—it was there, woven into the fabric of our lives.

The halls of Bedford [Hills Correctional Facility] were filled with women, the walking wounded, who asked the eternal questions that everyone asked; how and why did I get here and what reasons do I have to keep going, to keep living?[58]

The violence experienced by incarcerated people may be committed by other incarcerated people or by corrections staff. No matter who is responsible, the result is traumatizing to those who survive it and is typically met with impunity: very few acts of violence in prison result in meaningful responses, in part because reporting violence often exposes incarcerated people to more, rather than less, risk.[59] Violence is not an exception in prison—it is the daily, defining norm. Aside from the physical pain and injury so many people experience, the constancy of violence results in peak levels of hypervigilance, fear, and the pained, interminable alertness that surviving prison requires.

Prison violence is not limited to physical assault. The National Prison Rape Elimination Commission, a bipartisan effort by Congress to identify and address the extent of sexual violence in U.S. prisons and explore the adherence to the standards in the 2003 Prison Rape Elimination Act, found shocking rates of rape and other sexual violence in prisons across the country.[60] A 2007 Bureau of Justice Statistics study estimated that 60,500 people incarcerated in state and federal prisons were sexually abused in the prior twelve months alone.[61] Any survivor's experience of sexual violence requires a profound healing process, but first it requires at least a minimal level of safety. People who are sexually assaulted in prison are typically confined with—or, all too often, by—the very people who raped them. This means they live in the aftermath of their initial trauma in a context of continual threat at the very least, and more often with continual ongoing sexual violence.[62] The correctional officer with the key to the individual's doorway out of this pain is often the person who caused the harm in the first place. Added to that horrific dynamic is the reality that people who report experiencing sexual violence in prison, particularly when that violence is committed by staff, often face fierce reprisal, including beatings, the deprivation of privileges, and relocation to solitary confinement.[63]

Finally, an inability to meet one's economic needs drives violence.[64] Poverty contributes to neighborhood-level factors that make violence more likely, such as poor education, lack of mental health and substance-use treatment resources, inadequate housing, and counterproductive policing strategies. It contributes to interpersonal factors that exacerbate stressors within families and in other relationships, such as strain or discord resulting from unemployment, barriers to paying child care costs or child support, untenable housing arrangements, and unmanageable debt, and to individual factors that diminish self-esteem, nurture shame, and block pathways to education and gainful employment, such as poor schooling, limited work experience, limited availability of steady employment opportunities, untreated trauma and illness, child care challenges that interfere with employment, and poor health and mental health.

Inequity can be acutely painful and may result in resentment and hurt, as it exposes the difference between one's difficult circumstances and the relative ease that others enjoy.[65] Further compounding such circumstances, lack of opportunity suggests the permanence of these conditions, the blockage of any pathways out, and the futility of effort and sacrifice.[66] Too many people who choose violence as a means of meeting their economic needs do not experience it as a choice between genuinely available options; they experience it as the inevitable election of the one option available to them.

The context of all-consuming violence described earlier as a core feature of prison is made worse there by a toxic combination of economic hardship and few if any options for positive engagement and development. The options for work in prison are limited, and even when work is available, the wages are minuscule—typically not more than twelve to forty cents per hour.[67] These wages first go to pay required fines and fees, which in felony cases often amount to thousands of dollars.[68] Even in that context, many incarcerated people continue to try to support their loved ones back home, and will send the remaining meager funds they have to their family on the outside.

These barriers to economic stability and self-sufficiency continue after people are released, as many leave with obligations to pay outstanding fines and fees. It is widely known that a criminal record can be a barrier to obtaining gainful employment, so the prospects for formerly incarcerated people to earn a living wage are vastly reduced.[69] While "ban the box" and other efforts to prevent employment discrimination on the basis of a criminal record have gained traction in recent years, the barriers persist, and even in the absence of discriminatory practices, the fact that someone has not accumulated work experience for the duration of their sentence is often detrimental to their ability to secure economic stability.[70] This is problematic not only because it extends punishment beyond the end of a sentence, but because employment is demonstrated to help guard against recidivism.[71]

One underutilized strategy is demonstrably successful at preventing recidivism: college education in prison, which has been shown to dramatically reduce rates of re-offending and re-incarceration.[72] Still, only a minute fraction of prisons offer college education, and then only to a small percentage of the people incarcerated in those facilities. Because people in jail or prison are excluded from receiving federal financial aid available to all other college students, few incarcerated people can afford to participate remotely in higher education while they are imprisoned.[73]

Other educational opportunities are also rare. Few prisons have adequate basic education, vocational training, substance use treatment, mental health treatment, or other programs that would support people upon release to lead meaningful, productive, and law-abiding lives. These programs can work when they are available, but despite soaring investments in corrections across the country—and despite the relatively low costs of such programs in comparison to other spending on incarceration—those dollars have not led to an associated rise in the kinds of interventions that might truly contribute to rehabilitation.[74] Most people, then, have few outlets for personal development that could sustain their well-being while incarcerated and position them for success upon release.

The factors that drive violence and fundamentally characterize prison are all mutually reinforcing. Exposure to violence drives isolation, isolation drives shame, shame drives poverty, poverty drives exposure to violence, and so on. Far from being rehabilitative, prison all but guarantees the durability and continuation of cycles of violence, and in many cases increases the likelihood of further harm rather than reducing it.

Incapacitation

Incapacitation is perhaps the least disputed of the effects of incarcerating someone. It is the simplest: it just means that for the time people are imprisoned, they are physically incapable of causing further harm to others in society (other than those who are incarcerated with them). There is truth to that. And there are unquestionably people who cannot be in society without hurting others.

But even that seemingly straightforward benefit of incarceration turns out to be more complex. Take this situation as an example:

Pablo was riding the subway home from school when he looked up and saw a group of young men approach him.[75] He knew immediately it was trouble. Two of them had been harassing him for the past five years. When he first arrived in the United States when he was in the sixth grade, one of them said something to him after his first day of school and swung at him. (Pablo didn't speak English yet, so he still does not know what the boy said.) He fought back and—probably only because of the adrenaline that fear sent coursing through his body—won. Ever since then, these boys had never left him alone.

This time was worse. One of the young men in the group flashed a gun at Pablo. Pablo jumped off the train at the next stop and ran to the police. They apprehended the young man with the gun, but not the others. Even if they had, these boys technically hadn't done anything wrong.

At the time, Pablo wanted to be a police officer after he graduated high school. He hated the violence that plagued his East New York, Brooklyn, neighborhood and admired people who stood up to it. He saw the police as those people. When he engaged them for protection after the incident on the train, he expected to be safer. He was not.

Pablo made a report and the same week testified before a grand jury, helping the prosecutor secure an indictment of the young man with the gun—whose name Pablo now learned was Alberto. The court issued an order of protection requiring Alberto to stay away from Pablo's work and home.

The next day, Pablo came home from work and found his younger brother collapsed in the doorway of his apartment building. The boys from the train had come to his house (they had learned the address from the court's protective order) looking for Pablo, but when they did not find him, they beat his brother instead. Pablo felt a great responsibility to ensure the well-being of his family and was terrified and enraged about what had happened. He looked at his brother's injuries. He thought of his mother and younger sister upstairs. This time, he didn't call the police.

Pablo did not go out seeking the boys who did this, but he did stop attending school and work to stay home with his family regularly. Later, he would tell staff at Common Justice that he looked into the average police response time to his address and found that it was an hour and eight minutes. He asked what he was supposed to do for an hour and eight minutes if the young men who beat his brother were knocking down his door. He considered getting a weapon for the first time in his life—not to retaliate, but to be prepared to defend his family if they broke through the door and held that gun to his mother's head.

Pablo was unable to graduate from high school on time, his relationship with his girlfriend became strained as he withdrew from everyone but his immediate family, and his employment was tenuous because of all his absences. He could imagine a thousand ways the situation could escalate, ways he and others could lose their lives, but he could not see a way forward to safety.

When Common Justice reached out to him to tell him he was eligible for services and that, if he was interested, Alberto could participate in the program too, he asked a series of pointed, methodical questions and then offered an unequivocal yes. As he said then, "I'm not afraid of Alberto. He's not the problem. The problem is the short, loud one and the one with the braids." Pablo explained that he believed Alberto's incarceration would only exacerbate the tensions he'd had with those two young men and the larger group of people they were connected to. Pablo chose Common Justice because he thought it could help finally put the conflict to rest. He was not sure it would work, but it was the first thing that seemed as if it might. It was not that it made him happy. It was that it made sense.

Alberto seized the opportunity to participate. As part of his responsibilities in the program, he was required to do a wide range of things, including engaging in a violence intervention curriculum and attending school regularly. But perhaps most important to Pablo, one agreement required Alberto to communicate to those other young men that Pablo and his family should be protected from any violence, threat, or harm. It was not an agreement the court could require—but as an independent program, Common Justice could reach further into the community to get at the underlying causes of conflict.

Several weeks later, Alberto brought those young men to Common Justice's office and told them in front of staff, "I respect Pablo. And I respect his family. And I expect you to do the same. And if you can't respect them, then I need you to understand that if anyone touches a hair on any of their heads, the DA will come looking for me. And if the DA comes looking for me, I will come looking for you." He leveraged the best and worst parts of the reputation he had built with these peers to protect Pablo and his family.

At the time of this writing, more than eight years after the meeting, Pablo and his family have not been hurt or threatened. What's more, Pablo has gotten his life back—he moved out of his family's home, has advanced in his career, grown personally, and stopped living in the constant, legitimate fear that he or his loved ones would be harmed. And Alberto has honored his commitments—keeping a job, building his own future, and being a different kind of role model for the young men and others like them who followed his lead that day on the train.

About a year after the meeting with Alberto, Pablo asked me, seemingly out of nowhere, *How many cops are there in New York?* And I said, about 35,000.[76] And he said, *And how many people work at Common Justice?* I told him the answer at the time: Six. Pablo said, *That's hilarious.* I asked why. And he said, *Well, because it was y'all who could keep me safe.*

What is evident in this story is a reality that incapacitation fails to account for—that most violence is not about a single "bad" individual intent on causing harm. Most violence happens in context and in relationship—the context of alliances and rivalries, of history and conflict, of poverty and competition for resources, of drug markets and underground economies, of neighborhoods and of families. Although sometimes the threat to a person's or a community's well-being is a single person whose absence would make them safe, the vast majority of time that danger is about a larger ecosystem that made the harm likely in the first place.

The (usually temporary) removal of a person from that ecosystem unquestionably changes it—sometimes for the better. But just as often, the temporary removal of a person creates disruptions in that ecosystem, ones that can ripple out and lead to greater danger and violence: the abusive partner who returns from prison angrier and escalates his tactics of power, control, and violence to try to make sure that his partner never feels safe calling the police ever again; the person in the early throes of an emerging mental illness who commits a robbery and serves a prison sentence that exacerbates his trauma and solidifies his condition as a chronic and severe one, heightening his volatility when he comes home; the gang leader who committed assaults but also served to restrain the appetite for more senseless and severe violence among the young gang members who looked up to him, young men who, in the absence of his moderating influence, escalate from beatings to homicide; and yes, the young man who calls the police and comes home a few weeks later to find his brother beaten bloody on the doorstep and a once-diminishing conflict newly alight with danger and urgency.

Then we have to consider that the people who were committing violence were also doing more than that—they were being mothers and fathers to their children, caregivers to their elders, confidants to their friends, supports to their partners. Even people

who commit a great deal of violence spend the vast majority of
their time doing other things, many of which have value to their
loved ones and communities. They are workers, family members,
friends, neighbors. When they are "incapacitated," the benefits of
their participation in their lives are lost, often with great consequence for those left behind.

Perhaps the most salient example of this is what happens to
children when a parent is incarcerated. Research has shown that
children of incarcerated parents are more likely to experience
mental health challenges, traumatic stress, behavioral issues, stigma and shame, reduced educational prospects, and, in certain
cases, a greater likelihood of being arrested and/or incarcerated
themselves.[77] Separation from a parent can be extraordinarily difficult for a child. Ebony Underwood founded We Got Us Now, a
national movement grounded in the mission to engage, educate,
elevate, and empower children impacted by parental incarceration and to do the same with other stakeholders. While Underwood does not understate the devastating impact her father's
incarceration has had on her life, she also pushes back against
the stereotype that children of incarcerated parents inevitably lead lives of crime. Neither she nor any of her siblings has
been incarcerated—and that is obviously true of countless other
children who share a similar experience. Still, no success ever
resolved the pain of her father's absence. As she wrote:

> My father and I have a wonderful relationship. He calls
> me almost every day, sends birthday, holiday and even
> Valentine's Day cards. He's 61 years old and techno-
> logically savvy so nowadays he emails me. I can talk
> to him about almost anything and he will lovingly
> impart knowledge and wisdom. So you might expect
> that Father's Day would be a day of celebration for us.
> It is not. It's a day that's bittersweet. In April 2015, the
> NYT wrote that there are 1.5 million men missing in

the Black community because of mass incarceration. My father is one of them.

In 1988 . . . my father, William Underwood . . . received his first and only felony conviction, an extremely harsh mandatory minimum drug sentence of 20 years in prison, plus life without parole. . . .

I was 14 years old and hearing my father's arrest put me into a complete state of shock. If that wasn't enough, his sentence to die in prison was devastatingly, traumatizing and utterly confusing to me because my father was deeply devoted to my 3 siblings and me. . . .

Only through telling my story have I begun to realize how much my father's incarceration has not only taken an emotional toll on my life, but the lives of countless others. Even as now adult children of an incarcerated parent, my siblings and I endure a lot of emotional pain. Although my father has maintained a solid relationship with each one of us from behind bars throughout the years, we are all still numb. My hope is that by sharing my story I can show other children and families whose fathers, grandfathers, uncles and sons are part of that 1.5 million missing black men that they are not alone. There is no legislation to change my father's prison sentence. His only avenue for relief is through presidential clemency. . . . Whatever day that happens and he comes home will be considered Father's Day to me.[78]

As Underwood focuses on children of incarcerated people, Gina Clayton, the founder of Essie Justice Group, works to harness the power of women who have incarcerated loved ones, in the service of ending mass incarceration. Essie Justice Group speaks to the far-reaching impact someone's incarceration has on the people he or she leaves behind, noting that "an overlooked effect of mass incarceration is that today an astounding one in four women and nearly one in two Black women has a family member in prison. The sense of loss is painful, acute, and often borne in silence, leading to illness, severe depression, and even suicide."[79] This loss is what "incapacitation" of incarcerated people looks like in practice.

In the prisons themselves, incapacitation raises the question of whom we regard as deserving of protection, because while incarcerated people are separate from the free world, they still have regular access to a great number of people: other incarcerated people. When we value the humanity of those who are incarcerated and acknowledge that they are at risk when locked up with people who cannot or will not stop causing terrible harm, we have to become more honest about the benefits of incarceration. Imprisonment does not render people incapable of harming others. It only renders people incapable of harming anyone beyond those walls. That does not deny the value to some people of having those who harmed them and may continue to harm them separated from their communities. But it does demand our honesty in admitting who is and is not included within the scope of our protection.

The vast majority of people who are incarcerated come home, so we cannot talk about incapacitation without acknowledging that it is temporary and that, given prison's criminogenic qualities, it can actually serve to increase danger—including to crime survivors—in both the near and long term.[80] And although people desist from violence overall as they grow older, evidence shows that incarceration can interrupt the natural trajectory toward desistance, delaying rather than advancing a person's natural progression toward nonviolence.[81]

More broadly, the combined benefits and limitations of incapacitation should challenge us to rethink the place of prison in our culture as a whole. What if the question is not: who is dangerous and how should we punish them? But rather: who are we incapable of holding safely in our communities, and what would it take to be able to hold them?

If we ask the question that way, it turns our attention away from our obsession with identifying the worst among us and toward strategies that support the development of community capacity to prevent and address harm. This reorientation still allows for the fact that there are some people whose presence among us makes us all unsafe, but it posits that the problem is not simply their inherent dangerousness, but rather the limitations of the tools available to us to contain or change their behavior. If that is the problem, the solution lies in developing more tools, not in eliminating the person we fear. Given what we know about the lasting, damaging impacts of incarceration, it is our obligation to minimize our use of it to the degree possible. The pathway there will not simply be about identifying who is the "lowest risk" and minimizing their exposure to punishment, but also about expanding the range of strategies available to hold more and more people safely in our communities.

To offer an analogy to medicine: when a doctor estimates the deadliness of a medical condition, the severity of symptoms is certainly a factor, but what is far more significant in a prognosis is the availability of an appropriate treatment for the patient's condition. The question is not just: how sick are they? It is also: how capable are we of curing them? Doctors remain interested in the causes and symptoms of their patient's illness, but not simply as a means of identifying the extent of the sickness. They are interested because this understanding will help get the person well, and we will all be better as a result.

These same doctors would concede that a quarantine sometimes works, but they also would insist that it is a highly unsophisticated tool. We know that if we as a society found ourselves indefinitely quarantining more than 2 million of our members on any given day (and if that number were more than four times what it had been just thirty years earlier), we would understand it as a state of emergency and we would turn our attention to developing other strategies, if only because we could not tolerate—practically or morally—the separation of so many of our loved ones for so long without trying to do something different.

None of this is to say that our society is ready to do away with prisons today. Although they are limited in efficacy and dehumanizing to those incarcerated there, it would be irresponsible to pretend that the capacity exists yet to safely hold all people accountable in other ways. Even though punishment for punishment's sake runs contrary to the demands of accountability and to survivors' expressed desire for interventions that reduce the likelihood of further harm, that does not mean that incapacitation has no value in temporarily securing safety in certain situations. Some people who pose an immediate risk to others need to be separated from others, but confinement does not require degradation, and prisons throughout the world demonstrate that it is possible to take people's freedom without also taking their dignity and safety.[82]

We can acknowledge that incapacitation has its place. But we have to acknowledge equally its limitations, including its deficiencies in producing safety in both the short and the long term. We might think of it as a tool that is a blunt crude placeholder—one that at times accomplishes something no other tool in our toolbox can, but at a great price that is increasingly too high for us to pay. As such, it is a strategy from which we must earn—through advocacy, innovation, and rigor—our independence.

Retribution

The one thing punishment can always be relied on to produce is punishment. Advocates of retribution believe in the value of punishment for punishment's sake, in part as the one way a society can convey its unequivocal disapprobation of a harmful act.[83] Theorists also suggest that retributive justice can satisfy a society's desire for revenge, allowing the state to fulfill that emotional desire and thus resolving the individual's craving to do so outside the law.[84] The problem is what happens when the retributive impulse runs contrary to the well-being of a society. What if incarcerating someone increases the risk to the public safety and fails to meet the needs of the person who survived the crime? To what degree do we do something for "its own sake" when its impact is harmful, including to those who were harmed in the first place? Even if the state's job is in some ways to displace individual impulses to seek revenge, the state is not required to do so in a vengeful way. Surely, we can do better than a codified version of individual hatred, especially since we know that revenge fails to produce the kind of satisfaction we expect or hope it will in our moments of greatest grief and outrage.[85]

When we build policy that is based on an assumption of deficient morality in communities with high rates of violence, we betray a dehumanizing disrespect for the people who live there— who want the violence in their lives to stop more than anyone else does. But we also risk imposing strategies that run contrary to the very markers of morality that hold the community together, including humility, connection, mutual responsibility, and a prohibition against throwing anyone away.

Retribution becomes more complicated when we recognize that those we are punishing are almost invariably also people we have failed to protect. Nearly everyone who commits violence has survived it, and while that in no way excuses their actions, it reminds us that state-conducted retribution for violence is carried out almost entirely against survivors of violence.[86] We can develop respectful methods to hold people accountable that deny neither their culpability nor their humanity, but when our aim is simply to inflict pain, we end up hurting people our society failed to protect from victimization and harm in the first place.

Retribution sits uncomfortably at the intersection of two

aspects of our responses to harm: our desire for people to suffer
and our desire for people to change. When those desires are in
conflict, retribution always chooses suffering at the expense of
change. This is not just about a trade-off in values, though. Prioritizing suffering over change becomes even more difficult to
defend when we understand that the pain the state inflicts all too
often makes it more likely that others will suffer, and this means
the state is knowingly engaging in a form of punishment that
has been demonstrated to diminish safety and to generate future
pain. That is not what government is for.

But there is another option. It involves remembering that whatever moral basis for retribution exists does not lie in some inherent value of causing pain. Rather, it lies in the inherent value of
what and who was disregarded in the crime. This means the moral
requirement is not simply to convey our collective disapproval of
the harmful act, which is always only a negative gesture, but even
more so, to convey positively our respect for what that act damaged. Doing so demands that we do not just judge the person who
caused harm, we value the person who was hurt; we do not just
judge violence, we value safety and dignity. So the issue is not just
how we show our condemnation, but how we affirm unequivocally and powerfully the importance of what was violated—without
destroying the person who violated it. Seeking to express this
affirmation socially and structurally points us in a different direction than simple retribution (not coincidentally, one that crime
survivors point to as well): it points us toward accountability.

3

In Praise of Accountability

For all the faults of prison—the dehumanization, the prevalence of violence, the human and financial cost, the impracticality, the collateral consequences, the impact on families and other loved ones—it has another flaw that is rarely talked about: prison is a poor vehicle for accountability. This may sound strange in a country that has equated punishment and accountability, but the two are not the same.

When it comes down to it, being punished requires only that people sustain the suffering imposed for their transgression. It is passive. All one has to do to be punished is not to escape. It requires neither agency nor dignity, nor does it require work. It is undeniable that we as a country are tough on crime—particularly if we use the word "toughness" to signify acts of aggression. But in essential ways, prison lets people off the hook. No one in prison is required to face the human impacts of what they have done, to come face to face with the people whose lives are changed as a result of their decisions, to own their responsibility for those decisions and the pain they have caused, and to do the extraordinarily hard work of answering for that pain and becoming someone who will not commit that harm again. While incarcerated, people are brutalized, but they are also systematically protected and excused from all of those human burdens. Prisons render the most important kinds of human reckoning nearly impossible.

It is my belief that when we hurt people, we owe something, and one of the things we owe is to face what we have done. In that sense, when it comes to demanding that those who have committed wrongdoing pay that debt, there is nowhere softer on crime than prison. Our criminal justice system at once inflicts harms in ways that are inconsistent with human dignity and safety and, at the same time, is built precisely to excuse people from the obligations that *do* arise from hurting people.

When I was in my early twenties, I was teaching creative writing in a federal prison (with all the passion, commitment, hubris, and entitlement of a young white woman committed to changing the world). While I was there, I did something that I learned later is a widely recognized faux pas: I asked everyone what they did to get locked up. And the answers I got were explanations like: *I caught a case. I got hit with . . . I got slammed for . . . The DA did this . . . My lawyer did that . . . This snitch . . .* All of the answers were in passive tense; none exhibited real agency. It took until what might have been the one-hundredth person I asked before I got a response in the simple past tense: *I killed a man.* And it was when the man said that in no uncertain terms that I noticed the passivity and lack of responsibility in all of the other answers I had heard.

That is not because the people I asked were bad people. It is not even because they were not remorseful. It is because the criminal justice system is like kryptonite to accountability. If you are among the people who get caught for what you do, the one person who is formally on your side is your defense attorney, and the first thing that lawyer tells you to say (if you have an attorney who is good at the job) is "not guilty." So from the outset, those who have your interest at heart, those who see your humanity more than others do, those who have heard your whole story, stand on the side of denial. And then the process continues until, almost invariably in our system, you take a plea.[1] Almost invariably, this plea will be to something other than what you did—usually something less, though at times something more or just different. For instance, if you robbed someone and made a bargain with the prosecutor, you might take a plea to attempted robbery, even though you did more than attempt it. Similarly, if you and a friend robbed someone and your friend had a gun you did not know he had, you might take a plea to armed robbery, even though the gun was not yours and was never in your possession. You allocute—meaning that you describe in court what and when you did what you are admitting to—and the content of that is dictated not by what occurred, but by what your attorney instructs you to say, given the parameters of the plea you have negotiated.

And then you go to prison, where virtually no one talks to you about your crime—not the corrections staff, not the other incarcerated people, often not even your family on the phone or during visits. You may choose, in that context, to maintain your innocence. At the very least, you may deny or minimize or just obscure your guilt. And then you come home. And you have been supported to feel a lot of things, but remorse may not be primary among them. And when it is not, people see that in you—the way in which you are not fully settled in your responsibility—and they think you did not get it, that you should have served more time, that the sentence was not long enough to "teach you a lesson." And though that assumption is fundamentally flawed, their notion that something was missing is accurate.

For all the ravages of prison, it insulates people from the human impact of what they have done. While it is my belief that the people who commit harm do not belong in cages, should not be beaten, should not be sexually assaulted, should not be separated from everyone they have ever loved, it is also my belief that if we hurt someone, we have an obligation to face that pain, to face the person who felt that pain, to answer their questions, to hear how it affected them and their loved ones, to sit in that fire. That is in part because when we cause harm, we misuse our power, and accounting for harm therefore requires that we invert that misuse and put our power in service of repair. For all our fierce punitiveness as a nation, we do not require that of people. To the contrary: prison takes away the very power people should be obligated to use to make things right, thus rendering the possibility of repair nearly impossible. In that way, we let people off, and we let them off from exactly the thing the survivors of their crime need most.

It is hard to apprehend the full scope of what we have lost as a nation by allowing punishment to displace accountability. And although no new future ever erases history, we still have the opportunity to reverse that displacement, to reclaim what we have given up and what has been taken from us, and to begin the work of building the accountability-based culture we all deserve.

Often, people who recognize the harms caused by punishment seek to replace it with mercy. While mercy must have a central place in justice, on its own it is not an adequate substitute for punishment. Mercy alone often fails to acknowledge the suffering of those harmed or to take seriously the responsibility of those who caused that pain. That is in part because mercy is not precisely about the people who have caused harm at all—it is about those of us in a position to determine what should happen to them.

This is not an argument against the need for mercy. Mercy is essential. But we must be clear about what mercy is and isn't, and what it can and can't do. Most simply, mercy is "compassion or forbearance shown especially to an offender [sic] or to one subject to one's power."[2] It is, fundamentally, about the choices available to those in a position to punish. As Bryan Stevenson, one of the prophets of our time, teaches us:

> There is a strength, a power even, in understanding brokenness, because embracing our brokenness creates a need and desire for mercy, and perhaps a corresponding need to show mercy. When you experience

mercy, you learn things that are hard to learn otherwise. You see things you can't otherwise see; you hear things you can't otherwise hear. You begin to recognize the humanity that resides in each of us.[3]

Mercy is as much about those of us extending it as it is about those who receive it.

Choosing mercy can therefore be a moral and ethical act on the part of a country that is—as we almost certainly must be—obligated to a combination of gentleness and restraint in the face of the harm it has caused through the unjust exercise of its power throughout history. As such, mercy is a requisite element of justice. But mercy fails to replace punishment or constitute justice on its own because it does not include what is required (a) for the person who has been harmed, or (b) on the part of the person who has caused harm. Accountability offers both of these.

Just as mercy requires the right exercise of power on the part of those positioned to punish, accountability requires the right exercise of power on the part of those who have misused their power in causing harm. True accountability is not neutral—it is a set of actions as equal and opposite as possible to the wrongful actions committed by the person who caused harm. It is the active exercise of power in the opposite direction of harm; as such, it is a force for healing.

At its best, accountability completes mercy in generating justice. It does so by meeting a humane restraint of power (on the part of those in the position to punish) with a humane exercise of power in return (on the part of the person who caused harm). Justice, then, exists when all parties exercise their power in a way that is consistent with the humanity of everyone involved and in the interest of the greater good. In the aftermath of violence, mercy plus accountability equals justice.

Those of us who know that our current system of punishment is dehumanizing emphasize that people are more than their greatest mistakes. We are right to do so. But too often we arrive at that ratio by shrinking our estimation of the harm done; we minimize it so that it appears palpably smaller than the person who caused it. That instinct is wrong, in part because our minimization is often dishonest, and in part because in minimizing the harm, we shrink the space allowed for the pain of the person who survived it, someone who belongs to us, too. Instead, we should acknowledge that even when the harm is great, even when it is massive, the humanity of the person who caused it, even then, is greater. We get the ratio right not by shrinking our estimation of the harm but by growing our estimation of the person who caused it. We are misunderstanding Bryan Stevenson's teaching that "each of is more than the worst thing we have ever done" if we take it to mean that the harm we have caused is not so big, that it can be explained away, that it can be diminished. That is not the lesson as I understand it. He is not teaching us that the harm is smaller; he is teaching us that we are, each of us, larger: large enough for mercy, and large enough, I would add to his offering, for accountability, too.

Distinguishing accountability from punishment requires a rigorous understanding and shared definition of what accountability means. Accountability requires five key elements: (1) acknowledging responsibility for one's actions; (2) acknowledging the impact of one's actions on others; (3) expressing genuine remorse; (4) taking actions to repair the harm to the degree possible, and guided when feasible by the people harmed, or "doing sorry"; and (5) no longer committing similar harm. Each step has meaning and benefit for the responsible party, for the harmed party, and for the larger community or society. These benefits take work to produce. Unlike punishment, accountability is not passive. Far from it. It is active, rigorous, and demanding of the responsible person's full humanity.

Step 1: Acknowledging Responsibility
for One's Actions

Accountability begins with truth-telling. First, people who caused harm acknowledge what they did and own their responsibility for the choices they made. For the responsible party, this is at once a vulnerable and a powerful process. It is vulnerable in the way honesty is vulnerable: it requires abandoning the wide variety of defenses the person may have previously deployed, including denial, dishonesty, minimization, excuses. In relinquishing those defenses, responsible parties willingly expose themselves to judgment and to the consequences—emotional, interpersonal, and external—arising from that judgment. The escape hatch closes and they place themselves firmly in the space of accountability, where the only way out is through. In court, when responsible parties plead guilty, they are almost always certain what consequences will result: a plea bargain is typically negotiated before people take a guilty plea, so in telling whatever portion of the truth they tell in court, they know precisely what the price will be. The same is not true in an accountability process between people, whether that is a formal restorative justice process or a less structured interpersonal one. Telling the truth is an act of moral integrity, a relinquishing of a certain kind of control, even a leap of faith—and the outcomes that may arise are potentially vast and not yet settled, because it is the process of accountability itself that will determine them. In a culture where we so often associate protection of ourselves and others with secrecy and even deception, and where we have so few models for meaningful accountability, this exposure can be terrifying. Truth-telling trades the relative certainty of denial for the uncertainty of repair. While denial offers no future transformation and repair does, the choice to shift from one to the other is nonetheless often chilling for responsible parties.

Parallel to that vulnerability, which relinquishes one kind of power, is an equal assumption of a different kind of power. Anything or anyone whose roots are in dishonesty is never firmly planted. To deny our actions, we must deny both the truth and our own agency. We do that mostly because of shame and fear; we are ashamed of what we have done and afraid of the consequences we will face for having done it. In telling the truth, responsible parties stand up to shame and fear in a place of their own power. (Some might call it love.) It is the first step toward embodying the reality that they are more than the thing they have done. This becomes possible because acknowledgment of harm is also an acknowledgment of the responsible person's own agency. They are not passive, not invisible, not absent, not no one or nothing, not only someone to whom something was done. They are someone who did something. And people who did things are people who had—and have—power: the power to make choices and act on those choices. That power is a dimension of the responsible party's humanity, and it is that very same power that they will draw on to make things as right as possible. Someone who did something wrong is also someone who stands to make something right—because those actions draw from the same source. Someone in denial has no pathway to repair. Acknowledgment at once claims and creates one's potential to walk that road.

This truth-telling that marks the inception of accountability is also essential for the survivors of harm. For survivors who have great clarity about what happened to them or their loved ones, the responsible party's denial can feel deeply offensive, enraging, disrespectful, and dishonoring of those harmed. For survivors whose experience of the harm is more muddled, denial can induce all of that and more. It can shake their sense of certainty about what took place, a certainty that is already vulnerable to the distortions in memory caused by trauma itself. In doing so, it can feed their sense of self-blame: if they are sure only about their own actions but not the other person's, it becomes all too easy to focus on what they themselves did and didn't do.

In the aftermath of harm, survivors need to locate responsibility somewhere. When the person responsible for the harm is denying (or just not openly accepting) their role, it can be common for survivors to assign that responsibility to their own actions. The fuzziness of memory combined with the corrosive effect of self-blame can interfere with survivors' sense of entitlement to healing and can diminish the likelihood that they will talk about what happened to them and seek support to address their pain. At the very least, when responsible parties have not acknowledged what they did, survivors bear the unilateral burden of holding that truth. But when responsible parties tell the truth, they share the burden of holding what happened and validate the survivor's experience. This validation can help eradicate survivors' doubt, minimize or sometimes even eliminate their self-blame, reinforce their sense of reality, and give them a grounded basis for healing. For survivors whose memory of an incident is clouded or interrupted by trauma, the responsible party's recount of what happened can fill gaps in their memory and support them in the process of creating a coherent narrative, one of the most critical bases for recovery and healing.

The truth can also start to answer other questions about *why* what happened happened. So often that *why* is what creates the greatest disruption to a harmed party's sense of meaning, faith, and trust. In offering some clarity about *why*, the responsible party's truth-telling can offer the harmed party a tool to deploy in their effort to rebuild a narrative they can inhabit. This is sometimes true even when responsible parties are not (or not yet) insightful about their actions, and even (for this part of the process) if they are not fully remorseful. Survivors are often extraordinary at metabolizing just about anything into healing.

It is clearly preferable for harmed parties to hear from responsible parties whose truth is untinged by excuses or hate. But even in cases when the truth-telling is ugly, the fact of its honesty can be clarifying and steadying for harmed parties in a way that opens a door to transformation. The truth gives them ground on which to stand as they do the hard labor of healing. That ground need not be a bed of flowers—it need only be solid and real.

When responsible parties acknowledge what they did, they also strengthen the community's capacity to come through that harm. Violence rips something in the social fabric. Since a good society or community is supposed to be capable of shielding people from harm, incidents of violence implicate the society or community as a whole and damage people's trust in its capacity to protect them, its legitimacy as a binding force, and the group's ability to fulfill its responsibility to its members. Mystery or disagreement regarding what happened can make it impossible to fully mend the tear caused by violence. Acts of violence require resolution. When they are not anchored in acknowledgment, that resolution can take a variety of unhealthy and damaging forms. It can take the form of retaliatory or reactionary violence rooted in anger and fear. The resolution can involve the divestment from systems of support and protection—whether those are in family, in community, or with state actors such as law enforcement. It can ossify into a collective story of helplessness, lawlessness, immorality, and the inevitability of arbitrary loss and pain. None of these resolutions includes a pathway to mending.

When a responsible party tells the truth, that pathway is opened. Nothing becomes inevitable—truth-telling is not an act of magic that renders everything as it was or better. Rather, it allows a community to form a collective narrative and response that accurately assigns responsibility (including to actors other than the responsible party) and charts a way forward to repair. That repair may be about returning things to the way they were as much as possible. Or it may be about identifying forward-looking strategies that address the underlying factors that made violence likely in the first place. Regardless of how a community or society moves forward after harm, the shared basis in truth and responsibility opens a range of options that otherwise continually slip our collective grip.

Step 2: Acknowledging the Impact of One's Actions on Others

If the first part of truth-telling is about people acknowledging what they did, the second is about acknowledging what results those actions caused. While the first opens the floodgates, this part is often the flood. It is hard for any of us to acknowledge and live with the fact that we are someone who has hurt people badly. It is hard to face the pain we have caused honestly and openly. When that pain is not before us, we can underestimate and understate the impact of our choices. We can imagine the effects of our actions were not as bad as we may fear they were, diminish our estimation of how far those consequences reach and how deep they go for those we harmed, and imagine that we only affected the person we hurt directly, without seeing the pain we caused to those they know and love.

We can tell ourselves that things are not all that different because of what we did—that the world was already hard, that pain was already prevalent, that violence was already normal—and that our choices did not do much to change what is real. We can think of times we survived violence, minimize our sense of how bad those were, and tell ourselves a story that others must be fine. Even if we know, as we often do on some level, that what we did must have caused great harm, we can acknowledge that secretly without making our acknowledgment visible to anyone else. We do not have to see someone look at us as we hear them describe what we have done and search our eyes for an indication of what that information means. We can hide.

In this part of accountability, we give up that unearned right to remain hidden. We listen. When possible, we listen directly to those we harmed. We listen as they describe how they experienced the harm we caused and how we appeared to them in the moments we were at our worst. We listen as they tell us how they felt at the time, how they felt immediately after, how they have felt since. We listen as they tell us the way our choices have reverberated through their lives. We listen to their pain, to their rage (at us), to their disgust (with us), to their sadness, to their fear. We listen to what they have lost—what we took from them—and what they fear they may never get back. We listen to how they are changed, how their sleep and their appetite and their safety and their love are all changed—by us. We listen and we do not explain or deny or correct or diminish what they are saying. We just bear witness to what we have done. And as painful as it is, perhaps even *because* it is painful, that act of witnessing dignifies us in a way the harm we caused diminished our humanity.

It would be hard to overstate how hard that witnessing can be for people who have caused harm. At Common Justice, we worked with a young man who had been involved with a gang since he was no older than eight. He had witnessed all sorts of violence, survived all sorts of violence, committed all sorts of violence for which he had never been caught, and finally he had been arrested for a robbery and assault that landed him in our program. Three months into his time with Common Justice, he sat in a restorative justice process with the young man he beat and robbed, and with the man's mother. They were together for hours and reached agreements about how he could make things as right as possible. When the circle ended and everyone else had left, he turned to me and asked, *Can I stay in your office for a few minutes before I leave?* It was late and the office was closed. I asked him why. He said to me, *I just don't want to go back outside until my hands stop shaking.* This is a young man who I suspect could hold a gun without even a hint of a tremble. He said, *You know, for all I've done and all that's been done to me, I don't know if I've ever heard a real apology before. Do you think I did all right?* I answered, *I think you did great.* And he said: *Pardon my language, that is the scariest shit I ever did.*

In a fundamental way, what is required in acknowledging the impact of our actions can be harder—even scarier—than prison. It is not more violent, not more demeaning, not more debilitating to one's future. It does not expose people to greater degradation or pain. But it does require of people the one thing prison almost never does: facing the people whose lives they've changed, as a full human being who is responsible for the pain of others.

This acknowledgment, as difficult and powerful as it is for the responsible party, can be of great value to those harmed. Just as responsible parties telling the truth about what happened can shift the burden of holding the story from the harmed party alone to the harmed party together with the responsible party and the community, so can responsible parties' acknowledging the impact of their actions more evenly distribute the heavy weight of that burden.

Most often the experience of violence includes the responsible party being indifferent to, appearing indifferent to, or even taking pleasure in the pain they cause the harmed party. In accountability that dynamic is reversed, and the responsible party has to face that pain as someone who sees and experiences it as wrong. The truth that is told in this phase of accountability is not the technical truth of what happened, but rather the moral truth— that the responsible party had no right to hurt the other person, that the harmed party was undeserving of that pain, and that the pain was the responsible party's choice and therefore their fault. And if it was their fault, it was not the harmed party's fault.

That formulation sounds simple, but for survivors, knowing and believing that the pain we survived was not our fault is one of the hardest and most transformative things we can come to understand as we heal. This recognition of our pain and the responsible party's accountability for it can quiet something in us. For all of the ways we turn that pain inward, it can help quiet our self-blame. And for all of the ways we turn that pain outward, it can help quiet our appetite for revenge.

Some argue that the desire for revenge is a fundamental part of human nature.[4] It is certainly common among those of us who have been harmed. Like its sister, rage, it can have a variety of targets: it can be directed at the person who caused harm, at the people or society who allowed it, even at God. Rage is a more general feeling; revenge is action-oriented. It is the desire to inflict injury of some kind—whether physical, emotional, financial, or otherwise—on the people we perceive as responsible for our pain. We usually seek to inflict an injury we consider comparable to the one we sustained.

While I believe it is in the interest of survivors to move through and past the desire for revenge in time, and though I know that acting on revenge can create pain for everyone involved and fuel cycles of violence, still, I do not believe that the desire for revenge is pathological, unhealthy, or inappropriate. That said, neither the fact that it is none of those things nor the fact that it is common means that it is fundamental to human nature. I do not actually think that it is. Instead, I am persuaded that the emotion that *is* fundamental to human nature is a need for recognition, and that revenge is one form that recognition can take—and in the absence of other options, sometimes it is the only form available.

The desire for revenge typically resides between two people. But the feeling that underlies it is not just about an interpersonal relationship—it is about a loss of and betrayal by community or society as a whole. It is in our nature as people to need to feel connected to something larger. We identify as part of our families, our neighborhoods, our cities, our countries, our faiths, our races, our genders, our political affiliations, our organizations, our communities, our histories, our ancestors. We are who we are because of those to whom we are connected. The Bantu phrase *ubuntu,* roughly translated as "I am because we are," names this human quality. When we are part of something, that thing changes us, and when we change, that thing changes, too.

When we survive violence, we are transformed by it. The nature of that change varies widely, but the fact of it is nearly universal. And if we are truly a part of something, if our existence and membership in something larger than ourselves is real and matters, then that change in us should show up somehow in our world. When our pain is not acknowledged, the ways we are changed have no bearing on our world. Everything goes on as it did before. Here we are, fundamentally different than before, and here the world is, exactly the same. That disconnect can feel like unbearable isolation to survivors. As creatures of belonging and of community, it is not our nature as human beings to be so isolated. We fight it. And when what we are fighting is the invisibility and irrelevance of our pain to others, then in our fight we make that pain visible and we make it relevant.

One way we can do that is through revenge. When we enact revenge, the world is different because of what happened to us. Someone who wasn't hurting is hurting now because of us. That difference, ugly and largely unsatisfying as it may be, can feel like an affirmation of our connection and our influence on the larger thing of which we are a part. But though it may be a form of what we need, revenge is not itself the thing we need. It is not more pain that affirms us and quiets the terror and injustice of isolation. What we need is for something in our world to reflect what is different in us. What we need is to be *recognized.* As so many characters in movies say before carrying out retaliatory violence, "You see me now." Revenge is in part an inescapable demand to be witnessed.

The fundamental human need that can manifest as revenge,

particularly when it is otherwise unmet, is the need for recognition. Recognition affirms our membership in something bigger than ourselves and our importance to that larger group. It affirms that when we are different, so, too, is the world, and in that way recognition combats our isolation and the legitimate terror that accompanies it. When that recognition comes from the responsible person, and especially when it is witnessed by community, it can fulfill the need that underlies the desire for revenge and can, not always but often, release survivors from it.

In serving as a reflection of and contributor to connection in this way, responsible parties' acknowledgment of their actions' impact can form the basis for the mending a community must do in the aftermath of failing to protect one of its members. Just as the responsible party's acknowledgment reflects the interconnectedness of people, the community affirms its potential role in healing that pain and in transforming the conditions that made the pain possible in the first place.

Step 3: Expressing Genuine Remorse

Acknowledging the impact of one's actions does not in itself include recognizing the wrongfulness of those actions. That is where remorse comes in. Remorse is the sense of self-reproach, guilt, or distress arising from the wrongs one has committed. It is an acknowledgment that one was wrong, and at its best, that one is indebted as a result.

Professor Pumla Gobodo-Madikizela, who served on South Africa's Truth and Reconciliation Commission, has described remorse this way:

> [Empathy] is why a perpetrator can rise beyond guilt and shame to touch that place of remorse, which is a very vulnerable place. There, a perpetrator has to recognize their own brokenness, because for them to have violated and dehumanized a victim, they had

to dehumanize the self first. They rendered themselves inhuman in order to conduct their terrible deeds.

So remorse is a recognition of deep human broken-ness, and it is also the possibility—the place where it becomes possible for the perpetrator to reclaim their rights to belonging in the realm of moral humanity.[5]

In its overall place in the larger process of accountability, the expression of remorse is a critical part of the inversion of power that accountability requires. It is, to put it simply, a way for a responsible party to use his or her power for good. And because it is an exercise of power, it is rooted in agency, which in turn is rooted in the responsible party's persistent and always repa-rable humanity. It is an act of human grace and of goodness. Or as Gobodo-Madikizela puts it beautifully, "How does the other present their humanity? Through remorse. Remorse is a truly human phenomenon. Remorse cannot be evil."[6]

Remorse belongs to the world of accountability in ways it does not belong to the world of punishment, no matter how much our voracious appetite for punishment compels us to try to fit in there. Central to the problem with punishment is that it is inherently something that is done to us by someone else. One way we can approach being punished is to no longer engage in the behavior that resulted in our punishment. But we can just as easily continue that behavior and merely work to ensure that we are not caught. Forms of punishment that do not include the human reckoning of accountability and the human grappling of remorse rely exclu-sively on extrinsic motivation—a threat from outside. One of the effects of accountability is to help foster people's intrinsic motiva-tion, which manifests in part as remorse. Intrinsic motivation is always a more reliable driver of positive behavior than anything extrinsic. Because although we can sometimes escape the police, we can never escape ourselves.

The nickname of one of Common Justice's first participants before he came to us was The Enforcer—and not for enforcing high ethical standards. When he graduated, I was not sure whether he would continue to behave as he had with us or revert to his patterns before he started the program. So I asked him. We were walking back from court, where the felony charges against him had just been dismissed, and I asked, "Now that the threat of prison is no longer hanging over your head, are you just going to go back and do the same stuff you used to do?" He said, "Nah." (He was never much of a talker.) I asked him to be more specific. He looked me straight in the eyes and said, "No. It's just that, you know," and he pointed to his heart, "the judge is in here now."

This young man had done what social workers talk about as shifting from extrinsic to intrinsic motivation—from being driven by a fear of punishment to being driven by his own internal moral compass.[7] Intrinsic motivation has been demonstrated to be a more reliable and durable predictor of positive behavior than is extrinsic motivation, in part because of its inherent legitimacy to the person who experiences it—a legitimacy that can be undermined by external sources of control. As the restorative justice practitioner and teacher Kay Pranis puts it, "The use of authority undermines the development of responsibility and self-regulation."[8] Intrinsically motivated, the responsible party in this case was not motivated just by a desire to stay out of jail, but by wanting to feel at peace with himself, to go to sleep at night with a clear conscience, to be proud, to live in line with his values. He was remorseful. In that remorse, he was answering to himself. And when a person becomes someone who answers to himself, it means that he is never beyond the reach of the force that keeps him living an upright, ethical, and meaningful life.

For people who are harmed, the responsible party's expression of remorse can open more options to them about how they wish to relate to the person who hurt them. If they have been consumed by thinking of the person who hurt them, they can begin to do so less often and move forward with their lives. If they have been avoiding thinking of the person who hurt them, they can face him or her more directly and turn their attention to that person as the subsequent process of repair ensues; they can sit in their rage toward the person in a way that is reflected back to them by that same person as legitimate; and sometimes, depending on what we mean by the term, they can forgive that person.

Many people regard the expression of remorse, which sometimes manifests as an apology, as the gesture that opens a pathway to forgiveness. For some, remorse is not sufficient, and for others it is not necessary for forgiveness. For some, forgiveness is deeply interpersonal and resides between the harmed and responsible party. For some, it is a deeply spiritual process that lives primarily between the one forgiving and God. For some, it is solely personal and is largely about the forgiver's own release and reconciliation with what was done to them. For some it is highly pragmatic—some of these people have described it as "giving up all hope for a better past." For some it is a combination of these or something else entirely.

In my years doing this work, I have come to think of forgiveness rather simply as relinquishing our desire to see the person who harmed us suffer. I know that forgiveness does not require minimizing or even accepting the harm done; it does not require embracing the other person; though others would disagree, in my view it does not even require no longer being angry. At its most basic, perhaps it just requires separating one's well-being from the other person's suffering. That separation can be based on a profound sense of proximity—whether a literal connection and closeness to the person who caused harm or a broader sense of one's unalterable interdependence. But based on the healing processes I have had the honor to witness, I believe that the separation of well-being from another's suffering can also be based on a sense of distance—a feeling or belief that one will heal on one's own, in one's own community, without regard for what the responsible person says or does. It is beautiful when forgiveness arises out of intimacy and proximity, but that is not the only time it is beautiful.

If we act on the working definition of forgiveness as relinquishing a desire to see the other suffer, then forgiveness is deeply practical. However convenient it might be if it were otherwise, the truth is that someone else's suffering does not relieve us from our own. If it did, given our unprecedented use of punishment, the United States would be not only the safest nation in human history, but also the most healed. If causing pain relieved our own, then those of us who have hurt people would be steadied and eased by having caused so much suffering. But we are not. Violence begets violence begets violence. When we rely on the infliction of suffering as the solution to our hurt, whether by doing it or longing for it, we remain trapped in that pain, because the remedy we are counting on just will not work. When we break from that reliance, we can begin to pursue other pathways to the recovery and healing we deserve.

Regardless of the relationship remorse does or does not have to forgiveness in any given instance of harm, it is the turning point in the accountability process between the past and the future. The first two steps (acknowledging the actions and acknowledging the impact) are backward-looking and the last two (repairing the harm and never hurting anyone similarly again) are forward-looking. Remorse sits between these steps on either side. It is present and looks straight ahead, into the eyes of those who were harmed, and recognizes the wrongfulness of the actions and the legitimate pain the responsible person feels about the resultant harm.

At its best, remorse also includes acknowledgment of and sorrow about the impact a responsible person's actions had on his or her community or society. When remorse is broadened to include the larger network of those impacted, the opportunities for repair broaden as well. If the harm is solely interpersonal, all repair will have to happen solely between the people directly involved. But if the harm is broader, then the site of repair may be elsewhere: it may involve the responsible party "paying it forward," fostering the well-being of others who were or could have been harmed by the kind of choices the person made. And when the site of the repair is in the community, then community can join in that repair, and can be mended, too.

Step 4: "Doing Sorry": Taking Actions to Repair Harm to the Degree Possible, and Guided When Feasible by the People Harmed

The fourth step of accountability moves us into the future. It is the stage when people who have caused harm engage in the acts of repair to which the combination of their humanity and their actions obligates them. Punishment does not require such acts. Despite what we may assume, the fact that we insulate the people we incarcerate from these obligations is not merciful in any way, because it does not protect them from our power, but rather separates them from theirs.

Our failure to demand that people act on their accountability intensifies the overall dehumanization built into our approach to punishment. We tell our national story about violence and punishment almost as though we are talking about werewolves: *The moon comes out and their claws come out and they ravage people.* When we talk about people who commit violence as monsters (or "superpredators," if you prefer), we often viciously deny them the benefits we afford to people we consider fully human, but we also do not hold them to the obligations to which we hold people whose humanity we do not question. We never ask werewolves why they did what they did, never expect them to account for their choices or make things right. And the only tactics we have to manage werewolves' behavior are to kill them or put them in a cage. Those are frighteningly similar to the two main options available in our criminal justice system for responding to serious violence.

But it turns out that people who commit violence are not monsters. They are, in fact, fully human. Every one of them. They are not overtaken by the moon; they make choices, even if they are constrained ones. Committing violence is a choice we make that is rooted in our values, beliefs, expectations, and experiences, and constrained by our contexts. When people are given the opportunity to consider and transform those values, beliefs, expectations and experiences, even within the persistent constraints of harmful or oppressive contexts, they can make different choices. The upside of being fully human is that we can transform. The downside (or what initially may feel like one) is that we are accountable for what we do.

Accountability is not just a feeling. It is a way of behaving. In 2006, when I was planning Common Justice and serving as the deputy director of a program for young men coming home from a jail on Rikers Island, one of the participants asked me what accountability meant. Typically I would have loved this question, but I was busy that day and, admittedly, impatient. I barely looked up from my computer screen and said to him, "Accountability is doing sorry."

While I am not proud of my impatience that day, I think the definition I offered was right. Accountability is not just about *being* or *feeling* sorry—it is about a set of actions that demonstrate remorse in practice. And it is not the feeling of remorse that delivers us from our shame—it is the practice of accountability in action. It is *doing* sorry. That is in part because the inversion of the misuse of power requires not just the absence of negatively used power, but the presence of that person's power positively used.

In processes of repair, including restorative justice ones, that exercise of power is shaped by the acts of witnessing and acknowledgment, but also by the action-oriented agreements reached about how the responsible party can make things as right as possible. These agreements are not commitments to feel or be something—they are commitments to *do* something. The actions may include acknowledgment or restitution to the harmed party, service to the community, or the rigorous development of the responsible party to help ensure that he or she will not commit further harm. It is the completion of these agreements, not merely the formulation of them, that constitutes accountability. After all, we are not dignified by making a promise; we are dignified by keeping it.

Responsible parties know this. Many do not consider forgiving themselves for what they have done until they have fulfilled the promises they made to those they harmed. Time after time, when we ask responsible parties after a restorative justice circle with those they have harmed whether they feel some measure or relief, they tell us that they will feel relieved when—and only when—they have kept the promises they made in that room. For many responsible parties, the scope of commitments they make in these processes can be overwhelming, but nonetheless, they also bring about some measure of calm. That is because the agreements concretize repair in a way that makes clear to responsible parties that such repair is, despite what they feared, possible. Through these processes, they turn the corner, see down the long road to "doing sorry," and know they can walk it.

All too often, when people become persuaded of the value of accountability, they seek to cultivate it in people who have caused harm only by integrating a greater focus on remorse in prisons. This is not what a real understanding of accountability calls for. It is entirely possible to support incarcerated people in developing a deeper sense of responsibility and remorse, and a number of transformative and principled programs do so. But prison is not built for accountability—not only because of the nature of prison, but because of the nature of accountability.

First, accountability as "doing sorry" requires the right exercise of power, and prison is designed to restrict people's power—the very power they would be morally obligated to use in the service of repair in a culture based on accountability. But the disconnect between prison and accountability is even more than that. Accountability is multidimensional. A person is not just accountable *for* something, but also *to* someone. That is different from punishment, which is one-dimensional. A person is punished *for* something. Period. Nothing about the person to whom something is owed. In that sense, accountability is about relationship—and prison, based as it is on separation, is antithetical to relationship.

For many harmed parties, the opportunity to shape what repair looks like can be the most transformative part of the accountability process. Trauma is fundamentally about powerlessness, so having the power to direct the future that arises out of the past can contribute significantly to a person's healing process. Identifying acts of repair can also be the strangest part of the process for harmed parties. In our culture, most violence results in either retaliation (whether on the part of individuals or the state) or nothing. We are not used to getting to define what repair looks like. When one survivor, Ana, was asked what she wanted to see happen as a result of the harm she experienced, she answered, "That's the strangest question I've ever been asked." Countless others have reacted in the same way. The strangeness of such a seemingly basic and appropriate question reflects a long-standing failure in our country to meet the moral demands of understanding and answering to the needs of people who are harmed. Our failure is particularly damning because of how powerful it can be when we get right the process of seeking and acting on a harmed party's needs.

During Hanukkah, Ana was on the subway with a group of friends, wishing fellow passengers a joyful holiday and handing out candy. Suddenly, a group of young people began insulting them, claiming that the Jews had killed Jesus, and spitting in the face of one of Ana's friends. The verbal attack turned physical, and Ana and her friends were badly beaten.

The young man who initiated the attack had another open hate-crime case—for assaulting two black men—and was sentenced to prison. The friends who had played a more minor role in the attack were given probation and community service. Trish, the woman who attacked Ana, was somewhere in between. She didn't have a prior history committing crimes, but she had hurt Ana seriously—punching her, kicking her, and pulling out her hair. Ana suffered serious trauma symptoms following the attack, and she never rode the trains anymore. The change rippled through every part of her life.

This case came to the attention of Common Justice as a candidate for the restorative justice alternative to incarceration process we offer, and staff reached out to Ana to discuss what support she wanted and whether she was in favor of giving Trish the option to participate in the program. After careful consideration, Ana chose to do so, in part because of the role she would have in shaping the response to what she had survived. Ana wanted Trish to answer for and understand the impact of what she had done, so that she would never hurt anyone else again.

After extensive preparation, Common Justice convened a dialogue with Ana, Trish, and their support people to address the harm done to Ana and identify actions Trish could take to make things as right as possible. The group made quick, solid progress in shaping a wide range of commitments Trish would make—including work, education, apologies, reading assignments, and community service. Then we reached an impasse.

Ana's hair had fallen out after the incident, both because Trish tore much of it out and because hair loss is a common response to extreme stress and trauma, so much so that Ana finally had to shave it off. Now Ana wanted Trish to shave her head.

Chapter 4 explores restorative justice processes such as this one in much greater detail. For now, it is important to note that such processes don't allow agreements that are harmful or degrading to the responsible party. In this case, there was disagreement about whether this proposed commitment crossed the line. We took a break to see if we could find common ground. We talked to Ana about what this agreement meant to her. At first she said, "I want her to suffer the way I suffered." And while we empathize deeply with that, we cannot be in the business of replicating the suffering caused by violent crime. Ana added, "But it isn't just that. It's. . . ." She paused. She took a breath. And she said, "Everywhere I go, I think about this girl. When I wake up, I think about her. When I look at myself in the mirror, I think about her. And when I go to touch my head and my long hair is not there, I think about her. And when people tell me my short haircut is cute, I think about her. And when I get on the bus instead of the train, I think about her. And when I wait for the bus and I'm cold, I think about her. And when I go to sleep and can't fall asleep, I think about her. And I dream about her and I wake up and start it all over again. She's everywhere for me. I want to be everywhere for her. *I want to be on top of her head.*"

That, we said, we *can* try to do. We talked for hours, and the agreement that emerged from our conversation was that Trish was not allowed to ride the trains for the next year. Trish lived on the outskirts of Brooklyn, far from her school, the programs she was required to attend, and the job she had to maintain. The agreement we reached required her to stay off the trains and keep a daily journal in which she reflected about how Ana must have felt each day following the attack. At first her entries were short and even a little trite: "I think she felt angry." And "I think she felt mad." But after having to write these reflections day after day, finally something clicked: "I bet she felt so tired of waking up angry. I bet she was so frustrated that everything changed because of me, because of something she didn't even do, something she didn't even choose, something that wasn't meant for her. I bet she felt so sad because she didn't know if that feeling would ever go away. I bet she hated me for causing her that pain. I bet she hated hating me too."

Trish stayed off the trains. She had to spend two or three times as long getting to places. When her friends all hopped on the subway, she had to decide between making up a fake excuse or telling them the real reason she couldn't ride with them. She had to consider getting on the train, then imagine the possible consequence of doing so (the risk she would be terminated from the program and sentenced to a prison term), then would feel an overwhelming sense of panic and wait for the bus to come. And of course, these are all things Ana had been doing for a year as a result of the trauma Trish caused her.

Before engaging in this process with Trish, Ana experienced symptoms that rose to the level of PTSD, including flashbacks, anxiety, depression, and hypervigilance. She could not feel relaxed or safe anywhere. Within weeks of the dialogue, things changed dramatically for Ana: her symptoms subsided and she regained her ability to move through her life and to feel joy. Years later, Ana told us that the benefit of this process had persisted for her. And Trish kept her word, paying forward the generosity Ana showed her and living a healthy, productive, law-abiding life.

No court would have envisioned—or could have required—the kind of repair Ana imagined for herself. And the agreement she and Trish reached was certainly far from typical. The point of these acts is not that they are logical, though they often are; it is that they are meaningful and useful—to both parties. Harmed parties who get to shape the course of repair choose actions they believe will keep themselves and others safe from harm. Their sense of power in that process is critical, as is the sense of resolution that many experience when those promises are upheld. Just as many responsible parties cannot envision forgiving themselves until they have kept the promises they made to those they harmed, many harmed parties cannot envision forgiving those who harmed them, feeling closure, or feeling safe until the agreements are fulfilled. As one harmed party put it, "I can't forgive you based on what you say, but I can forgive you based on what you do. That's because people won't be safe based on what you say. They'll be safe based on what you do."

Many harmed parties question the truth of a responsible party's apology or expression of remorse—or question whether that remorse will affect what the person does going forward. They are moved instead by the times when responsible parties fulfill their commitments to obtain and retain employment, when they study for and obtain a GED, when they complete hundreds of hours of community service at a site meaningful to the person harmed, when they pay restitution from the income they have earned at work, or when they speak publicly to younger people to help steer them down a better path. The clarity and objectivity achieved when the responsible party completes agreements gives harmed parties a degree of confidence in the change they are owed that no verbal commitment alone could ever provide.

When responsible parties "do sorry," the benefits accrue not only to the harmed party and to themselves, but to the community as a whole. The acts of repair, at their best, give back to that community and strengthen it from within. Accountability as a set of actions can also satisfy a larger society's need for recognition that its tenets were violated and can go a great distance toward restoring what was lost or damaged because of that violation. The visibility of such repair offers a critical counterbalance to the visibility of harm and its impacts. People in the community need not hope or believe in a difference: they can see it carried out before their eyes.

Step 5: No Longer Committing Similar Harm

It is not easy to become someone who will not commit harm again. Most of us are not yet those people. But accountability requires that becoming. This is particularly challenging when we understand that violence is driven by structural and contextual factors that are not changed by an accountability process. Still, it is the work of accountability to transform as much as possible within those constraints so as not to cause more pain to others.

This requires, in part, that responsible parties develop a greater sense of self-worth and dignity, develop empowered relationships to the obstacles in their lives, believe they can lead long lives and be determined to live, set short- and long-term goals, and create new avenues toward acquiring authentic and life-affirming power. It requires that they demonstrate respect for those they encounter; become conscious about their respective histories on individual and structural levels; begin to understand their emotional, psychological, physical, and social responses to their experiences past and present; identify what they are responsible for in their everyday lives and to whom; and ask for help when needed and collaborate with those in their support system to meet those needs. No longer committing violence requires that responsible parties understand the roles of violence in their lives; foster reciprocal relationships by sharing knowledge and experiences; communicate effectively, including expressing what they need to say; develop or strengthen empathy for others; develop self-awareness about and strategies to handle anger effectively; acknowledge the impact their actions have on their own lives and those around them; build durable strategies to cope with stressors; and, for many, develop a healthier sense of masculinity and manhood.[9]

No longer committing violence also requires developing coping strategies to deal with factors that underlie much violence, such as economic and housing instability. People with nowhere to live or not enough to eat will always have a harder time refraining from causing harm than will people with the benefit of that stability. These factors are never solely within a responsible party's control, so they demand the fulfillment not only of the person's promises, but of our larger societal responsibility to create the conditions that make violence less likely.

And no longer committing harm requires healing—not as a replacement for responsibility, but as a dimension of it. Research unequivocally shows that one of the most surefire predictors of violence is surviving it.[10] Nearly everyone who has committed harm has survived it, and few have received any formal support to heal.[11] None of the violence people have experienced excuses what they go on to do. But it is unquestionably a factor in why they caused harm. I believe when we hurt someone, we incur an obligation. Period. Nothing changes that obligation—not our own history of pain, our unhealed trauma, nothing. That is true because the obligation we incur arises out of our humanity, our agency, and our dignity—and each of those things are fully present in everyone who commits harm.

So what happens when we come to understand that part of why we caused harm is because of our own unhealed pain? Our insight does not erase that first obligation. Instead, we incur a second obligation: to heal through that pain so we no longer pass it along to others. And then the larger "we," as a society, have an obligation to meet people in that process and provide them with the resources and the support they need to come through their pain. That means that our history of surviving violence does not get us off the hook, but it does beg the question of where societal supports were when we were hurt, and thus puts the larger society on the hook as well.

Our healing also supports our ability to be accountable by strengthening our capacity for empathy. Accountability requires that people who commit harm consider how the people they harmed felt during and after the crime. Fairly often, responsible parties will say some version of "they felt fine." They will express that they believe the people they harmed were likely unaffected by the violence and that it did not matter much. For some people who hear this, the response sends off the sociopathy alarms. They read into it an elemental incapacity for empathy. They see the person's minimization of the impact of the harm caused as an indicator of their disconnection from others' feelings and suffering. They see in that a pathological inhumanity—one many people believe may be innate—or if not innate, at least irreparable.

That conclusion fundamentally misunderstands how empathy works in context. The basic emotional gesture of empathy works something like this: we listen to someone else's experience, mine our own experience for the closest corollary we can find, remember how we felt at that time, and extrapolate from that information to reach some understanding about how the other person must feel. That effort of reflection and extrapolation is empathy. It seems quite simple: You get punched. I think about a time I got punched. I ask myself: How did I feel? I answer: I felt afraid, angry, and later, sad. I assume: You probably feel afraid and angry and sad. The problem for people who have committed harm isn't that they are not engaging in empathy. The problem is what they find when they mine their experience, because what happens if what they find there is—nothing?

It is not only true that many people who commit violence are survivors of it. It is also true that many of those survivors belong to groups of people whose pain our society devalues—whether they are young men (whom our society tells that they should be tough and impervious to pain), young women and gender nonconforming people (whom our society tells that they provoked the harm done to them), or people of color (whom our society tells that their pain is neither as substantial nor as important as white people's pain). So what happens to empathy in this context? If I draw on my own most comparable experience and think back to how I felt, what if I had told myself (and my culture told me) that I felt fine? That it was normal? No big deal? To be expected? What if someone later asked me, "How do you think he felt when you put your gun to his head?" What if I did what empathy requires and asked myself, "When a gun was placed to my head, how did I feel?" And what if the only answer left to me after the minimization of my pain had been "Fine"? That is what I would have assumed that the person I hurt had also felt. It is not that people whose pain has been devalued are not enacting empathy. It is that when they mine their own experience, they often find our culture's answer about their pain and tell it back to us: they tell us it doesn't exist, and that even if it does, it doesn't matter.

In order for survivors who have gone on to commit harm to become more consistently capable of practicing empathy in the way so many people (including survivors themselves) seek, we have to begin by validating their pain, terror, and suffering as real, and by validating what happened to them as wrong. We have to say, "This thing you said was no big deal? It *was* a big deal. It mattered. You mattered. It was wrong, it shouldn't have been done to you." When that happens for survivors, they become capable of owning the fact that what happened to them was wrong and acknowledging the full range of emotions they felt at the time.

At times, responsible parties will struggle to take accountability for what they have done and may struggle in particular to acknowledge the impact it had on the victims of their crimes. They reach a limit to the insight they are able to develop. Often the intervention that enables them to break through that limit is an engagement with their own trauma and healing. When our attention turns there, we typically find underestimated, ignored, and unhealed pain. When we create the space to validate that pain and allow it to be spoken about, responsible parties become capable of decisively naming its impact on them as more than nothing. With support, they can speak to their hypervigilance, insomnia, digestive problems, flashbacks, and night terrors. They can tell the truth that they were hurt and that it mattered.

Then when it comes to empathy, they can do the same thing they have always been doing, which is to see the corollary between their experience and that of others. Only this time they find something different when they mine their own experience. This time they infer that the person they harmed probably couldn't sleep for days, that their stomach didn't feel quite right for years, that their dreams were horrifying. This time they infer that after what they did, the person they hurt didn't trust their girlfriend, didn't trust their family, never felt safe in the street. This time they infer that nothing felt the same or ever would again.

That conclusion becomes a solid basis for accountability, which includes seeing, acknowledging, and answering to someone's pain. Being able to fully regard the depth of that pain is an essential component of being fully accountable. To the degree that unacknowledged and unhealed pain is a barrier to that regard, it is an enemy of accountability. We need to commit to healing in its own right. But we also need to commit to healing because of the way in which unhealed pain guts accountability and, in so doing, all but guarantees that cycles of violence continue. Healing, then, takes its place among the most pragmatic priorities of a culture that values safety. And accountability takes its place among that culture's moral demands.

For harmed parties, the transformation of the people who hurt them into people who will not hurt anyone in that way again can constitute the most meaningful and useful conclusion to an accountability process. That is in part because it ensures their future safety as it relates to the person who harmed them. But it is more than that: it is to the great credit of survivors that they are typically as invested in other people's safety as they are in their own. So any process that protects only them from future harm is incomplete, both morally and as a contributor to their healing. Only a process that extends the same protection to others truly meets their needs. When that happens, the impact is palpable. When the person who harmed them changes in a positive way, the benefit of that evolution accrues to survivors and their healing.

Of course, that benefit accrues to the community as well, as the transformed person becomes a contributor to the social fabric rather than an impediment to it. Communities capable of improvement are places where people can be well. That is because healthy communities are not defined by perfection, which does not exist. They are defined by the potential for change. In embodying that potential, people who repair harm not only mend the particular tear to the social fabric for which they are responsible, but strengthen the fabric as a whole.

There is wide agreement that survivors deserve to have the people who harmed them held accountable to them—and to other people affected by their actions. This process can help satisfy the moral demands of a culture, facilitate the survivors' healing, and validate that what happened to them is wrong. All of that is true. But we also have to understand that people who commit harm also deserve accountability, in the toughest and most generous sense of the word. They deserve to have to pay in a meaningful way for what they have done. They deserve the difficulty of that reckoning, and even the fear and pain it may cause. But they also deserve a process that will allow them a way out of shame and its associated violence. Accountability, as outlined here, is as essential for those who cause harm as it is for those who survive it. That is because, when practiced well, it is not just an obligation, but also an avenue to dignity.

In our culture, we have many reference points for healing processes. We know that when we survive harm or suffer a loss, there is a process we undertake to come through it—whether we think about those as stages of grief or phases of healing, we know there are things we have to do and can do that help us recuperate our sense of dignity, of self-worth, of connectedness, and of hope. Many of us are familiar with the "stages of grief," widely regarded as some variation of denial and isolation, anger, bargaining, depression, and finally, acceptance.[12] Our understanding of these stages not only helps us navigate each one, but helps us experience even the hardest ones as part of a longer trajectory toward healing.

I believe that when we cause harm, we are affected by what we have done. We are damaged by it in ways we rarely talk about. I often ask people interested in accountability work to take part in a brief exercise, which goes like this:

> Think about a time you did something wrong and then repaired that harm as much as possible. Pay attention to how you feel when you remember that. Pay attention to where you feel it in your body, how it feels in your mind and heart.
>
> Now remember a time when you did something wrong and did not repair it—because it was too late, because you did not know how, because by the time you were ready, the person you hurt was gone—and pay attention to how that feels in your body, your mind, your heart.

Having done this exercise with hundreds of people, I have not encountered a single person who has said that the two memories felt the same. The first—the one we repaired—is typically something we can think of with relative comfort. We can hold the feeling and still feel like ourselves, can still feel deserving of love, can feel proud of the way we are in the world, can feel connected to those around us in a positive way. The latter, though—the feeling of harm we have caused and not repaired—sits differently. The best word I know for it is shame. It is not a perfect word, but it is the closest I have found. That second feeling, for most of us, is much harder to hold. It rubs up against our dignity, our self-love, our pride, our connectedness. For many of us, it feels much closer to the parts of ourselves where we hold the things that have been done to us and have not been repaired. It is a hard feeling, an uneasy one, even a painful one. It is what it feels like to be human beings who have done wrong.

This is especially problematic in light of Dr. Gilligan's work that concludes that the greatest driver of violence is shame. As he sees it, the relationship between violence and shame is in part about eradicating witnesses to our failings, our incompleteness, our flaws, and our weakness. Whether in our homes or in the streets, violence as a vehicle to overcome shame is about damaging or destroying those who have seen us as limited, afraid, or incapable. It is about insisting on our power by inflicting pain so as not to be seen in our vulnerability or powerlessness.[13]

If Gilligan is right, and if committing violence causes us to feel shame, then committing violence becomes a risk factor for committing more violence. We hurt people, we are ashamed of it, we act that shame out as violence—and repeat. As human beings, we find shame intolerable, and we are moved to act to escape it. Absent a healthy avenue out of that shame, one of the core tactics we turn to is violence.

I have long been persuaded that the only avenue out of shame is accountability.

It is answering for what we have done and making things as right as we can that transforms shame. So often our instinct is to hide or deny the things for which we are accountable. There may be a feeling of safety in that avoidance, but it is detrimental—not only to the harmed party and members of the community, who suffer from our dishonesty, but to ourselves when we are the ones responsible for harm. Shame thrives on secrecy; it grows in the dark. It is only the bright light of day that can evaporate it. In telling the truth, responsible parties give up the comfort of denial, which insulates them from knowing the full impact of their choices. They also give up the relative security of privacy, which insulates them from the feeling of exposure and vulnerability. But they gain something in return: a pathway out of the shadows in which shame thrives.

In expressing remorse, responsible parties acknowledge the harmful impact of their power and the damage done not only to others, but to themselves, in exercising that power wrongfully. In owning the impact of their actions, they own their power and the fact of their connectedness to others. However painful it is to sit with the distress of what they have done, that distress is evidence of their humanity, their empathy, and the persistence of their relationships with others, even in the aftermath of harm. These qualities—humanity, empathy, and relatedness—are the sweet enemies of shame, because they reveal shame's impermanence by lighting the pathway out.

Then, in repairing harm—by "doing sorry" and engaging in the labor of transformation, responsible parties reclaim their deservedness of respect. If shame is in part about eradicating witnesses, the best counter to it is to become someone who can be proud to be seen. By exercising the power responsible parties used to harm in the service of repair instead, they become legitimately and positively reconnected to their own power. By healing through their own histories of trauma, they become people anchored in resilience and change. In integrating their past into their present and future, they become people whose imperfections are human and whose failings are reparable. They become people who no longer seek secrecy or find comfort in it; rather, they seek to be witnessed because what they are doing is worthy and they know it in their bones.

In this way, accountability does for those of us who commit

harm what the healing process does for us when we are harmed: it gives us a way to recuperate our sense of dignity, our self-worth, our connectedness, and our hope—the things we lost when we caused harm. It is like grieving, too, in that it begins with an emotion that feels impossible to bear and ends in a place of resolution and integration. I am therefore persuaded that accountability is the corollary to grief for when we cause harm, and it is as essential as a grieving process is in restoring us to our best selves. We would do well to develop our methodologies for supporting people through accountability as thoroughly as we have developed our methodologies for supporting people through grief. It is no less necessary for a healthy society, and no less possible.

If accountability is the avenue to dignity, that means that in replacing accountability with punishment, we have denied those responsible for harm precisely the process that would allow them to recuperate their dignity, transform their lives, and halt the cycles of violence they are otherwise at enormous risk of perpetuating. This is not unlike or unrelated to the way we deny survivors what they need most, by allowing punishment—which offers them almost nothing—to take the place of accountability, which they so richly and fully deserve. We also pay the price for this loss on a larger scale: we become a culture mostly incapable of repair, so that every rip in the social fabric compounds the last until we can barely see ourselves as part of a whole. But we are capable of inverting this reality, and of making accountability, and the justice it promises, the norm for our nation. We can do so not just by ending incarceration, but by displacing it.

4

Displacing Incarceration

Elijah was riding the bus home one day, when someone across
from him asked where he was from. He was nervous. He knew
that a young man from another housing project had been killed
that week where he lived and expected someone was planning
to retaliate. But he was proud, and he had had nothing to do
with the killing, so he answered: "Livonia." When the bus pulled
into the next stop, a group of about a dozen young men rushed
into it through the front and back doors. The young man Elijah
had spoken to nodded, and the group surrounded him, beating
him to the ground. Then they jumped off the bus and ran. The
bus driver kept driving and Elijah got off a few stops later at his
house. He walked to his apartment and through the front door
and collapsed. His brother Donnell was home and saw Elijah fall
to the ground. His face was already swelling and his shirt was
stained with his blood.

Donnell considered calling an ambulance, but when his brother regained consciousness and did not appear to have any life-
threatening injuries, he did not consider calling the police. He
had had plenty of encounters with the police (it was the height of
the stop-and-frisk era in New York City and he was a black man
in America), as had his friends and family, and before that, his
parents and ancestors—and few if any of those stories ended with
people being safer. That said, he knew that if no one was made

to answer for the harm done to his brother, Elijah would only be in more danger—for not defending himself, not retaliating, not being "a man."

Donnell, who had a bit of a name for himself in the streets, was deeply protective of his brother, who was, even in his own words, a "nerd." He was afraid for Elijah's safety. So Donnell helped his brother off the floor and walked toward the door. "Come with me," he said. And Elijah did. As they left their building, several of their friends joined them for the walk. They saw Elijah's face and knew where they were going.

The brothers and their friends approached the bus stop and saw Elwin standing there. Elwin was on the phone with his girlfriend, who was on her way home from work on the approaching bus about two blocks away. He turned and saw a group of five young men walking toward him. Donnell and Elijah stopped, the other three young men standing behind them. Donnell turned to his brother and asked, "Was he with them?" Elijah mistakenly thought he recognized Elwin's face from the mob, could picture it from where he looked up from the floor of the bus, and answered yes. Elwin didn't know what they were talking about, but right as Elijah said yes, he saw one of the other young men flash a gun. Elwin had buried two of his friends in the past two months. He was consumed with grief, but the main feeling he had wasn't sorrow, but fear. He had come to think that his death by violence was imminent, maybe even inevitable. But he was not ready to die. He looked at this group that outnumbered him five to one, looked at the gun and its promised death, reached in his pocket for the knife he carried, swung the knife at the person closest to him, and ran.

Elijah did not feel the cut at first. He just saw his shirt turn red. When he touched his hand to his cheek, it met his teeth. He was cut from his jaw to the corner of his mouth. He felt in shock. He joined the others as they took off running after Elwin.

They chased Elwin into a store. They fought there, and Elwin eventually locked himself in the store bathroom. When he thought one of the young men was finally going to succeed in breaking through the door, he pushed himself out, swinging and heading for the door. In the scuffle, someone got ahold of his knife. He ran outside, where his sister and the police were arriving at the same time.

Donnell, Elijah, and Elwin were all arrested. Elijah would get a bandage for his face, but no stitches or real care until he made bail days later, after the wound had partially, clumsily closed. The scar on his face is as much a testament to that lack of treatment as to the cut itself. Donnell would spend much longer on Rikers Island—his family could afford to bail only one of them out, and he insisted that they release Elijah first—where he would spend some time in the infirmary as the result of an acute health issue.

The paramedic checked out Elwin cursorily before putting him in handcuffs. She said he was fine. His sister looked at her brother and knew something was wrong and insisted that the paramedic check again. On second review, the paramedic found a small wound in his back where the knife had entered and broken off in his lung, puncturing it. Still handcuffed, Elwin was put in the ambulance rather than the police car, where he was made to ride the whole way on his back, the blade digging further in. He would have one surgery in the city hospital before he was transferred to the hospital on Rikers Island, where he would spend another eleven months.

One of the challenges in addressing violence without prison is the belief that we do not have other options available to us. That is simply not true. There is no single answer, nor a perfect one, but throughout the country, formally and informally, people are tackling violence in ways that reflect the core values of honoring those harmed and holding those responsible accountable with dignity. Many of these strategies are working. Many are imperfect, but we cannot measure their success against perfection, because what they stand to displace is, to put it mildly, far from perfect.

Mass incarceration as a strategy to address violence is failing. Punishment as our core mode of responding to violence is failing. We as a nation are failing. When we admit to that failure, we become responsible for trying something different. We are not a people who are taking a medication that is working and considering an experimental new drug. We are a people who are taking a medication that is barely scratching the surface of our symptoms and generating compounding side effects that are becoming increasingly unbearable. In this context, when we decide to try something different, we are not taking much of a risk. We are acknowledging that the risk associated with the status quo is not one we can continue to assume, so we choose something different, not out of innovation or bravery or curiosity, but out of responsibility to what remains of our democracy.

Perhaps one of the greatest harms the criminal justice system has done is persuaded us that we do not know how to solve the problems that arise between and among us. We have been taught that our experience is inconsequential in comparison to the evidence the "experts" present, and that the strategies we gravitate toward instinctively—calling each other's families first instead of the police, addressing the underlying causes of people's behavior, requiring people to give back to those they harmed—are somehow not only wrong, but socially irresponsible.

But our experience is invaluable. Those of us who have been harmed, who have lost loved ones, who have caused others pain and repaired it as best we could—we know something. And that knowledge we possess is pragmatic, it is firmly grounded in reality, and it can become the basis for expanding approaches to violence that stand a chance at keeping us safe.

Communities have long had the capacity to address the pain that arises within them. When we combine the inherent ability of human beings to participate in transforming harm with some of the centuries-old tools for doing so, we open pathways to safety and justice that are otherwise unavailable. Restorative justice is one such pathway. With its roots tracing back to a wide range of indigenous practices, much of restorative justice as we implement it in the United States today has its origins in circles practiced by the Plains people in North America, the Maori in New Zealand, and, as Dr. Morris Jenkins has taught us, a variety of African communities.[1] The lineage and application of restorative justice practices raises complex questions about cultural appropriation that are beyond the scope of this book, but it is unquestionable that the approach's central lessons are deeply held across diverse cultures, passed down in a wide variety of ways, and, at their best, nurtured and changed by the people and communities implementing them.

These practices persist because they work. Substantial research in the United States, Australia, Canada, and the United Kingdom has demonstrated that restorative justice can be an effective response to violent crime, reducing recidivism rates by as much as 44 percent and helping to break cycles of violence.[2] Restorative justice will not fully replace incarceration; it is not a panacea. But for an enormous number of cases in the criminal justice system, its existence does mean that we can no longer pretend we do not know what else to do.

I know restorative justice best through the work I have been part of at Common Justice, where we operate an alternative to incarceration and victim services program for serious and violent felonies. Guided by restorative justice principles, we offer a survivor-centered accountability process that gives those directly impacted by acts of violence the opportunity to shape what repair will look like, and, in the case of the responsible party, to carry out that repair instead of going to prison. We work primarily with gunpoint robberies, serious assaults, shootings, and other acts of street violence committed by sixteen- to twenty-six-year-olds. (We do not work with cases of intimate partner

violence, though we respect those who do.) Com-
ce's fifteen-month intervention for responsible parties
includes an intensive violence intervention curriculum that runs
concurrently to the restorative justice process. Participants who
complete the program and fulfill all of their commitments to
those they harmed are not incarcerated and the felony charges
against them are removed from their records. At the time of this
writing, fewer than 6 percent of Common Justice participants
had been terminated from the program for being convicted of
a new crime, and in the six years from 2012 (when the program underwent substantial refinement) to 2018 (the time of this
writing), only one person had been terminated because of a new
crime. At the same time, we provide wraparound services to a
broad range of survivors of all demographics, nearly all of whom
are members of groups typically excluded from most services
and support for victims: a full 70 percent of our survivors, for
instance, are men of color.

Common Justice's experience is offered here not as the epitome
of these processes, but as a source of examples that can reveal what
this work can look like in practice, how it can align with the values that should guide our justice strategies, and what outcomes
it can be expected to deliver. Our work at Common Justice is
only one way of applying these principles—there are countless
other interventions in communities, schools, and criminal justice settings across the country that look different in fundamental
ways and show great promise. These include Project NIA and
the Community Justice for Youth Institute in Chicago; Restorative Justice for Oakland Youth (RJOY) and Community Works
in Oakland and San Francisco; the Community Conferencing
Center in Baltimore; the Insight Prison Project in San Quen-
tin; restorative justice projects growing throughout the country
in partnership with Impact Justice, and many more. Common
Justice's flaws and limitations should not be understood as the
flaws and limitations of restorative justice, but rather as openings

for others to do better. At its best, our efforts advance this work down the field and help move us closer, collectively, to being within striking distance of the goal.

Restorative justice is a decision-making process that involves those most directly impacted by a given harm in identifying the pathway toward repair—and then carrying out the actions to get there. That sounds straightforward enough, but it is markedly different from the criminal justice system as we know it.

The question of who should be involved in decision-making about repair is a fundamental one. If I am hurt, I am changed by it. And the people in my life are changed by it, too. The crime may change how I can show up for them; it changes what I am available for, what I am capable of, what I need from them. It changes their level of fear and safety sometimes as much as it changes my own. They carry the burden of my pain, too, and it often touches on their own pain. The criminal justice system defines very narrowly who has a stake in the outcome of a case. If you walk into a courtroom, you will see a defendant surrounded by a lot of other people who had nothing to do with what happened. You will almost never see the victim in that room. You will almost never see the victim's or defendant's loved ones. You will just see someone who has caused harm in a room full of people who are disconnected from that harm and making a decision about what to do.

Restorative justice inverts these exclusions, acting on the belief that transformation depends on the involvement of those who have the most on the line. In most restorative justice approaches, the central method of that involvement is a dialogue process, often called a circle, that includes the responsible party, the harmed party, and support people. In this process, people identify the harm that was done and begin to define a pathway to repair.

These processes benefit from (and I would say require)

thoughtful preparation. In robust preparation processes leading up to the circle, participants have the opportunity to secure their basic safety and stability; gain an understanding of the restorative justice process and their options for taking part in it; identify the emotional and physical impact of their experience and begin to address those impacts; situate their experience in the context of their own history, family, and community—as well as those of the other party; develop the tools to communicate their experience; foster a readiness to engage with the other party in whatever way feels right; begin to think through possible agreements for what meaningful repair could look like; engage their community and support people in the process in whatever way makes sense; and make connection with therapeutic, medical, employment, educational, or other services to support their own healing and recovery.

When everyone is prepared, the circle provides a framework and opportunity for accountability on the part of the responsible parties and healing on the part of those harmed. These processes are consonant with harmed people's most pressing needs—to ask *why*, to describe the harm they endured, to regain control and a sense of agency relative to the incident, to begin assembling a coherent narrative regarding what took place and thus plant the seeds of recovery from trauma, and to have that harm repaired in a way that is responsive and meaningful to them. At the same time, the process helps the responsible person to feel and take accountability, engage support from their existing networks, reach a dignified resolution with those harmed, develop a strong sense of responsibility, empathy, and capacity, and plan for and demonstrate follow-through. By providing not only an outlet for witnessing the human consequences of harm but also an opportunity to regain a sense of dignity and self-worth, the process addresses key driving forces behind violence.

In the circle, all parties decide on agreements other than

incarceration to hold the responsible party accountable in ways meaningful to the person harmed. These may include responsible parties providing community service at places significant to those harmed, pursuing their education, completing job training and/or obtaining employment, paying financial restitution, making apologies, learning about their own culture and the culture of the harmed parties, becoming positive role models to younger people in their lives and communities, addressing any harmful reliance on alcohol or other drugs, developing their skill sets as parents, or any number of other creative commitments particular to each case and the needs of the people affected by it.

In shaping these agreements, some harmed parties want no further contact with the people who hurt them once the circle concludes. Others do. One man who participated in a circle at Common Justice had had to walk daily past the place where the responsible party stabbed him. Every time, he was overcome with fear, which subsided only into anger. As part of the circle, he asked the responsible party to meet him a handful of times at the place where the stabbing occurred and to greet him respectfully and shake his hand. It seemed simple enough, but for the harmed party, this allowed him to overwrite the experience of trauma—which was situated for him in a specific place—with an experience of reconciliation, safety, and respect. Another harmed party wanted his children to meet the responsible party's children. He said: "I want you to look in the eyes of the small children whose father you almost took from them that night with your gun. And after today, I believe in the father you can be to your baby girl, and I want to say that to her face." In another case, the harmed and responsible parties did a speaking tour in their neighborhood, talking to younger people about the impact of violence on their lives and the options other than retaliation and prison that could be available to them. Many harmed and responsible parties start correspondences of some sort, and many

harmed parties find that witnessing the trajectory of the responsible party's growth can contribute to their own healing. For
others, they prefer to leave the responsible party's transformation
fully to the restorative justice program and to be given few if any
updates. For these harmed parties, their trust in the program to
engage that process allows them to be released from it in a way
that can give them the space they need to heal their own pain
and live their own lives.

Just as not all harmed parties want ongoing contact with the
people who hurt them, not all of them want to participate in a
circle. And they never have to; they do not incur an obligation for
being hurt. Harmed parties who do not want to attend the circle
can be represented by a surrogate—someone who will take their
seat in the circle and stand for their perspective. The surrogate
can be someone close to them or can be someone who has been
through something similar. Harmed parties can talk at length
with the surrogate or can say they want no part in revisiting the
harm they survived. They can decide how they want their voices
heard—they can simply entrust the surrogate to represent them,
they can write a letter and have it read aloud, they can record a
video or audio statement, they can provide a list of questions, they
can attend the first half of the circle but not the second (or vice
versa); they can, essentially, do what works for them to participate
in shaping the repair they are owed.

This emphasis on repair reflects restorative justice's primary
concern with harm rather than with broken rules. Restorative
justice contends that crime causes harm to people, relationships,
and community—and this is different from thinking of crime
primarily as a violation of the law. If the primary understanding
of crime is about a legal infraction, then the most urgent concern
is to reassert the power of the state through the enforcement of
the law. But if the core concern is that people have been harmed,
the priority is to repair that harm.

Restorative justice requires a fundamental belief in the humanity of those who have been harmed and those who caused harm. People who have been harmed have to be regarded as worthy of care even if they are imperfect, even if they have caused harm themselves, even if they owe repair to someone else for what they have done. It is not the harmed party's innocence that entitles them to repair, it is their humanity.

Similarly, people who commit harm deserve and owe it to repair the harm they have caused. That seems obvious, but our criminal justice system not only fails to require repair, it often prohibits it. Other than financial restitution, which is notorious for how ineffectively it is managed, the system creates obstacles to the ways responsible people could make right for what they have done. Prisons, for instance, typically disallow communication among victims and incarcerated people. Victims who seek dialogues with those who hurt them or killed their loved ones face enormous and often insurmountable legal and bureaucratic barriers. These barriers are rooted in the ways that the standard criminal justice process profoundly underestimates the degree to which the people who have committed harm can be contributors to healing. The system treats them as though their only capacity is to cause greater pain to those they have harmed, and as though its only job is to keep "those people" away from survivors and—depending on the scale of the harm—from the rest of us as well. What we know is that the truth is messier. Some people unquestionably pose an ongoing risk, whether physical or emotional, to those they have harmed. Others can offer something meaningful to a survivor's healing process, whether that is information, recognition, or repair. And many people belong to both of these categories at once.

Restorative justice also contends that it is not only the harmed and responsible parties that have a role in identifying and carrying out the repair, but the community as well. What that means is that a sense of urgency about solutions requires that we involve those whose lives are at stake in the problem. In restorative justice, that includes the people who raised the people in the circle, those who see them day in and day out, those who will reap the benefit or pay the price for whether or not they change. The approach is based in a belief that support people have a central role in the necessary transformation of the harm. Addressing what happened requires not removing the harm from their support people, but rather locating the harm more closely among them and giving them the room and the tools to address it.

As described by Howard Zehr, one of the early leaders in the modern restorative justice movement in the United States, the questions those people aim to address are *Who has been hurt? What are their needs? Who has the obligation to address the needs, put right the harms, and restore relationships?* Those questions are in stark contrast with the more standard criminal justice questions: *What rules were broken? Who did it? What do they deserve as a result?*[3] As with any problem, the way we frame a question plants the seeds of how we will answer it. So restorative justice requires us to reopen a core question in our society: when harm has been done, who owes what to whom—and why? It is a question whose current dominant answer is baked into the fiber of our criminal justice system as we know it, into our disciplinary practices in schools, and even into our neighborhoods. And when we ask it again, we get the option to answer differently—and that includes the option to reconceive of justice as getting well rather than getting even. As Fania Davis, the former executive director of Restorative Justice for Oakland Youth and a visionary in the restorative justice field, has written:

> My dream is that restorative justice might help move us from an ethic of separation, domination, and extreme individualism to an ethic of collaboration, partnership, and interrelatedness. In that sense, I would say that this movement is more subversive than

any of the revolutionary movements in which I have
been involved since the 1950s.[4]

Restorative justice's transformative potential does not arise
from its newness, but rather from the way in which it draws
entirely from insight, power, and capabilities that already exist
wherever harm occurs. It is because of its alignment with these
capabilities that it stands to help solve the problems incarceration
cannot.

It is worthwhile in this context to revisit the four-part test that
any approach to violence should pass: it should be survivor-centered,
accountability-based, safety-driven, and racially equitable. People
who are hurt deserve a process that will help them heal. People
who are responsible for harm deserve to be held accountable for
that. All of us deserve responses to crime that make us safer. Those
responses must be equitably available. The promise of restorative
justice can be understood through each of these four principles.

A Survivor-Centered Approach

Elijah came home after being bailed out, trying to settle into his
new life. His sense of self was reduced to the evidence of what he
had survived. It consumed every other way he might see himself. He avoided mirrors, he disliked brushing his teeth or going
to the dentist, he wouldn't let anyone take pictures of him—at
least not from that side, and whenever people looked at him, he
imagined that all they were seeing, and all they were thinking
about, was his scar. As a young man of color, he knew that in
job interviews he was more likely to be perceived as someone
who had engaged in street violence, not just someone who was
hurt. He knew he might be asked about it, and then would have
to tell (or avoid telling) the story he liked least in his life. He felt
a range of seemingly conflicting emotions—at one moment an
acute, overwhelming sense of fear; at others, a sense of numbness

and detachment. He lost his appetite; he couldn't sleep and had nightmares when he did; he was furious; he was shivering. It would be more than a year until he would hear about the concept of trauma and assemble all these feelings into a single group. At the time, it was just chaos.

Elijah, Donnell, and Elwin's case was relatively atypical for Common Justice because of the overlapping roles each person played. Donnell was only a responsible party in the case. But Elijah was both harmed and responsible. Although Elwin sliced his face, causing the scar Elijah still bears to this day, Elijah was also part of the group responsible for assaulting Elwin. Elwin, similarly, was responsible for harming Elijah, but he was also stabbed in the lung and fought his way back from death's door as a result. Fortunately, restorative justice is capable of acknowledging and holding people's multiple roles as at once harmed and responsible, at once owed and in debt.

In their capacity as survivors, during the preparatory process and then more fully in the circle, Elijah and Elwin each spoke about the pain they experienced and its lasting impact on their lives. It was in the circle that Elijah identified himself as "a scar," where he shared the strategies he had developed to avoid mirrors, admitted to his new aversion to going to the dentist, to the way he had become more reluctant to leave his home or talk with people face-to-face. It was there that Elwin shared how close he had felt to death, how terrified he was at the time, and how shaken he had remained since. Their pain was the center of gravity for the circle: it was the very thing the process was responsible for repairing.

Restorative justice is not the only way to meet survivors' needs, nor can it provide survivors with everything they deserve. To begin with, survivors need services and support that have nothing to do with the person who hurt them, such as therapy, relocation resources, and services related to mental health and substance use. We need a social fabric that provides survivors with the wide range of supports they deserve over their lifetime and exists independent of whatever is done with or for the person who caused harm. But we also need strategies to address that harm, and restorative justice stands out as one of the most promising ways to do so.

When these processes are held with integrity and genuinely center the survivors throughout, they pay off. Restorative justice has been shown to leave those harmed more satisfied with outcomes: survivors who have taken part in restorative processes in the United States have reported 80 to 90 percent rates of satisfaction, as compared with satisfaction rates of about 30 percent for traditional court systems.[5] More recently, restorative justice programs have also been shown to significantly reduce post-traumatic stress symptoms in survivors. A study by the University of Pennsylvania that examined restorative justice programs found that robbery, assault, and burglary victims who took part in them reported 37 percent fewer symptoms of post-traumatic stress than those who participated in standard court processes.[6]

Those impacts are in part attributable to the fact that these processes include precisely the things survivors want and don't get from the criminal justice process: answers, voice, control, repair, and a belief that others will be protected from the harm they survived. For many survivors, the circle is a particularly powerful contributor to their healing, in part because it can help transform power. No one is at the head of the table in a circle; no one is at the top. While the harmed party's voice is central, its centrality in no way diminishes the value or importance of the responsible party's voice—or the voices of support people who are present. Responsible parties are asked to answer for what they have done from a position that affirms and reorients their personal power, rather than one that aims to constrict it. And harmed parties are brought into an equitable power dynamic with the person whom they did not have the power to stop from hurting them. For some harmed parties, the circle itself can provide substantial relief from the pain, rage, confusion, loss, and fear that so many survivors feel after they have been hurt, and it can form the basis for the ongoing healing work they undertake formally and informally. For others, the benefits of that transformation come later, as the agreements are completed—both those the responsible parties complete on their own and those that involve the survivors in some way.

Accountability

Donnell's, Elwin's, and Elijah's agreements emerging from their circle were similar, with adjustments that reflected each of their respective levels of responsibility and each of their goals and areas of growth. Donnell's commitments, for example, required the following: he had to keep a weekly journal, take the GED exam, complete a medical assistant certificate training program, complete his résumé, and seek employment. He had to conduct community service, share reflections about his experience with a group of his peers, and plan one activity every month to take part in with his children. He had to get all of his necessary documentation, identification, and paperwork in order; dress professionally for court and when he completed his public speaking engagement; and go to the doctor and receive a full physical exam to gain an understanding of the current status of his physical well-being.

Donnell had to read and watch a combination of ten books, sets of articles, and films that gave him insight into himself, his community, and his history, and share his reflections on what he read and watched; write reflections about his experience with the police and at the hospital when he needed medical attention; write a letter to himself that he read when he was losing focus, to help him regain his momentum and commitment; write a letter of apology to Elwin and his family, expressing his responsibility and remorse for the harm caused and his reflections about how the circle affected him; write a letter to his children telling the story of what happened; write an anti-violence pledge, share it with the other responsible parties at a community meeting, and invite them to take the pledge, too; write a journal entry with images that represent how he saw himself and his community; and learn about what is required to publish a book and investigate options for self-publishing and recommendations to new writers.

He had to spend time listening to other harmed parties to learn about their experience and share his own as appropriate; write an essay about the impact of violence on individuals, families, and communities, and about how young men of color behave when they are afraid; participate in a group session quarterly with his brother and the harmed party so that they could get to know each other as men and mend the harm among them; attend at least three counseling sessions so that he could talk about and heal through the pain and trauma of what happened; meditate six times for at least fifteen minutes each time; and help create a memorial or message to be placed at the bus stop where the incident occurred.

Finally, he had to attend the MOVE (Men Opposing Violence Everywhere) groups at Common Justice, which focus on the development of healthy masculinity. More than six years later, at the time of this writing, Donnell is now on staff at Common Justice as an intervention manager. Among his responsibilities is the facilitation of the MOVE groups.

At a recent event, Donnell reflected on his experience as a participant in Common Justice:

> I got into Common Justice because I committed a violent act. . . . When I went to Rikers [Island jail], automatically I'm thinking of all the horror stories [about the place]. I'm doing push-ups in my cell. I'm

not taking food from people. I'm doing all that stuff just thinking to myself, *I'm going to have to go through this thing that I heard so many other black men like me were being inducted into.* . . .

Then, instead, I get to Common Justice and meet the person that I harmed. Now . . . it's not just about me. It's like I had to go through something to feel a connection to anybody being hurt. I had to go through my own hurt too. I had to deal with that part of myself, because, like they say, hurt people hurt people. . . .

You don't have to tell me I did good by going in a store and doing something I thought was protecting my brother. It wasn't, but I want you to acknowledge the pain that was in it for me, too. When you do, you watch the magic of something happen where you start to give that same care back to the person that you have harmed. That's what meeting that person has done. . . . We've been different places sharing our story. I'm sitting here looking at this person like, you're so similar to me. You're so much of who I am. Your dreams are like mine. Your mother's dreams for you are like my mother's dreams for me. We are so connected and we didn't even know this thing.

If I knew that before, I wouldn't have moved the way I moved. I wasn't connected. I don't know when we lose our connection. I can't tell you that, but I was disconnected from something that was already here for us way before this. The one thing that I can say is this process is yours. It was already here. This is your thing. This is of your culture. That made me feel powerful. I also felt mad because something was held back from me, but I felt powerful that I knew it now.[7]

When asked to define accountability, Donnell said, "It was answering to the people of the community that surrounded the person I harmed. It was answering to the community of people that surrounded me. It was basically being able to answer to all points, and you can't do that when you're locked up. You can't speak to all points. You can't answer for that. You don't get a chance to do so."

The day before the circle, when asked, another responsible party described what he hoped to get out of it: "The way I think about it, I owe him twice: once for what I did, and once for him giving me this chance. And both those debts will take my lifetime to repay." The grace of restorative justice is that there is dignity in paying those debts—and the lifetime it takes to pay them stands to be longer and more fulfilling as a result.

After the circle, we asked that young man what struck him most. He said that he would never forget the way the harmed party "reached out his hand—not to punch me, not to shoot me, not to give me the finger—he reached out to shake my hand like a man. I've never seen anything like that in my life."

It has been more than six years since Elijah, Elwin, and Donnell sat together in that circle. Donnell works at Common Justice, and the other two young men are also employed, safe, and thriving. It is hard to imagine what their lives would have been like otherwise. They would each have come home from prison in 2017 after serving five years upstate, a setting that would have presented no opportunity to heal through their trauma. They would be saddled with violent felony convictions and would almost assuredly still blame one another for their pain. Donnell does not believe they would all be alive today if they had been incarcerated. It seems certain they would not all be doing so well. So well and so useful to others. So present in their children's lives. So valuable in their communities. So oriented toward the future. So capable of repair. So capable—dare

I say it and risk being accused of being "soft on crime"?—yes—
of love.

Safety

The most legitimate function of prisons in our society is to hold
people we cannot safely hold in our communities. The challenge
that arises for those who want to see the end of mass incarceration, then, is to develop more and better community capacity to
address harm so that we can break our reliance on prison without
compromising our obligation to secure safety. While restorative
justice achieves this in part by reducing recidivism, it is crucial
to also conceive of safety as something broader than just reduced
recidivism. Safety includes the cessation of violence, of course.
But it also includes the presence of healing. It is based on connection. And it thrives not on the suppression of power, but on the
rightful exercise of it.

One night, a young man robbed an immigrant named Federico of his week's wages as he came home from a fifteen-hour
shift at the restaurant where he worked in the kitchen for cash.
The incident changed everything for Federico, who experienced post-traumatic stress symptoms in its aftermath. He had
trouble sleeping, withdrew from his relationship, and could not
concentrate on studying for the GED test he had planned to
take. He started taking taxis home, which consumed a huge
portion of his already small income. He became afraid of walking on the street. He would say that whenever anyone came up
behind him, "even a little old lady," his mind would race, his
heart would race, his stomach would turn, and his whole body
would freeze up.

Several months after Federico's case came to Common Justice,
we convened a circle with Carl, the young man who robbed him.
After hours of talking about what happened and its impact on
Federico, we brainstormed ways that Carl could make things as

right as possible. After the group suggested (and Carl agreed to) some typical actions—going to school, apologizing, doing community service—Carl added, "Every man older than me in my family has been in prison. My older brother served a long time, and he won the prison boxing league championship when he did. He is the one who taught me how to fight. I showed you the wrong end of that on the street that day. But he is also the one who taught me how to defend myself—and if you want, I will show you that, too."

Then it was Federico's turn to speak, and he said, "I would love that."

A few months after the circle, Federico and Carl went to a local dojo. Supervised by a seasoned martial artist, Carl first stood in the position of the person being held against his will and Federico held him there. Carl demonstrated multiple ways to escape the hold. Then, they switched positions. Federico was in the same position he was in the night he was mugged—and being held by the same man. Only this time, as he practiced the techniques Carl taught him with increasing skill, he was repeatedly able to free himself from Carl's grasp.

The next day Federico called me and said, "I'm calling to tell you nothing happened." "What?" I asked. Federico explained: "Nothing happened. A six-foot-tall man passed me on the street and nothing happened." His mind did not race. His heart did not race. His stomach did not churn. His body did not freeze.

Federico had a little while before he had to be at work, and he went to Times Square so he could walk by as many people as possible. He looked for the tallest people, the biggest men, to walk past. At each one, he said to me on the phone, "Nothing!" "Nothing."

That is not an outcome that a standard criminal justice process, particularly one constrained by our dependence on mass incarceration, could have produced for him. Carl's and Federico's experience stands as a stunning refutation of the myth that survivors' safety always depends on separation from the people who harmed them. Not everyone could do what Carl did—or, for that matter, what Federico did. But for survivors whose healing could be aided by a restorative justice solution, we would be hard-pressed to come up with a legitimate ethical justification for denying them that path.

Racial Equity

Years ago, in a park in East New York, Shawn shot at Daquan. They had been friends until a recent disagreement had torn them apart. Shawn would later describe going to the park with the intention of just scaring Daquan, but as he arrived he "went in and out" of consciousness and the next thing he knew he had shot the gun. Daquan saw the gun pointed at him, heard the shot, and, not knowing whether he had been hit or not, ran for his life. Shawn's shot thankfully missed, but the bullet hit a bystander in the foot. Shawn ran out of the park in the opposite direction from Daquan. Daquan's eight-year-old sister, who saw it all happen, froze, shaking like a leaf. Eventually a neighbor walked her home.

When Daquan's mom heard the news, she ran to the park. "My son wasn't there," she would later say, trembling at the thought of the memory, "and no one could tell me where he was. . . . I have never felt more afraid in my life." The time between then and when she finally heard her son's voice felt like an eternity.

It would take Daquan some time to decide to tell the police: he did not believe they could keep him safe, and his fear that they would treat him as a suspect rather than a victim was sadly confirmed when he ultimately reported the crime. Feeling no promise of real protection, Daquan moved on a moment's notice to live with his older sister in Philadelphia, changing his sister's life as well. And because until then Daquan had been his younger sister's primary child care provider while his mother was at work, this move upended the entire family. The loss was always imbued with the threat of what it could have been. His mother said, "I almost lost my child. Every day I say to myself, 'he's still here, he's still here.'"

Shawn was arrested and charged with the shooting and, months later, the case came to Common Justice. It was only then that Shawn told his mentors, Mr. and Mrs. Miller, about what happened. Shawn had been friends with their son, Kenny, and the year before, he had been beside Kenny when he was fatally shot. Shawn became close with the Millers in the aftermath of Kenny's death, which affected him deeply. "I was next to Kenny when he was killed, not even two inches away," he said. "After that, I would see it replay in my head every day, over and over, like it just kept happening. I would cry at home, by myself, but could never cry when I was with other people. Nothing made it stop. Sometimes at school it got too quiet and it'd just start playing in my mind again—it got to the point I couldn't stand being in class because it was too quiet." Though he didn't make the connection when he first came to Common Justice, Shawn would later draw a link between his own trauma and his decision to shoot Daquan, including identifying the dissociation he felt in the park that day with what he experienced whenever he remembered Kenny's death. Making the connection haunted him. As he would later put it to Daquan directly in the circle process Common Justice convened: "After being through that—after losing Kenny and everything I felt after—if I almost did the same thing to you, Daquan, and your family, then I must be the biggest fool in the world."

It was the Millers who would help Shawn figure out how to hold all these truths at once. They became involved in the circle process, where Mrs. Miller turned to Daquan's mother and said: "That feeling you felt before you found your son, I feel that *every day*. It never stops. I'm here today because I believe this is a way to help Shawn, because I hope it will help you, Daquan, and you, his mother, but also because it's part of my healing, and all of our healing, to stop these young boys killing each other, and I think what we're doing here can help do that."

What they were doing in that circle was in part facing each other and the pain between them. But they were also crafting the response to the harm in the form of the commitments Shawn would have to fulfill. These commitments reflected the group's shared vision of the kind of man Shawn could become and involved college, work, restitution, trauma-focused therapy, apologies, peace offerings, public speaking, and more. They required him to complete a significant number of hours of community service, divided among the Millers' church, Daquan's family's church, and a variety of projects happening in honor of Kenny. These projects all held him closer to the community he had damaged through his actions rather than casting him away.

Over the nearly two years following, Shawn worked through the program diligently, responsibly, and with consistent and unfaltering respect and focus. He is the young man referenced earlier who said, "the judge is in here now." He is now employed as a welder and is obtaining further training to advance his career and secure membership in a union. He has not been arrested for any new crimes, has become a role model to his peers and to younger people around him, and has taken on a leadership role in the Millers' nonprofit community and anti-violence efforts. Daquan has completed college and his symptoms of trauma have subsided. His family has found peace, too.

No one involved in this situation believes the court and prison could have produced such an outcome. It was the people whose lives were at stake who could do so. As Mr. Miller put it when Shawn graduated: "*We* did it."

———

Daquan and Shawn, Elijah, Elwin, and Donnell, Carl and Federico—all of these young men are young men of color. Their loved ones who participated in the process are people of color. That sounds simple enough, but it is rare that solutions to violence are led by the people whose lives are at stake because of it. One way that racial inequity manifests is in shaping who gets to decide what happens in response to harm. These men and their support people together centered the experience of those among them who had been harmed, defined and practiced accountability, and carved a new pathway to safety. They accessed an exit ramp from the courts and the road to mass incarceration and instead built a thing they were always capable of from the start: a reconciliation that honored the past and made possible the future each of them deserves. Mass incarceration's disproportionate impact on communities of color is even more reprehensible when we are honest about how capable the members of communities are at solving their own problems when they have the space to do so.

People who commit harm have in themselves what they need to transform. Common Justice sees this daily, in part because our curriculum is entirely inquiry-based. Our staff does not tell people what is true. We do not believe people are vessels into whom we are pouring empathy and good values. Rather, we believe people are fundamentally capable of insight and transformation and regard it as our job to help dismantle the barriers to those things being fully present and expressed. People who commit harm know more about why people commit harm than do the rest of us. Responsible parties are almost all survivors of violence, so they know all too well about the lasting impact of actions like the ones they took. Young people of color know concretely about the daily impacts of structural racism and have the information they need to arrange their experience into a structural analysis. It is only when embedded in such a structural context that real, lasting change is possible.

At its best, restorative justice challenges and allows us to hold seemingly contradictory truths at the same time. On one hand, we recognize the reality of this country's inequitable conditions and how and why they have arisen; and on the other hand, we recognize the reality of individual agency. Restorative justice allows us to acknowledge that the context in which harm takes place is almost never right or fair, and still, even within that context, each one of us is responsible for carving out the most ethical, most righteous lives we can. It honors each person's dynamism and self-determination while never pretending we exist independent of our context or our (often unjust) constraints.

We are a long way from these kinds of solutions being universally available. But fortunately, we do have an example of what non-prison-based solutions to crime look like at a systematic level: it is what we do for white kids, and for middle-class and rich white kids in particular. We could reasonably describe whiteness as the oldest alternative to incarceration in America.

We begin diverting privileged white children at an early age. Most of the time (though certainly not all), we hold them close (keeping them after school) rather than throwing them away (sending them to jail). We ask them what is wrong. We believe that what they have done by the time they are twelve is not indicative of everything they can and will do with the rest of their lives. We treat them like the children and young people they are. We typically worry about them rather than fear them when they act up. We provide pathways out of the chaos and idiocy of adolescence and into adulthood. White people who are being honest will admit how badly we needed exactly that. And we deserved it. The problem is, so did the kids of color who didn't get the same opportunities.

I would like to say that the restorative justice movement has been immune to this kind of racial bias. But like most broad movements in this country, it has not been—at least not in the parts of the movement led primarily by white people. Believing in the potential of restorative justice for addressing violence requires believing unequivocally in the humanity of all the people involved, including the responsible parties. Racism diminishes white people's ability to believe unequivocally in the humanity of people of color. This means that until white people grapple with the ways we have internalized racism—and anti-blackness in particular—we will not fight for the expansion of these practices as we are morally obligated to do, and instead will create, knowingly or unknowingly, barriers to their advancement.

We are moving in the right direction. The restorative justice movement is growing in the United States, under the leadership of people of color and their anti-racist white accomplices, in a way that is becoming more aligned and intertwined with the struggle for racial justice. The movement is using its tools of repair to grapple with its own omissions, dishonesty, and disregard. Increasingly, people are carving a way forward that reflects the fundamental values of humanity and answerability that lie at the heart of restorative justice.

In my view, one of the most profound effects of this shift (and there are many), is that unlike before, many people in our movement now consider ourselves part of the struggle to end mass incarceration. It may seem strange that these movements have not been previously aligned or interconnected on a large scale, but they have not. That is partly because the movement to end mass incarceration has been largely focused (with essential, notable exceptions) on critiquing and shrinking the reach of jails and prison, not on displacing them. That movement's focus on the drug war has also drawn its attention away from cases of harm between and among people, which is where restorative justice does its work. On the other hand, the broader restorative justice movement (also with essential, notable exceptions) has largely shied away from tackling violence, has often taken a "we are all human" approach to equity rather than steering into the realities of historic and present oppressions, and has criticized the movement to end mass incarceration as too combative—or perhaps more often, people have not thought about it at all.

That division is ending. The increased focus on racial equity in the restorative justice movement has brought the carnage of mass incarceration squarely into the center of our attention. And the movement to end mass incarceration's increasing recognition that it will need to expand its focus beyond low-level and drug-related crimes and include interpersonal harm in its scope has created a sense of urgency about identifying alternate ways to address crime and violence. The potential of this emerging alignment is enormous. When the struggle to end what we can no longer withstand meets with the struggle to advance what we can do instead, we might just stand a chance of winning.

5

Policy and Power

The work of creating a world in which pathways to repair are the norm rather than the exception is fundamentally the work of culture change. It will require not just new programs or new resources, but also new ways of thinking and acting with one another. We make a grave error if we mistake policy change for culture change—changing the law and changing hearts and minds are not the same. And on the whole, policy flows from culture, not the reverse.

But we will make a comparably grave error if we wait for the culture to change before changing our policies—or if we underestimate the ways in which policy, when deployed accountably and strategically, can remove barriers, foster supports, and be mobilized as a force for larger shifts. Policy, then, will be but one dimension of how our nation extracts itself from the cycles of interpersonal and institutional violence that have become as American as apple pie. But it will be a crucial one.

All of the recommendations here would result in reduced rates of incarceration. These shifts are likely to raise concerns that less prison will mean more violence. Fortunately, the evidence demonstrates unequivocally that it is possible to reduce incarceration and reduce violence at the same time.[1] A recent Justice Strategies and Harvard study documented the phenomenon in New York City, where serious crime fell by 58 percent from 1994 to 2014, while at the same time the combined jail and prison incarceration rate was cut by 55 percent.[2] And other places have seen similar trends. When California reduced its prison population by 25 percent, reports of violent crime dropped by 21 percent.[3] When New Jersey reduced its prison population by 25 percent, reports of violent crime dropped by 31 percent.[4] Although scholars will debate the causality in these changes, the correlation is irrefutable and the result makes sense, given the conspicuous limitations of incarceration as a primary safety strategy. And we stand to do even better than we have done.

To build the political will to develop and expand these solutions, we have to stop talking about alternatives to our current policy as though they are alternatives to something that works. The question of whether to embrace a more dignified and humane approach to violence than the current system might be complicated if the current system were working. But when that system is failing, the burden of proof shifts. We should not be asking whether there is an appetite or opening for something new. We should be asking whether there is any moral or practical basis whatsoever for continuing with the old.

Thus far, only a tiny fraction of our policy reform efforts has dared to touch the question of violence. It is time for that to change. I believe we are ready. But if we are not ready, then perhaps it is because we will never become ready other than by beginning. So let us begin.

Righting Our Sentencing Policies

Any policy change that seeks to address the long-standing history of racial inequity in the United States and the intergenerational impacts that arise from mass incarceration will have to contend with the way the criminal justice system sentences people. This cannot be solved through tinkering; it will require a large-scale overhaul of how we approach crime and punishment.

Acting on a national commitment to reduce violence will require inverting the logic that has driven our sentencing policy for the past several decades. We will have to restructure our punishment codes to allow for accountability, repair, and restoration. Excessive sentences are the enemy of those aspirations. Lengthy sentences offer diminishing returns at increasing costs to the people incarcerated, their loved ones and communities, and the public. Evidence even suggests that such sentences can reach a tipping point at which both individually and broadly they can become risk factors for violence rather than protective factors against violence as intended. Lowering the maximum allowable sentences will be an essential step toward uprooting the excess of punishment we have baked into our statutes and toward creating a boundary, aligned with reason, morality, and evidence, beyond which our laws should no longer go.

This will include eliminating the most severe penalty available: capital punishment. We can do this because of a moral approbation of state-sponsored killing, because of concern about the practical and financial drain it places on the system throughout the necessary appellate process, because of its inefficacy as a deterrent of any kind, or because we have been persuaded of the imperfection of the criminal justice system and know that any time we have the death penalty we will inevitably execute some people who are innocent.[5] For whatever reasons we reject the use of capital punishment, a criminal justice system that opposes violence cannot have killing as its maximum penalty and still achieve its aims.

Similarly, we will also have to lower minimum sentences for crimes, including crimes of violence. This means, first and foremost, the elimination of mandatory minimums. Mandatory minimum laws are the flagships of a criminal justice orientation we have to outgrow, and no large-scale change will be possible if we remain constrained by laws that are increasingly understood to be archaic and draconian. The elimination of mandatory minimums will also require eliminating or rolling back the host of "three strikes" laws that compound penalties exponentially for people with multiple convictions. These laws place some of the narrowest and most illogical constraints on the sound exercise of discretion and will have to be removed for any system to be empowered to act as humanely and rationally as possible.

When sentencing guidelines still recommend (even if they do not require) a minimum sentence of jail or prison time, those guidelines should allow consideration of public safety, the needs and wishes of survivors, the age and circumstances of the person responsible for harm, the social and financial costs to community and society of incarcerating the person, and the availability of other options (such as diversion programs) that may be capable of producing better short- and long-term results than imprisonment can. These alternatives to prison must be available even for the most serious crimes when a reasonable set of criteria are met. The criteria might include the wishes of the survivor, the availability of diversion programs with a demonstrated record of success, the willingness and capability of the responsible person to engage in a meaningful accountability or treatment process, and any remaining risk to public safety not managed by the alternative to incarceration. Ultimately, these solutions have to become the default from which we deviate in exceptional circumstances—not the exceptional opportunity available to only a few.

In this way, incarceration has to be rendered an option of last resort, so that ultimately, we would talk not of community-based interventions as "alternatives to incarceration," but of incarceration as an "alternative to community intervention," one we deploy sparingly and reluctantly with full awareness of its drawbacks and risks. We have seen substantial movement in this direction in the juvenile justice arena, where arrest rates are plummeting, incarceration rates are down from their peak by more than half, and systems increasingly rely on responses other than incarceration to address even serious harm.[6] But on the adult side of the system, even where broad networks of alternatives to incarceration, intervention, and treatment programs exist, few jurisdictions make these options available when someone has committed violence. Many people assume—incorrectly—that incarceration is the "toughest" response to crime, when in fact some dignified, humane alternatives to prison turn out to be more difficult and more effective, perhaps in part because of what they require of the people who participate. This is true of some substance use programs that have demonstrably reduced recidivism more effectively than incarceration.[7] Although these programs do not subject people to the isolation and indignities of prison, they require participants—whether mandated by the courts or, even better, engaged voluntarily—to go through the enormously challenging work of battling addiction. In New York City, numerous alternatives to incarceration that address a combination of nonviolent crimes and lower-level violent crimes have demonstrated better safety outcomes than prison has.[8] These programs in New York and across the country often include education, mental health treatment, community service, and vocational training as ways to help hold people accountable. New responses to violence can build on the lessons learned from these programs (which thus far have focused primarily on nonviolent offenses) and from violence intervention efforts that have not yet been deployed as alternatives to jail or prison.

One of the ways mass incarceration has grown has been through the classification of an extraordinarily wide range of crimes as felonies, including as violent felonies, even when they do not involve what most people would consider serious violence—or violence at all, for that matter (such as someone stealing from the residence of a person who is not home). Reclassifying a wide range of felonies as misdemeanors will put those crimes into a sentencing range more proportionate with the harm caused and will reserve the censure of felony sanctions for the harm our society takes most seriously.

Along with this reclassification, it will be important to roll back the variety of enhancements that have been legislated to increase the penalties associated with certain crimes. Prime among these are gang enhancements, which add additional penalties (or upgrade the classification of a crime from a misdemeanor to a felony or to a higher-level felony, for example) for people believed to be gang-involved. The information gathered on gang involvement is notoriously inaccurate, and the databases in which this information is held raise serious concerns about civil liberties.[9] Information about people can be placed in these databases without their knowledge. People are often included based solely on their social connection to others in the databases who have criminal histories. There is no standard mechanism to remove people from these databases and no way for a person to contest being included in these lists.[10] These lists and the enhancements they power have been demonstrated to be inequitable. What they have not been demonstrated to be is effective.

Finally, any changes to sentencing statutes should be applied retroactively. It is important to remember that these changes are not simply reform—they are a form of societal repair. There is arguably no one more entitled to that repair than someone who has paid—and is continuing to pay—the price for our misjudgment and mistakes. This means that sentencing reform can and should include releasing people who are currently incarcerated, as well as supporting them when they come home.

Reshaping the Power of U.S. Prosecutors

Substantially reducing mass incarceration will require demanding that prosecutors use their discretion to rely on jail and prison as a last resort, constrained by values of fairness and parsimony and only to the degree necessary to ensure safety. For instances of violence that result in arrest, no amount of building effective responses will matter unless prosecutors throughout the country become different kinds of partners in the overall effort to produce safety.

Prosecutors exercise an extraordinary degree of power and discretion in the criminal justice system.[11] They decide whether to file charges against people who are arrested—and in so doing, they can increase, reduce, or dismiss the charges brought by police. Prosecutors have a leading role in determining bail, both through the recommendations they make at arraignment and through the charges they bring, which shape a judge's determination. Unlike at trial, where the judge and jury are the decision makers, prosecutors retain the lion's share of the power in the plea bargaining process—the process through which 94 to 97 percent of all cases are decided. This process is rife with racial disparities.[12] What is more, the outcomes of this process are shaped by the bail the prosecutor had a hand in setting, given that people who are detained pending trial are more likely to accept a plea bargain.[13] Disproportionately, these are poor people who cannot afford the cost of their freedom.

Prosecutors' discretion can have a greater impact on incarceration rates than almost any legislative reform. But to put it mildly, prosecutors driving decarceration is still not the norm. Much of that has to do with politics, culture, and incentives—not just policy. Prosecutors' offices and the public typically measure a prosecutor's success—whether an elected district attorney or an entry-level assistant district attorney—by the number and severity of convictions and sentences he or she secures. Prosecutors' practices will change substantially only if they define success differently and if their constituents join them in doing so. This includes prioritizing more nuanced results like fairness, parsimony, rehabilitation, and safety over the blunt outputs of lengthy sentences.[14]

This shift is not unthinkable, and in some places, it is under way. For instance, Law Enforcement Leaders to Reduce Crime & Incarceration, a group of more than 150 current and former law enforcement leaders, align around a platform that includes increasing alternatives to arrest and prosecution—especially diversion to mental health and drug treatment; restoring balance to criminal laws; reforming mandatory minimum sentencing laws; and strengthening community–law enforcement relations.[15] Some prosecutors' offices are taking the lead in embracing and implementing diversion programs across a wide range of charges.[16] In 2017, voters elected new local prosecutors who ran on platforms that included the promise of reducing the overuse of incarceration in places including Illinois, Florida, and Texas.[17] In 2018, Eric Gonzalez was elected Brooklyn district attorney with a campaign that promised the continuation and expansion of District Attorney Kenneth Thompson's progressive legacy.[18] Larry Krasner, a well-known civil rights attorney and public defender, was elected district attorney of Philadelphia on an unapologetic reform platform that same year. And a number of new candidates are right behind them. This new wave of candidates stands to have a transformative effect on criminal justice practice and policy. In recent years, 85 percent of prosecutor elections went uncontested.[19] This means that the actors with the most power in the criminal justice system are rarely held to account by their constituents. The increasing momentum around and attention to elections of prosecutors suggest that these types of candidates and these types of victories are positioned to become far more common and to redefine the justice landscape in America.

Crucially, prosecutors will not act better in office simply because they are better people, or even because they hold better beliefs. They will act better when their constituents make different demands of them. These demands can shift in two main ways. First, a newly educated, preexisting constituency can demand different outcomes than it did previously. The potential for this is particularly strong in places with active voter education and/or places where it has been a long time since a prosecutor's seat was contested; the values that a prosecutor holds might be outdated or out of sync with constituents.

Second, new voters can participate. This does not require changing the opinions of people who are already actively engaged in the democratic process; it requires activating those people who care deeply about these issues but have not taken that concern to the voting booth. The most important constituencies that can be activated in this way are the communities most impacted by crime, violence, and incarceration. These are the communities to which the district attorney's office should ultimately be held accountable, since they are the ones that will reap the benefits or pay the price of the office's practices. The group Color of Change, among others, has done formidable work to activate black voters around prosecutor elections with this reality in mind. When district attorneys are elected by the people whose lives are at stake in their choices, we see results that are far more aligned with the principles of representative democracy: district attorneys better reflect the values of their constituents, take risks their constituents can tolerate, and make the shifts their constituents demand.

This shift in accountability changes practices. Prosecutors who are working to truly serve their constituents who are most affected by violence recognize that long sentences do not always produce safety and sometimes even run contrary to that goal. These prosecutors, then, often forgo the harshest punishment they can secure in favor of the fairest and most effective one. They rely heavily on proven alternative to incarceration programs, favor probation or conditional discharges over prison sentences when it is safe to do so, respond to victims' requests for restorative justice processes, support measures to meet young adults with developmentally appropriate interventions, and do not always seek the maximum penalty.

These prosecutors are more likely to develop fair and reasonable practices regarding bail and charging decisions, commit to transparency, shift their internal and external measures of success so as to incentivize different behavior, seek to reduce collateral consequences of convictions whenever possible—including those related to immigration—and hold themselves accountable to the communities harmed by crime, violence, and incarceration. When they reorient their standard practice in this way, these prosecutors can play a leading role in ending the overuse of incarceration as a response to violence.

This matters profoundly in our local jurisdictions, but it can also have an impact on policy more broadly. District attorney associations typically play an active and influential role in the state capitol, and prosecutors who take different positions on legislation—even if that means that the group expresses multiple conflicting positions rather than one unified draconian one—could dramatically accelerate the pace of legislative change across the country. The recent elections of progressive prosecutors have also demonstrated how deeply people care, when they are fully informed, about their local prosecutors. This means that prosecutor elections stand to be a lever for broader voter engagement. There are undoubtedly jurisdictions where people are relatively indifferent about their senator but care deeply about the DA who sets bail in their case, who arrested a loved one in front of their children, who overcharged their friend for an honest mistake. When people come out in support of progressive candidates, they are likely to also support other progressive candidates on the ballot—including the senators they might not have otherwise bothered to come vote for. As we consider the contested terrain in elections throughout the country, the potential for these races to activate an engaged constituency should not be underestimated or underutilized.

Transforming Our Responses
to Young Adults

Emerging adults from the ages of eighteen to twenty-four make up only 10 percent of the overall U.S. population, but represent 30 percent of the overall arrest rate and about one in five admissions to prison.[20] They are also disproportionately responsible for violence, have the highest rearrest rates upon release from prison, and are imprisoned in the most racially disparate rates.[21] Even as (and in part because) they are still developing, young adults are capable of causing serious harm. As we continue to learn, they are also particularly capable of change: as a group, their arrest rates plummet once they reach the age of twenty-five.[22] Our challenge, then, is to identify strategies that increase the likelihood of positive transformation.

Much of the recent research on adolescent development, largely from developmental psychology and brain science, has taught us what most parents of adolescents already surmised: adolescents are still growing up, and their capacities for consequential thinking and impulse control in particular are still in development until they are twenty-four years old.[23] These findings have led to calls for mercy for young adults who cause harm and have influenced Supreme Court decisions about sentencing young people who commit crimes.[24] But the implications of the research require more than just principled and sensible mercy: they require serious, functional, and dignified methods to hold young people accountable.

Deploying these methods will require a greater emphasis on rehabilitation (and on employment and education in particular); measures that help young adults separate early on from the justice system (like diversion); steps to reduce the likelihood of returning to the system once emerging adults have left it (like confidentiality of records); and on the creation and regular use of developmentally targeted interventions.[25]

The juvenile justice system (also called family court in some states) on the whole is better equipped than the adult system to meet the needs of younger adults. Restructuring our courts to ensure that most younger adults (up to the age of twenty-one—or even twenty-four, if we are using science as our guide) are seen in these courts would position us to identify and employ the appropriate interventions to ensure accountability and safety. These juvenile systems, though far from perfect, are not bound in the way adult systems are by the same mandatory minimum sentencing requirements; often have access to a broader range of community-based programs to which they can refer young people who have broken the law; and give judges the discretion to consider the young person's maturity, circumstances, and development to determine a fair and safe sentence.[26]

When young people cannot be moved to or kept in the juvenile justice system, strategies should be employed to allow judges in the adult system more discretion, similar to the judges in family court. Some states have "youthful offender" statutes, which typically waive minimum sentencing requirements and allow for the sealing of young people's records at the end of the case and/or their term of incarceration.[27] These statutes recognize the value of greater flexibility in the sentencing of younger adults and the ways in which a permanent record can create barriers to them growing up and out of their negative behaviors, in part by making it more difficult for them to secure employment and higher education, both of which are associated with reductions in crime and violence.[28] Similarly, the expansion of confidentiality protections more broadly (including sealing and expungement options for young people in both juvenile and adult courts) can allow people a pathway out of their youthful mistakes and into mature and responsible adulthood.

Jurisdictions can be motivated in this arena, as in others, through fiscal incentives that promote the development of rigorous community programs rather than the imprisonment of their youth. A wide variety of such structures exists (a subject that exceeds the scope of this chapter to explore), but all create mechanisms by which jurisdictions pay a price—literally—for electing to imprison people and receive resources to deploy other options. In reversing the financial structures that accompanied the rise in "tough on crime" policies on local, state, and federal levels, policy makers can redistribute resources toward effective interventions by leveraging budgetary considerations in the interest of justice.

Similarly, people should be given incentives to participate in programs with proven track records of success. Emerging adults can be particularly responsive to restorative justice, cognitive behavioral, educational, substance use, mental health, and employment programming. By creating incentives for this participation—as alternatives to incarceration, pathways to "earned" or "merit" time for young people who are in detention, or conditions for shortening probation sentences—our sentencing practices can better align with the lessons of science and the interests of safety.

And finally, even when young people are incarcerated for long terms for committing very serious crimes, they should still be given a chance at redemption. The Youth Offender Parole Legislation in California has required that individuals given long sentences as youth must have parole hearings at which developmental issues are taken into account. As scholar and well-known justice reformer Vincent Schiraldi testified in 2017, "while 36 percent of all releases from California prisons return to prison within the first year, no one paroled under the youth program has been either convicted of a new crime or sent back to confinement since the law's enactment."[29]

Releasing People from Prison

When prison is used as the means of holding someone accountable, its use should still be bound by parsimony—which means that no one should be incarcerated longer than necessary. Despite conditions that make transformation difficult, many people who are in prison for violence become people who will not hurt others again. For some, the pathway to this is through reflection and remorse. For others, it is through time—people mature, engage in classes and activities that support them in changing, and get older. It is widely documented that after a certain age, the risk that people will hurt others diminishes vastly.[30] And the severity of one's crime does not affirmatively predict risk: in fact, people who commit homicide and sex offenses, for instance, have some of the lowest re-offense rates of anyone returning home from prison.[31]

The limited use of parole throughout the country—so that only a small fraction of eligible people are granted it—also has the detrimental effect of providing disincentives for positive behavior, given that the promise of parole is a primary vehicle in prisons to reward people for engaging in constructive activities and refraining from violence.[32] Pragmatism and fairness therefore point to the value of providing people with real opportunities for parole based on their actions while incarcerated and a current assessment of their risk to others.

Although many parole boards also attempt to gauge subjectively whether someone expresses adequate responsibility for past actions—in addition to objective measures of the person's behavior while incarcerated—it is extraordinarily hard to do that effectively. Even in the context of intimate relationships, it can be hard to tell the degree to which someone truly feels remorse. It is unrealistic to expect a group of strangers in a high-pressure context to make such a nuanced discernment over the course of an hour or two—or in some cases, as few as ten or fifteen minutes. Parole should therefore be more focused on actions than impressions of remorse, and it is also important to have other mechanisms for early release (including "earned time," "good time," and "merit time") to further encourage positive change.[33]

The sound and consistent use of all these mechanisms is sub-stantially strengthened, where available, by educational and other programs that give people in prison an opportunity to change and are demonstrated to reduce the likelihood that someone will cause further harm upon return from prison.[34]

In New York, support for the greater use of parole has emerged from what is perhaps a surprising source: the Downstate Coali-tion for Crime Victims. The group has recently become more supportive of the expanded use of parole, and in 2017 opposed a bill that would have extended the period between parole hearings from two to five years for certain crimes.[35] In this case, coalition members understood that the proposed legislation would signifi-cantly diminish incarcerated people's opportunities to be grant-ed parole when they had earned it. As such, it risked subjecting incarcerated people to unnecessarily lengthy terms of imprison-ment even when they had met the standards for release consistent with their court-imposed sentences and with the judgment of the parole board. This was particularly worrisome to the group, giv-en the number of incarcerated people who are themselves crime survivors and the prevalence of sexual violence in prisons.

The coalition's opposition was based on the recognition that although some victims do oppose parole of the people who hurt them, for many survivors, the rehabilitation of the person who harmed them may be far more meaningful than that per-son's ongoing punishment, and the granting of parole can serve as a marker of that change.[36] What is more, victims and their advocates know that the possibility of parole can motivate par-ticipation in programs, accountable reflection, and behavior change—all key elements in the change many survivors want to see. As the group put it in a letter to New York legislators, "Victims' families deserve whatever peace they can find. Rather than investing in punitive practices that may not guarantee either safety or healing, law-makers committed to that peace should make a commitment to ensuring all victims have access to necessary supports at every stage of their healing process." When we no longer treat incarceration as a victim service, it frees us up to make both sounder decisions about people's release from prison and sounder investments in survivors' healing.

We all stand to benefit from such a shift. In thinking about safety on a community level, it is crucial to remember that people who have transformed are assets to society—and we lose their contributions when they remain incarcerated. So granting parole is not only about assuming a responsible risk in consenting to a person's release. It is also about bringing an asset back into the community, someone who stands to contribute to the larger social fabric of well-being through their participation, their relationships, their accountability, and their healing.

Reducing Collateral Consequences

In 2014, between 70 million and 100 million people in the United States (or one-third of the adult population) had criminal records, and a full 13 million people (or 6 percent of its adults) had felony convictions.[37] Felony convictions result in more than just sentences to incarceration, probation, and/or parole. They also come with a host of additional restrictions or "collateral consequences." The reach of these collateral consequences is vast, and depending on the nature of a person's conviction and the place where it occurred, they can include denials of public housing, limitations of parental rights and access to child support, exclusions from the job market, restrictions on access to welfare benefits (including food stamps), barriers to higher education, increases in deportation, and disenfranchisement.[38]

In addition to exclusion from public and Section 8 housing, many people with convictions also face discriminatory practices in the private housing market, which either denies them housing or forces them to pay above-market rates for substandard living conditions.[39] Compounding the impact of locking people into long-term housing instability, these laws also make it more difficult for people with convictions to keep their families intact. Some state and federal statutes allow the termination of the parental rights of people convicted of felonies; others disallow the approval of people with certain convictions as foster and adoptive parents; and others create barriers to formerly incarcerated and convicted people's access to child support.[40]

Despite the benefits that would arise from formerly incarcerated and convicted people being able to support themselves and contribute to the tax base, statutes across the country put up substantial barriers to gainful employment. Some laws bar people with convictions entirely from jobs as teachers, child care professionals, and even barbers or morticians.[41] For others, the exclusion comes due to the proliferation of background checks that are regularly deployed—both legally and illegally—as a reason to deny employment to people with convictions. The national movement to "ban the box," arising from a range of campaigns and advocacy, most notably the leadership of Dorsey Nunn and the organization All of Us or None, aims to limit an employer's ability to discriminate based on people's criminal history by restricting when the employer can ask questions about criminal convictions and how they can use information gained through background checks. Far-reaching though these efforts are, they still leave most of the job market rife with inequity and untouched by antidiscrimination regulation. For people who aim to overcome these barriers through education, doors close there, too. The Higher Education Act of 1998 suspends eligibility for a student loan or other financial assistance for people convicted of certain offenses.[42] In the 2007-2008 academic year, thousands of students were found to be ineligible under this provision and many more were deterred from even applying.[43]

People who face barriers to education and employment become more dependent on the social safety net, but our practices also limit access to that for people with convictions. Riding the "tough on crime" wave, Congress's 1996 welfare reform package permanently bars some people convicted of felonies from receiving Temporary Assistance to Needy Families (TANF).[44] Although states may opt out of the lifetime ban, thirty-seven states either fully or partially enforce the TANF ban, still imposing substantial restrictions on people's access to welfare and even food stamps.[45] The number, reach, and restrictions associated with sex offender registries skyrocketed at the same time.[46]

For people who are not U.S. citizens, the consequences of convictions—or even arrests—can include deportation. In our current environment of heightened, overt anti-immigrant sentiment, these laws, including the Immigration Reform and Control Act of 1986 and the Illegal Immigration Reform and Immigrant Responsibility Act of 1996, are being deployed to remove thousands of people from their homes and families, even those who have been home from prison for years or even decades.[47] This intersection with immigration law promises to be among the most devastating and contested terrains in the criminal justice arena in the years to come.

In addition to barriers to people's ability to stay in their communities and remain healthy and productive contributors there, our statutes also restrict convicted people's access to our democracy by denying their right to vote. The United States has reached record levels of disenfranchisement: 6.1 million people are barred from voting as a result of their convictions (as compared with 1.17 million in 1976). These policies differ from state to state, with the most restrictive states limiting people's voting rights permanently and only two states (Maine and Vermont) not restricting these rights at all.[48] The impact of these policies is not evenly distributed and affects communities of color disproportionately. According to the Sentencing Project, "one in every 13 black adults cannot vote as the result of a felony conviction, and in four states—Florida, Kentucky, Tennessee, and Virginia—more than one in five black adults is disenfranchised."[49] This is not, to put it mildly, the first time America has blocked people—especially black people—from voting.

The exclusion of so many people from our democratic process has far-reaching effects. First, it means that by definition our criminal justice policy is not shaped by the people most impacted by it. Formerly incarcerated and convicted people have not only some of the highest stakes, but also among the deepest insight into what constitutes sound policy. What is more, ongoing disenfranchisement runs contrary to the notion that people who have finished their sentences have paid their debts to society. The resolution of that debt can and should include a pathway to full participation in our democracy. The principled choice here is also pragmatic, as higher civic participation has been demonstrated to be associated with lower recidivism.[50]

The exclusion of these voters has had substantial impact on the outcomes of elections nationally. A 2002 study identified seven United States Senate races from 1970 through 1998 that would probably have resulted in different outcomes had people with convictions not been banned from the polls. If Florida had allowed people with convictions to vote, it is likely that the 2000 Bush–Gore presidential election would have ended in a different result.[51] At the time of this writing, Desmond Meade and the Florida Rights Restoration Coalition, along with countless others in the movement, are in the process of reversing this inequity and are leading a groundbreaking campaign to secure the vote for formerly incarcerated people statewide.

These efforts are right and winnable. The exclusion of people from democratic participation runs contrary to public opinion, and efforts to restore people's rights have gained some traction, with twenty-four states since 1997 changing their policy to allow more people access to vote. The Sentencing Project estimates that 800,000 citizens have been re-enfranchised as a result of these successful reform efforts.[52] Still, the overwhelming pattern nationally remains one of disenfranchisement, and the reversal of that pattern is crucial to becoming the fully participatory democracy America claims and aspires to be.

Transforming Policing

We will not be able to transform our responses to violence without transforming policing. This means enacting major changes in how police respond to harm, but also changing how our society responds to harm committed by police. The complexity and breadth of this topic far exceeds the scope of this book, but it is useful to note some particularly essential shifts that will be necessary to the transformation of violence.

Poor communities, and communities of color in particular, suffer from a combination of over-policing and under-protection. Homicide clearance rates (that is, the portion of cases that are solved) in black communities are often as low as 20 percent, and while those murders go unsolved, often members of the same communities are policed aggressively for low-level infractions that have no bearing on safety.[53] Wherever this disconnect occurs, it is devastating to any sense of legitimacy a community might have about its law enforcement, as these police practices betray a serious misalignment with community priorities and can engender a sense of deep disregard on the part of law enforcement for the lives of residents. A police department that is not trusted will never be an effective agent in securing safety. Police depend on the cooperation of witnesses and victims, particularly in cases of serious harm, and a divestment in the outcomes of policing on the part of those whose lives are at stake makes it impossible for law enforcement to make the contributions to safety that everyone deserves.

Narrowly, the inversion of this trend means, on the one hand, insisting that murders in low-income communities are taken seriously and solved, and, on the other, an end to "broken windows," "stop and frisk," and other approaches that result in broad-scale surveillance, excessively frequent police contact for minor infractions, and grave inequities. But more broadly, inverting this long-standing history will require dealing with the history itself.

Community leaders and scholars with deeper expertise than mine can chart a number of forward-thinking reforms to policing. But accountability work teaches us that none of those reforms will have a transformative effect without an acknowledgment of the underlying causes of distrust of police, particularly in communities of color. The racially inequitable legacy of policing stretches back to the formation of this nation, and police have not only failed to protect communities of color from harm, but they have enacted enormous levels of harm. This is not simply or most importantly about individual police officers, many of whom have the best intentions and even behavior in their work. It is about an institution with a history of enabling and enforcing the worst disparities in our country's history. It is about officers who returned escaped people to the plantations they were fleeing, officers who publicly announced the times of lynchings to be carried out in the backyards of their own precincts, officers who drove black residents out of neighborhoods where they had bought homes, and officers who continue to arrest, assault, and shoot black people at glaringly disproportionate rates.

People do not (and to be fair, should not) trust institutions with such a past or present, particularly if that past or present is unacknowledged. Any substantial shift in police-community relations will require a direct acknowledgment of and grappling with that history. Groups ranging from local community leaders to grassroots movements to more resourced efforts like the National Network for Safe Communities (NNSC) all regard police legitimacy as essential to safety: they understand that police cannot keep a community safe if its people lack trust in them to do so, and they acknowledge that communities have had and continue to have a sound basis for their distrust. Many of these efforts aim to repair breaches between communities and police, in part by recognizing the history of harm that law enforcement in America has caused—and engaging police in making that recognition. When police departments around the country have made explicit statements acknowledging the harm their institutions have caused, the speed at which change has been possible has been accelerated by that practice of honesty.[54]

Acknowledgment alone will not be enough. There will also have to be a shift in power. Creating stronger mechanisms for community control and oversight over law enforcement will demonstrate the seriousness of a police department's commitment to admitting past harms and ending current and future ones. The value of civilian oversight of police is widely recognized by parties across the political spectrum.[55] The policy platform for the Movement for Black Lives is clear on this issue:

> By requiring all civilian oversight agencies to retain the power to hire and fire officers, determine disciplinary action in cases of misconduct related to excessive and lethal force, determine the funding of agencies, set and enforce policies, and retain concrete means of retrieving information—such as subpoena power—from law enforcement and third parties as it pertains to circumstances involving excessive, sexual and lethal force; communities will be able significantly to reduce the number of Black people impacted by police violence.[56]

The collaborative development of functional mechanisms to

ensure true accountability by police officers who commit harm will be an essential dimension of changing communities' relationships with the people who police them. Impunity guts legitimacy, and so any effort to bolster the legitimacy of law enforcement will require that its members be held to at least as high a standard of behavior as that of the people they are authorized to police.

Finally, a great deal of what police can and should do is to *do less*. We have asked and empowered police to play an impossibly, unsustainably, and unreasonably wide range of roles. They are charged with addressing mental health crises, addiction, and other social challenges that are beyond the scope of their training, expertise, or fundamental responsibility. Emerging efforts that divert cases at the point of arrest, including LEAD (Law Enforcement Assisted Diversion) and a wide range of other local and more grassroots endeavors, suggest a way forward to radically reducing the scope of police responsibilities by creating conduits to support and off-ramps from arrest and prosecution before the process even begins. Getting policing right will require less policing. As with preventing and responding to violence more broadly, more of the responsibility for safety has to be given and entrusted to the communities most capable of bringing about the outcomes everyone seeks and deserves.

Prevention

Safety and community well-being are supported by efforts and structures that prevent harm from occurring in the first place. Because violence is contextual, most effective prevention efforts include the broad distribution of the social supports that make violence unlikely and healing accessible, including quality schools, housing, jobs, health care, mental health and substance use treatment, and after-school programs. Recognizing the degree to which mental health and substance use challenges drive substantial portions of crime and violence, for instance, compels us to develop a robust and accessible treatment infrastructure that does not require a court mandate as a prerequisite for help.[57]

That said, the concept of "prevention" can be misleading. We cannot prevent our way into safety while keeping our responses to existing violence the same. Prevention is appealing: what better response to violence than to keep it from happening in the first place? But an emphasis on prevention all too often includes a narrowing impulse that discards anyone who has already committed harm or been harmed. It rings like a longing for some kind of clean slate, as if we could say: we will start with these children here, and we will do right by them in ways we have not done right by the ones who came before, and they will grow into happy, healthy adults, and all of this violence will be behind us.

It is an understandable wish, but also a fundamentally dishonest and unaccountable one: it betrays our longing to avoid facing the impact of what our current policy choices have produced. There is no world where we can raise safe children without supporting the well-being of the teenagers and adults in their lives, and the desire to do so is dangerously ahistorical. Moreover, focusing on prevention, particularly with an emphasis on early childhood, often betrays an implicit racial bias in our estimation of who constitutes a child. Studies show that white people consistently misperceive the age of children and young adults of color—often overestimating their age by nearly five years.[58] White people's inability to see the *child* in older children of color is matched by an increased perception of dangerousness of adolescents and adults, particularly adolescents and men of color.[59] Unexamined, those biases will steer us toward dangerously narrow conceptions of prevention—ones that are focused only on young children who have not yet committed harm or been harmed. What is more, prevention allows us to evade the issue of repair—as if we do not have to own the harm we have caused to people who are already hurt, to face their pain and our responsibility for it.

But every five-year-old lives in a home with adults, and many live in homes with teenagers, often with teenagers who have been in trouble or caused harm or both. Children's parents are incarcerated, their older brothers are shot, their sisters and brothers are sexually assaulted, their aunts and uncles are treated unfairly by the police, their grandparents get inadequate health care, and their ancestors' losses live in their bones. We cannot isolate the children we perceive as innocent from the other people in their lives whom we hold responsible somehow for their own suffering. This means that a true focus on prevention requires an intergenerational approach to community well-being. Prevention at its best and most honest is rooted in an awareness of the interconnectedness of different segments of a community—of the ways in which that interconnectedness can be a source of pain, but also one of the ways in which it is the very fabric that can hold a healthier community together.

Relocating the Locus of Control
to Define and Secure Safety

There is no single proven model that can replace the current failing approach to violence, nor will there ever be one solution to the wide variety of interlocking challenges that produce violence in communities. But there are crucial lessons from promising interventions for violence that, given sufficient investments to develop them and others at anywhere near the scale of investments in incarceration, could diminish violence in ways punishment alone never will. Central to these lessons is the fact that law enforcement alone will never solve the problem of violence and that the locus of control to define and secure safety must be relocated into the hands of the people whose lives are at stake.

One strategy common to a variety of interventions that show the greatest promise is the engagement of "credible messengers" in the work. Credible messengers are people who leverage their

moral authority and experience to support people involved in
violence in transforming their behavior, ceasing violent activity, and becoming safe. Credible messengers often belong to the
communities where violence is occurring, have survived and/or
committed violence themselves, are familiar with and often have
been a part of the street culture, and have authority rooted in
their experience in that culture, their subsequent cessation from
violence, and their role as leaders in their neighborhoods. While
the term credible messengers may be new, the concept is not—
neighborhoods across the country have, for generations, been
relying for leadership on the wisdom of what Albino Garcia calls
the BTDTs—the "Been There Done Thats." Countless grassroots violence intervention programs work in just this way.

The Cure Violence model, which has been replicated nationally and has demonstrated significant contributions to the reduction of shootings in neighborhoods where it has been deployed,
has formalized the deployment of credible messengers as a defining feature of its strategies. These messengers work day and night
and run toward violent conflict as it occurs. They stand—literally
and figuratively—between people on opposite sides of a dispute and
work to defuse situations that could escalate into deadly violence
and to halt cycles of retaliatory harm. They mobilize their lived
experience to create peer-to-peer (and sometimes elder-to-youth)
connections that can interrupt violence as it occurs. They do not,
notably, work closely with the police.

The efficacy of these strategies makes sense, as we know that
people tend to trust the counsel and direction of people who have
shared their experience more than that of those who have not
(there is a reason why AA sponsors are people who have struggled with alcoholism). However logical the successes of these
formal and informal models may be, it is important to note that
they invert the long-standing presumption that people who have
committed violence should be separated from others rather than

given the opportunity to lead others to more peaceful resolutions of conflict.

Even those programs that do not stand in the crossfire when violence arises have succeeded by engaging the people most likely to cause or survive harm (who are almost always the same people). The community-based Roca programs have produced extraordinary results in their work with street- and gang-involved youth outside of Boston. A central facet of the Roca model is the engagement of young people at highest risk of incarceration, injury, and death. They work by developing trusting relationships and use restorative justice strategies rooted in connection, persistence, and a belief in all people's capacity to change. They have demonstrated substantial success in helping young people stay out of the justice system, obtain and retain employment, stay involved in the lives of their families and children, and develop durable connections to the program and their communities. Community-centered approaches like these, when adequately supported, hold out a degree of promise that prison never will—in part because they stand to produce stronger results, and also because, unlike prisons, they can reach people law enforcement does not and can engage them in change voluntarily.

A central feature of some of the most successful violence intervention efforts is the creation of ways to access support that are separate and independent from the criminal justice system. Given high levels of distrust of law enforcement, particularly in low-income communities across the country, any reliance on police as the primary or exclusive pathway to care and intervention will inherently fall short and will miss those at greatest risk of harming others or of being harmed themselves. Knowing that, the programs in the National Network for Hospital-Based Violence Intervention Programs—including Healing Hurt People in Philadelphia, Kings Against Violence Initiative (KAVI) in Brooklyn, Youth ALIVE! in Oakland, and Detroit Life Is Valuable

Every Day—create conduits to support through the emergency rooms where people are treated for injuries resulting from violence. Research shows that one in five survivors of shootings will later be killed in another violent incident.[60] Deploying a mix of credible messengers and/or trained social workers and engaging emergency room clinicians as partners, these projects seek to halt cycles of violence by managing immediate risks of retaliation in the short term and engaging the survivors of violence in trauma-focused care in the longer term. Ranging from therapeutic groups to employment support and safety planning, the services these programs provide aim to reverse the trend wherein surviving a shooting places someone at far greater risk of future involvement in violence and instead use that event as an opportunity for intervention and transformation. The project earns the trust of the communities they are part of, and that trust positions them to be a force for safety and reconciliation when needed.

Decoupling Victim Services from Law Enforcement

The expansion of the victim services field, with its focus on intimate partner and sexual violence, holds lessons of all kinds about what it will take to make these services equitably available to survivors in this country. On the one hand, the field has taught us the extraordinary impact a movement can have on a culture. Thirty years of advocacy for victims has brought about lasting, paradigmatic change in our culture's response to domestic and sexual assault and has reached millions of victims of these and other crimes. This work has taught us that healing can be brought to scale, and that a culture can be brought along in doing that. The field has developed models for safety planning and support that have transformed survivors' lives, and the movement has ensured access to those supports.

But this service infrastructure teaches other lessons, too.

Despite the formidable work of many to ensure otherwise, the victim services field has not achieved equity in service delivery.[61] Far too many victims are far too often left out of the scope of care. Whether because of limited resources, lack of information, implicit bias, or an emphasis on partnership with law enforcement, the field has struggled to reach many survivors, including immigrants; young people of color; people with disabilities; women of color; lesbian, gay, bisexual, transgender, and queer people; and other historically marginalized communities. When people belong to more than one of these groups, they are even more likely to be excluded from services.[62] And aligning victim services too closely with law enforcement—whether by requiring a report to police as a condition for receiving victim compensation, co-locating victim services within law enforcement agencies, or encouraging survivors to report the harm they survive to police without first understanding the implications for their safety—will always exclude survivors when they or their communities have fraught experience with police.

We see this perhaps most clearly in cases of harm within families. Even criminal justice practitioners who believe the system is effective in addressing street or "gang" violence will typically admit how greatly the system struggles to address intrafamilial harm productively, including domestic and intimate partner violence and child sexual abuse. This kind of harm represents a substantial portion of the violence that exists mostly out of reach of the criminal justice system—and is far too often unresolved or even worsened on the occasions when it is addressed within it. The solutions to these kinds of harm are beyond the scope of this book, but not beyond the scope of what is possible. What is perhaps most important to note here is the degree to which experience suggests that the best answers to intrafamilial harm will almost always come from within communities, not outside them.

Speaking from her experience as a survivor of child sexual

abuse, sujatha baliga attests to not only the inadequacy but the danger to her and her family of the alignment of support and law enforcement—what she calls "the crimmigration Child Protection System clustermuck of South Central Pennsylvania."[63] She says it was this system "that was the reason my father got to continue sexually abusing me." She has explained this concept in greater detail:

> What I mean by this is that I had no interest in my father being incarcerated or my mother being deported or in being taken away from my family. Even as a child I knew that if I told anyone what was happening in my home, any of these things could have happened, especially because, for much of my childhood, we were the sole immigrant family in our rural patch of America. This is really important for us to understand, that the systems designed to protect us are actually doing us harm because they disincentivize truth telling and help seeking.[64]

Sujatha's experience is shared by an enormous portion of survivors for whom, for a variety of reasons, the engagement of law enforcement is regarded as likely to increase rather than diminish the threat to their safety and the safety of their families. Although its work is not limited to intrafamilial or intimate partner violence, Creative Interventions is a leading force in imagining better solutions to these types of harm, aiming to build the capacity of everyday people and communities to end and prevent interpersonal violence; and to shift the anti-violence movement away from individualized social services and criminalization and toward community-based responses. These and other aligned solutions draw on the experience, power, and ingenuity of communities to address the wide range of harms and violence that persist through generations, poison relationships, thrive on silence, and remain painfully unresolved by the often counterproductive intei ꭣꭣꭣꭣꭣ of law enforcement and the criminal justice system.

A wide range of programs embody the insight that responding to violence must also heal those who survive it. Most of the beacons of promise in this work are grassroots, neighborhood-grown organizations led by and for the people who are most directly impacted. These programs include Fathers & Families of San Joaquin in Stockton, California, which promotes strong, healthy families and communities in which youth are nurtured and fathers are engaged in their children's lives; Life After Uncivil Ruthless Acts in Los Angeles, which takes a holistic approach to victim services, offering support and resources to the families of both the victim and the person responsible for a crime (in doing so, they work with their partners at the Reverence Project, which develops comprehensive wellness centers in urban communities to support those suffering from trauma); Mothers of Murdered Children in Detroit, which offers self-help groups, help for survivors and their loved ones in navigating the criminal justice system, grief counseling, and support with funeral costs, basing its work on the idea that grief must be shared in order for people to heal; and countless others.[65] Across the country, the National Compadres Network draws on culturally rooted healing practices to treat survivors of violence to help ensure that they do not pass their pain on to others. And while not always grassroots-based, the successful Trauma Recovery Center in California, notably, have been broadly replicated nationally through funds that come from reducing criminal penalties.[66]

The direct availability of these healing supports in community runs contrary to the pattern of exclusion that arises when victim services and law enforcement are too linked and is critical to reaching the full range of crime survivors, including survivors with complex lives. Our media, our culture, and even some of our statutes continually reinforce the idea that to be deserving of care, a survivor of crime has to be "innocent." Sometimes innocence is tied to some intangible yet narrow notion of purity that our culture uses to assign value and recognize vulnerability. Sometimes innocence is a matter for the courts—the opposite of legally determined guilt. And sometimes innocence sits in statute, as with the regulations that guide the distribution of federal Victims of Crime Act (VOCA) funds. These funds help certain victims address the financial impact of the crime they experienced by reimbursing victims for costs associated with the crime, such as hospital bills that insurance did not cover, the replacement of essential property, emergency relocation expenses, some therapeutic services, and, in cases of homicide, burial expenses.[67] The federal statute that guides the distribution of these funds—which are disbursed to states, which then disburse them to eligible victims—requires that the funds go only to "innocent victims of crime."[68] In almost all cases, the statute also requires that those victims of crime report to the police and cooperate with the investigation fully.[69] In spirit and practice, both intentionally and inadvertently, this idea of "innocence" and the requirements of reporting and cooperation exclude a wide range of people from services and limits the options and resources available to people who survive serious harm.[70]

Victims who do not choose to participate fully in a police investigation or prosecution of the person who hurt them can and often do have their applications for compensation rejected for "failure to cooperate." Still other victims are rejected for what is called "contributory conduct"—essentially an assessment on the part of the state that the victim was at least partially responsible for the harm they sustained. The problem with these restrictions stems from the fact that survivors' experience with reporting the harm they survive can be fraught. Survivors often say they felt blamed or met with disbelief when trying to report the violence they experienced.[71] These barriers to reporting are intensified for people from marginalized communities, including lesbian, gay, bisexual, queer, transgender, and gender nonconforming people, in part because of outright and implicit biases, and in part because first responders are often not trained to understand their identities or their relationships, and thus cannot assess these types of violence as effectively and accurately as necessary.[72] We also know that many other groups of victims, including people of color and members of immigrant communities, have had negative experiences with law enforcement that affect their sense of trust and safety when reporting—and may encounter bias when they report the harm they survive. Similarly, people too often experience bias and/or barriers to accessing law enforcement based on language, ability, HIV status, and other facets of their identities.

Tying compensation and services to cooperation with law enforcement limits access to critical healing services, inequitably excludes the most vulnerable survivors, and is distinctly not survivor-centered: because it prioritizes the apprehension and punishment of the person who caused harm over the needs and preferences of the person harmed, it is a decidedly defendant-centered approach to addressing crime. Re-centering healing services around the survivors to whom they are owed will require no longer treating victims as mere instruments of police and courts, and instead decoupling services from enforcement in a way that enshrines in policy our belief in their deservedness of care. This reorientation will be entirely consistent with the relocation of the locus of control from law enforcement to communities more broadly.

Among the people who will lead the charge to make the changes outlined here are not only formerly incarcerated people and their loved ones, but also crime survivors—a broader range of survivors than those whose voices we are used to hearing. Among those whose voices are typically excluded from the public understanding about violence and the best responses to it are not only survivors who are not "innocent" enough, but also survivors who are not deemed to be who they are "supposed to" be and survivors who do not want what they are "supposed to" want—those who are inadequately or inappropriately afraid, too silent or too outspoken, too angry or not angry enough, too forgiving or not forgiving enough, too political or not political enough, insufficiently "innocent," too addicted, too violent, too volatile, too complicated. These are survivors who are concerned not just with interpersonal violence but with state violence as well, not just with their own trauma but with the trauma passed through generations, not just with themselves but with the people who hurt them, not just with their own safety but with what will make everyone safer. These are survivors who want revenge and compassion at the same time, and who change, constantly but not linearly, as they heal. These survivors' stories are messy, conflicted, and uncontained. Almost all of us are these survivors.

Developing adequate responses for these survivors, like achieving any of the policy shifts described above, will require a fundamental reorientation toward violence—toward those who commit it, those who survive it, and what it will take to end it. Some of those reforms will be fought and won in statehouses around the country. But much of the terrain of this battle will not be only in the law. It will be in our culture. And the battle we will fight will be for a country that no longer regards violence as normal. It is only that country that will make the changes outlined here.

6

The Opposite of Violence

Identifying policy platforms that stand to increase safety and reduce our failed reliance on mass incarceration will be fruitless if we do not change the culture that drives and constrains those policies. The stories we tell and what we believe they obligate us to do will determine the scope of what is possible in our shared future.

We are starting from a hard place. Our nation's culture is notoriously celebratory of violence. We see this in our military, our militarized local police forces, our leadership in the international weapons trade, and our popular culture. It is hard to think of a single blockbuster movie, for instance, in which the hero wins without using violence. Our stories of glory, of manhood, of bravery, and of strength almost all include violence as their central method. In *The Matrix*, a film about the pliability of reality and the expansiveness of what is possible, the lead character is in a large empty room where he can conjure up anything he can imagine—anything at all—to help him secure justice. His answer? "Guns, lots of guns." Our American heroes beat people, shoot people, and detonate bombs. They are lethal weapons. They terminate. They die hard.

We imagine our culture to be one that condemns certain forms of violence, particularly against those we consider "innocent." We condemn sexual violence against children. We condemn murder. We condemn rape, particularly the rape of white women. Of course, we also tolerate these forms of violence in countless ways—including treating intrafamilial sexual abuse of children with willful ignorance, murder as acceptable when the victims are poor people of color, and rape as a territory of "gray area" replete with bragging rights. But somehow we think of these patterns as exceptions to an overall moral attitude of condemnation and righteousness about violence. Still, we do not valorize all forms of violence, not every victim's pain is considered commonplace, and not all people who commit harm are portrayed as indifferent to others' pain. There are people whose pain still outrages our mainstream American culture, people who are not meant to be hurt, people we are meant to protect. Most of these people, it turns out, are white.

America has a long history of disregarding the pain that people of color experience. I say "America" cautiously, knowing that the term actually includes a whole continent and not just the United States. But I use the term to mean this country alone because I am not exactly talking about the United States here, not in the sense of its geography or even its government. I am talking about America as an identity and a force—as an accumulation of history and narrative and ways of behaving in the world. I am talking about the America Langston Hughes evokes, the America James Baldwin evokes, the America, frankly, that Donald Trump evokes. I am talking about the cultural terrain that is so deeply contested in our current climate, the terrain we have to fight for if any of what is suggested here is to be possible, the terrain our opposition knows it has to control in order to win. There is a reason the hats do not say "Make the United States Great Again." The fight is for "America."

This America's origin story (not to be confused with the land's) is one of the genocide of Native people. Christopher Columbus and his men murdered, raped, tortured, poisoned, beat, shot, and starved people to death, and we take a day off every October to celebrate his exploratory spirit. We are a nation that could not exist but for a group of people's willingness and capacity to cause unimaginable harm. Forget George Washington—our true forefathers are violence and pain.

Then came the Middle Passage and all that followed. The vicious violence that characterized slavery—including whipping people with leather straps studded with nails, hanging people by their wrists for days while repeatedly beating them unconscious, raping people with wooden poles and broken glass, castrating men, cutting off people's fingers or hands, burning people to the brink of death and then reviving them only to hurt them further, dragging people by their ankles behind horse-drawn wagons—was treated as a natural and necessary part of business. What is more, as we inflicted this unthinkable pain, we promised the people we were harming that we would do the same to their children and to their children's children. As the visionary social worker Dr. Anna Ortega-Williams puts it, in this act of spiritual and psychological brutality, slavery promised enslaved people that we would inflict violence against "all the versions of you that will ever be." We have never reckoned with that history; passing an amendment that outlaws slavery "except as punishment for a crime" does not constitute reckoning. Our centuries-long silence continues to reinforce the normalcy of the extreme violence that characterized what we euphemistically called a "peculiar institution." And slavery *was* peculiar, not in the more colloquial sense of "strange or unusual," but in the sense of being one's own, something distinctive to or characteristic of a particular place or people. It was anything but strange—it was ours, America's. It became the definition of normal, and so did the violence on which it depended.

Of course, the way slavery normalized violence was entirely racialized and gendered. It treated white violence against people of color as not only a common practice, but even an aristocratic one. To the extent that a white man's slaveholding was a reflection of his success, his status was defined in part by how many black people he had the power to hurt with impunity. The violence became so normal as to be called something else—discipline, management, control, even education.

This normalization of violence against black people was held in place in part by the conjured fear of sexual violence against white women by black men. Any nation's self-definition includes defining who belongs and who poses a threat to those who belong. In the United States, a core part of our formative sense of ourselves included a story that white women were in danger and black men were dangerous—and that it was the job of white men to protect their women. Black men raping white women was extraordinarily uncommon (and still is), but the mere specter of this form of violence reinforced two inextricably intertwined myths: the danger and hypersexuality of black men and the helplessness and purity of white women. It is a story that allowed Roy Bryant and J. W. Milam to brutally beat a teenager named Emmett Till, drag him to the bank of the Tallahatchie River, shoot him in the head, tie him with barbed wire to a large metal fan, and shove his mutilated body into the water—all for allegedly whistling at Carolyn Bryant, a white woman. It is a story we still live today, having never done the work to uproot its distortions. Black men in the story are capable of horrible harm, but not vulnerable to pain or deserving of care. White women in the story are only vulnerable, cannot possibly be responsible for harm, and depend on their subservience to white men for protection and survival. White men are the supposed authoritative arbiters between the two, commanding fear and insulated by impunity (not only for violence against people of color but also even for violence against white women) as the power-holders in the very institutions that could in theory hold them to account. And black women—both their pain and their power—are all but erased from the story, as though their bodies and experience are somehow outside of and irrelevant to the justice equation. In that arrangement, none of us gets to be fully human, none of us has what we need to heal (both vulnerability and power) or to repair harm (both accountability and dignity), and none of us is positioned to fully regard our own or one another's humanity.

It will be a great but essential labor for America to move from a story that regards violence against people of color as not only acceptable, but necessary and noble, to a story that regards it as immoral and illegal. It is not a transition we, the descendants of Emmett Till and of J. W. Milam and of Roy and Carolyn Bryant, have yet made. We see the persistence of the age-old story in police killings of black men, in the public silence over killings of transgender women of color, in the presence of armed police officers in predominantly black elementary schools, and in seemingly simpler places, like doctors' offices and emergency rooms, where care is distributed inequitably and withheld cruelly.

One of the capacities white people will have to develop out of the ravages of our history is our capacity to believe in the existence and importance of black pain. We will have to do it historically and politically—but we will also have to do it literally. A 2012 study looked at racial bias in perceptions of others' pain and found evidence that "people assume *a priori* that Blacks feel less pain than do Whites." Four of the experiments conducted "show that White and Black Americans—including registered nurses and nursing students—assume that Black people feel less pain than do White people."[1] Studies about the treatment of sickle cell—a disease that disproportionately affects black people—have revealed this trend writ large, as sickle cell patients have to wait 50 percent longer in emergency rooms to receive care, their pain is vastly undermedicated, and their mortality rates remain unconscionably high, even in the presence of effective treatment options.[2]

This is no small thing. People's belief in someone else's capacity to feel pain has enormous implications for empathy and treatment. Our vulnerability is a dimension of our humanity and is part of what entitles us to protection and care. We have to ask: How could it be possible that black people feel less pain than white people do? What would people have to believe to believe that could be true? In the justice system, we can imagine that if system actors seem impervious to black men's pain, it has to do with the setting—that they are before them as defendants—or even as victims—in a larger context of criminal activity. What we learn from the medical research on pain management is that the basis for the disregard for black pain isn't the narrow frame of the justice system; it is the much larger context of our culture's narrative about who can hurt and whose hurt matters. That narrative is at the heart of our ability to address all crime survivors equitably, because in a basic way, to believe you are a victim, we first have to believe you can hurt. Most of the stories we have told thus far have compromised rather than nurtured our ability to do so. It is time to start telling other stories.

Let us start with a familiar story and tell it differently: the story about how a person becomes capable of committing violence. Our current approach often goes as follows: we look at arrest records—particularly for adolescents and young adults—and home in on the stories of young people who commit more and more violent crimes over time. The story we tell to explain this trend is one of children developing into "violent criminals." We narrate the way that each offense paves the way for the next, that the punishments for the lower-level ones are inadequate deterrents, that the people who commit these crimes are hardened in the process (or that they were inherently hard to begin with), and that they will inevitably go on to commit more and more violence.

The story commands a broad audience. And it is wrong, the way all incomplete stories are. It suffers from the distortion our larger cultural normalization of violence promotes. For starters, even in a story that is entirely about violence, nowhere in it do we talk about the young people's own experience of victimization. While there is a great deal of research linking a child's maltreatment and exposure to violence to future violent behavior, far less research examines the reasons for the causality between the ongoing experience of violence and the decision to commit further or escalating harm: we do not lay the chronologies on top of each other. The U.S. Department of Justice and Centers for Disease Control and Prevention's National Survey of Children's Exposure to Violence estimates that as many as one in ten children in our country are "polyvictims"—people who have survived multiple kinds of victimization.[3] Such experiences can have a cumulative effect. According to the final report of the United States Attorney General's National Task Force on Children Exposed to Violence, "the toxic combination of exposure to family violence, child physical and sexual abuse, and exposure to community violence increases the risk and severity of posttraumatic injuries and health and mental health disorders for exposed children by at least twofold and up to tenfold."[4] These experiences play a central role in young people's development—particularly as it relates to violence.

It is important to ask: *what if part of what makes violence "normal" is surviving it?* A decade of engaging responsible parties in Common Justice in an exercise that charts their experience of witnessing, surviving, and committing violence yields two key lessons: first, almost all people who commit violence report witnessing and/or surviving violence before perpetrating it for the first time, and most report ongoing incidents of surviving harm interwoven with incidents of causing it.[5] In other words, the experience of committing harm and the experience of surviving harm advance concurrently. For example, a young person may ditch school one day and be beaten up while outside. He may then affiliate with a person or group of young people he believes can protect him from further harm. He may participate in hurting someone with that person or group. He may then be retaliated against for his actions, survive a serious assault, and decide to carry a weapon. On his rap sheet, he will have advanced from truancy to a serious violent felony. As a victim, he is a survivor of multiple potentially traumatic assaults over a short period. And of course both of these realities require a response. But what it comes down to is this: almost no one's entry point into violence is committing it.

Trauma symptoms themselves can become drivers of cycles of violence. Hypervigilance exaggerates survivors' sense of threat—so that a minimal threat can legitimately feel like a substantial and potentially even life-threatening one. How endangered one feels depends in part on the baseline of danger that exists. So for survivors who are hurt in the context of relative safety, their exaggerated sense of danger may result in simple self-protective actions like crossing the street when they get a bad feeling about someone approaching, holding their keys as they approach their apartment, or carrying pepper spray in their bag. For people who live where there is a more widespread, regular threat of violence, where day in and day out, they are making decisions that will affect whether or not they get home safe and alive, perceiving threats as more immediate than they are may mean that the self-protective actions people choose are graver. Not all survivors cope in this way, but many do.

The way in which survivors cope—particularly in the early aftermath of harm—is not usually a matter of choice. Trauma, after all, has a way of pulling rank. Say a young man is suffering from hypervigilance and lives in a neighborhood where several people have been shot in the past week. He is walking down the street and hears someone approaching behind him. Before his traumatic experience, he was able to wait until that person was closer, get a feel for that person's intentions, adjust his body language to convey that he was not looking for trouble, and let the man pass. But now his mind and body are telling him that the danger he perceives is more substantial and more immediate than it is. If he believes that the man approaching him from behind means him harm, he cannot just wait for the person to reach him. He has to protect his life. So he turns. He says something aggressive to try to indicate that he is not someone this man should consider hurting. He throws the first punch. He shoots the first bullet. He does not experience this as an act of unprovoked aggression; he experiences it as self-defense. And his body tells him that is exactly what it is.

All too often we conflate cycles of violence with retaliatory acts—as though people only go out and hurt the people who hurt them. But that is not how these cycles work. We see this, for instance, in the literature about child abuse. People who were abused as children are more likely to pass that violence on—not to hurt their parents who abused them, but to hurt their own children. Cycles of violence are not primarily about giving pain back to its source—they are about paying that pain forward. Similarly, the young man who was nearly killed last week and is now walking down the block may be thinking not of retaliation, but of survival. And he may still cause harm.

The second lesson is that the experience of surviving harm often is the most significant factor in contributing to a diminished sense of how serious violence is. This may be surprising to some of us, but only if we underestimate the larger-scale normalization of violence against so many survivors.

When someone survives violence, the range of options available is culturally determined. Those options have everything to do with what is accessible, what is sanctioned, and what is regarded as normal. When we look to the cultural basis for responses to violence, too often we look only as far as the neighborhood level, and typically end up blaming communities of color and poor communities for some supposed amorphous deficit in values that somehow makes them unusually indifferent to violence. Pretending that culture is ever that local, that isolated, or that ahistorical is naïve and dishonest—and it insulates the broader American culture, including white people, from our responsibility for setting and reinforcing the norms that disregard black pain. That's because the culture that sets the norms about violence is broader than any neighborhood. That culture includes the larger economic structures that constrain what is possible in a given neighborhood, most of which are located and controlled far beyond that community's geographic or political reach; the larger context of media and its depictions of those involved in violence, whose locus of control is also not within the communities being represented; and the historical realities that endure through generations and legitimately infuse a community's understanding of itself.

It is in this larger cultural context that survivors seek out strategies to cope with trauma, pain, and loss. People who are harmed have a range of coping strategies available to them, from seeking help, doing exercise, and going to therapy to alcohol and other drug use, violence, and minimization or even total denial of the harm they survived. In deciding among these, whether consciously or unconsciously, people are more likely to choose coping strategies that are consonant with their culture's norms. For example, for many white women (particularly straight, cisgender, able-bodied, middle-class white women), this most often means a culture that says their pain is of importance, that they are in need and deserving of care and protection, and that their fear is legitimate. Hard as it still may be to do so, many of these women, then, do what those norms would suggest: acknowledge fear, express sadness and hurt, ask for help, and seek protection (often by any means necessary on that last count). For other survivors whose pain has been devalued by our society, there exists a set of norms insisting that their pain probably does not exist, and even if it does, that it does not matter. The coping strategy most consonant with that set of norms is clear: many survivors survive by minimizing.

Minimization involves rationalizing and downplaying the significance of an event or emotion. Those harmed may tell themselves, "It doesn't matter. It's okay. It happens to everyone. It's not a big deal. It's nothing." And that strategy may prove at least partially effective in helping them manage some of the symptoms of trauma they experience.[6] But minimization also has downsides. First and foremost, it creates immediate and lasting barriers to acknowledging pain and fear and to seeking help; one cannot seek help for something that is "nothing." This—coupled with the systemic denial of their trauma that drives minimalization in the first place—means that survivors whose experience of violence is normalized are less likely to seek or receive support for their trauma, more likely to live with unaddressed pain, and less likely to recover.

Many young men of color involved in Common Justice, asked how they felt when they were robbed or assaulted, respond, "Fine." Some of these young men are knowingly understating the intense emotions they felt when they were hurt. Our culture teaches men that their feelings should be limited more or less to fine, angry, aroused, or happy their team won. It does not make space for pain and vulnerability. But other participants are not obfuscating the pain they felt. Rather, they are essentially reporting a common trauma symptom: numbness. Numbness and minimization as symptom and strategy go hand in hand, and both allow people to not feel pain. The problem is that as human beings, we are not built to shut down only negative emotions. It's like a breaker switch in the basement of a home—either the whole thing is on or the whole thing is off. Numbness cuts the power to the whole house, not just the room where sadness is. So survivors who experience numbness often experience a diminished capacity for joy, for fulfillment, for excitement, and for giving and receiving love. The depression many survivors feel in the aftermath of the harm they survive is not just about the presence of sadness—it is also about the inaccessibility of joy. Numbness is often a factor in making that joy unavailable.

Despite the vast odds stacked in favor of cycles of violence, it is essential to remember that most people who experience violence do *not* pass it along to others. But minimization also increases the risk of a survivor passing that harm on to others, in part because it can diminish a survivor's sense of the seriousness of the harm they are causing.[7] Once we determine that something is "not a big deal," it becomes something we can justify doing to each other.

Many people who commit violence do so only after having developed a decreased sense of its seriousness. Some of that response has to do with individual experiences of surviving harm and minimizing that pain. But a decreased sense of violence's seriousness is never entirely individual. It is also cultural. The coping strategies available to people are socially determined, and the choices survivors make reflect society's overall regard or disregard for their pain. When we look for the underlying source of the normalization of violence, we cannot look at just one person's trajectory. A person does not make something normal. Only a culture can do that. And when it comes to violence, our culture has firmly established it as our American way of life.

Making violence normal is always entangled with inequity. It is fairly straightforward to see the ways in which the normalization of violence sustains such inequity: brutality on plantations has to be normalized by those in power for slavery to persist, domestic violence has to be considered commonplace for people to stay in homes where they are beaten and controlled, police violence has to be rendered as standard practice to enable the broad and brutal criminalization and punishment of whole communities, and so on.

What is perhaps less obvious and less central to our public discourse is the way the normalization of violence not only generates and secures inequity but depends on it. A society cannot normalize violence entirely. Its people cannot say that anyone can hurt anyone else at any time. They could say that no one can ever hurt anyone (though we don't say that in America). Rather, as sociologist and criminologist Nils Christie grapples with in his scholarship, our society says that some people can hurt other people some of the time for certain reasons.[8] The function of a society is in no small part the containment of violence. The state reserves its right—to the exclusion of others' rights—to commit certain violence. In theory, this authority is meant to replace vigilante justice, for instance, with police and courts and prisons, so as to protect a society from individualized, unpredictable, uncontained violence. The problem with that frame in this country is, first, that the government is responsible for a great deal of violence that exceeds the permissions legitimately granted to it by the people; and second, that our culture continues to tolerate, condone, and even celebrate a wide range of violence committed by people other than their government. The only way to defend that arrangement is to tell a story (and by a story, I mean a thousand stories told over and over again for centuries) about the people against whom violence is being committed—a story that explains why the violence they sustain is acceptable and, even more important, why others should still feel safe in a world where people are being harmed.

These stories always fall along fault lines of power: race, gender and gender identity, sexuality, national origin, and other dimensions of identity that enable us to explain why certain violence has a place in our otherwise allegedly safe and moral nation. In a country where we were all truly equal, danger to another person would mean I am at risk. It is only in a place where we are unequal that danger to another person can be irrelevant to me, or even protective. The problem for people on the receiving end of oppression is obvious: the framework allows for unthinkable harm to go unaddressed. But even for those of us in positions of greater privilege, this normalization has consequences. Once our story is no longer "violence is wrong and it matters every time" but "violence is sometimes wrong and that sometimes matters," then even those of us who co-signed and benefited from one form of inequity and the violence it generated can all too easily find ourselves on the wrong side of the power line, faced with violence that our culture will not say is wrong. In that way, there can be no lasting safety for anyone in a society that has inequity at its core.

"When I was six, I was playing with my pet turtle," Hyunhee said, "and I was all of a sudden surrounded by our neighborhood teens." She continued:

> They were a bunch of poor white kids who didn't have any other outlet. We lived in a really poor town. We were one of the only folks of color in our community back at the time. They had their hands on my underwear, and I didn't know what they wanted. . . . I was confused. I was scared. When you are a kid, and you have strangers violating you for no reason, it's confusing, it's scary. When I look back, I don't know if the police would have believed me. A group of white kids, a little Asian kid—who are you going to believe?
>
> A lot of what's available to survivors is tailored to white women, a lot of the public narrative about who a survivor is is white women, and when you're not a white woman, you think that: "I don't get to be a survivor, I don't get to access these resources. They're not for me."[9]

Whether based in human dignity or sexism or a little of both, mainstream American culture has a robust narrative about the importance of protecting women. But when America talks about women, we are usually talking about white women, and cisgender, straight, middle-class white women at that.[10] Contrary to this dominant narrative, however, the range of people who are harmed by crime is vast—including women of color, immigrants, people with disabilities, young men of color, LGBTQ people, and the working poor.[11] Of course, many survivors belong to more than one of these groups, and for most, their victimization happens in a larger context of structural inequity, poverty, and disenfranchisement. This context means that the newest trauma is likely to amplify previous traumas, exacerbating the impact and making healing more complicated and elusive.

Women of color live at this intersection—and they survive violence, including homicide, at extraordinarily high rates.[12] These disparities are even greater for queer, trans, and gender nonconforming people, who suffer homicide with extraordinarily high and often greatly underestimated frequency.[13] But despite the relative erasure of these murders in comparison to the murder of white people, homicide is actually the most visible kind of violence. Other nonfatal forms of violence are all too often hidden from view, and their history is long and their prevalence vast. Ranging from the legacy of sexual violence and genocide against Native women to the trafficking of women from Asian and other countries, violence against immigrant women attempting to cross the U.S. border, neighborhood-based violence, and brutality in this country's prisons, the violence women of color experience is far-reaching and often entwined with the very systems that are supposed to protect people from harm.

Women of color are also more likely than their white counterparts to survive intimate partner violence.[14] An estimated 29 percent of black women report experiencing this type of violence in their lifetime (including rape, physical assault, and stalking), but when they are harmed they are less likely than white women

to receive the support of social services, battered women's programs, or hospitals.[15] This violence is not, of course, limited to
black women. Studies show that Asian and Pacific Islander wom-
en, Latina women, Native women, and countless other women
of color experience inordinate levels of violence.[16] And across
cultures, trans women experience intimate partner violence at
unusually high rates.[17] These trends also hold true for sexual violence; women of color are disproportionately likely to be survivors of rape.[18]

Formidable work by thousands of women over the span of
decades has ensured that there are formal services for women
who survive violence (particularly sexual assault and domestic
violence). Still, women of color—even those who built and sustain those services—experience significant disparities in accessing them. Some of the barriers to access arise from our dominant
narrative. Too often we do not tell women of color's stories at
all. When we do tell them, we do so in a distorted way, regularly portraying women of color as uncommonly or even super-
humanly resilient, to the point of obscuring their vulnerability
and diminishing their need for care. This narrative is central to
locking in our disregard for women of color's pain: it is designed
to excuse us from the obligation we would otherwise have to
fulfill if we were to contend fully with the impact of violence on
women of color's lives.

For women of color, their access to support in the aftermath
of violence is also diminished by the same structural factors that
made that violence likely in the first place.[19] The pathways to
healing and protection for women of color are limited by bias—
against them and, when the people who harm them are men
of color, against these men.[20] The Women of Color Network
describes the pattern:

> Non-arrests of suspected abusers of African American
> women and a fear that police will exercise an abuse of
> power have contributed to African American women's

reluctance to involve law enforcement. Stereotypes amplify the complexities African American women encounter when trying to seek help services. Myths that African American women are "domineering figures that require control" or that African American women are "exceptionally strong under stress and are resilient" increase their vulnerability and discourage some from speaking out about abuse.[21]

These women's vulnerability to harm therefore results not only from the people who commit violence against them, but from the failure of the systems that are supposed to protect them to acknowledge their pain and to see them as fully human and deserving of care. This is not a new insight: countless scholars and leaders who are women of color have been teaching these lessons for decades, and we would do well to hear and heed them.[22] As Andrea Ritchie, author of *Invisible No More: Police Violence Against Black Women and Women of Color*, said in an interview:

> We think of police as being there to protect the vulnerable or protect people who are targeted by violence. If you show police officers consistently—where Black women, women of color, or LGBT people of color are concerned—ignoring violence, telling people that they deserved what happened, assuming that they're a threat, that they committed the violence, or perpetrating violence against them, then the myth that they're about protecting victims of violence or vulnerable people starts to unravel. And we get a clearer picture that actually they don't change their stripes when they're responding with violence. They're still policing race, they're still policing gender, they're still policing sexuality, they're still policing poverty. They're saying victims of violence who are outside of

a very small group—middle-class White women who
are not trans—are not deserving of protection.[23]

Not only do police too often fail to protect women of color,
they are also likely to cause them harm. "Although Black wom-
en are routinely killed, raped, and beaten by the police, their
experiences are rarely foregrounded in popular understandings of
police brutality," writes Kimberlé Crenshaw, director of Columbia Law School's Center for Intersectionality and Social Policy
Studies.[24] She continues: "Inclusion of Black women's experiences in social movements, media narratives, and policy demands
around policing and police brutality is critical to effectively combatting racialized state violence for Black communities and other
communities of color." It is in part for this same reason that the
group INCITE! Women of Color Against Violence concludes
that "strategies designed to combat violence within communities . . . must be linked to strategies that combat violence directed
against communities."[25] It is only when we treat interpersonal
and structural violence as related that we will develop solutions
that work for people who live at the intersection of the two.

Such integrated approaches are especially critical when both
the people harmed and the people causing harm have little or no
basis for trusting law enforcement. When the people who harm
women of color are men of color, for example, the broader context of white supremacy sets a trap: women of color are placed in
the nearly impossible situation of seeking regard for pain caused
to them by people whose pain they know has also been disregarded. It might seem to some that our broader culture's indifference to the pain experienced by men of color would mean that it
would hold the men unequivocally accountable when they cause
pain to women of color. But this doesn't happen. To the contrary,
the disregard of men of color's pain only tightens the constraints
around safety and healing for women of color, cutting off path-

ways to the transformation of harm. Self-identified healer and alchemist Fatimah Muhammad has described her experience:

> As a little girl, I adored my father. Our time together was full of games we'd invent, and his affirmations that I am valuable to him and the world.
>
> And, I saw my father beat my mother. I saw him caked in blood following bad drug deals. I witnessed in horror as the police barged into our home and took him away in handcuffs.
>
> For 20 years, there was a vast silence between us held tight by the criminal justice system: restraining orders, my father's ongoing spells of prison time, and a belief fortified by the world that this black man could only ever do me harm. I had no access to him, and no access to the part of myself that longed to be connected to him.
>
> In my twenties, I decided to find my father to release the anger, fear, and grief. In my healing journey with my father—a journey we leapt into immediately and with deep urgency—he confessed stories of the harm he had done to me, my brother, my mother, and others. I also learned about my father's recovery from addiction, his faith, and his own childhood abuse. And, though my mother never saw or spoke to him directly, she accepted a gift he sent her—and accepted it with laughter.
>
> People of color carry the impossible burden of transgenerational structural harm alongside transgenerational interpersonal harm. The labor women of color toil through in these realities is glorified and vilified, without ever being understood, off-loaded, resourced, or elevated accurately.

Who but us carries the work of redemption and
healing for our loved ones who have harmed us? Who
but us breathes through layers of unspeakable trauma
only to get crushed by systems that render our full
experience invisible? Who but us can testify that these
systems that never give us the support or resources we
deserve to heal, rest, and harness our power to actual-
ize new visions—for us, for our loved ones, for our
communities?[26]

Our failure to address the harm women of color survive has to
be understood both as its own independent wrongdoing requiring repair and, simultaneously, as inextricably intertwined with
our failure to address the harm men of color survive. This second failure often begins in a denial of the possibility that men of
color's pain even exists.

Daquan was shot at in a public park by someone he knew. It
was broad daylight. He was playing basketball. He looked up
and saw a friend he had had an argument with approaching him.
Then he saw the gun and saw it fire. His friend missed. He ran
for his life across four lanes of traffic and eventually, after much
hesitation and consideration, decided to report the crime to the
police. When he did, he told the officer, "I was shot at in the park.
My baby sister was there and I don't know where she is. And I
know who did it." The officer's response: "Where's your gun?"
Daquan paused in silence. The officer added. "Well, he didn't
shoot you for nothing." Our culture's denial of the pain men of
color experience shows up in the widespread portrayals of them
as violent, but almost never as survivors of harm.[27] A robust body
of research documents the distorted representation of black men
in the media. This includes underrepresentation overall (they
are simply not shown); the exaggeration of negative associations
including criminality, unemployment, poverty, and violence

when they *are* visible; limited positive associations (for instance, seeing successful black men only when they are sports heroes, not when they are businessmen or fathers); and the decontextualization of the challenges they face (for example, the problem of violence in Chicago being told without the historical context of redlining that helped create it).[28] This decontextualization is an important dimension of the distortion of public images of black men, and includes erasing "how the lives of black men and boys are affected by larger contexts, such as historical antecedents of black economic disadvantage, persistence of anti black male bias, and relative disconnection from the social networks that help create wealth and opportunity."[29] This decontextualization can also exacerbate bias and blame.[30] As the social justice communication lab Opportunity Agenda contends in its report on the subject, "Public perceptions and attitudes toward black males not only help to create barriers to advancement within this society, but also make that . . . seem natural or inevitable."[31]

When it comes to violence, black men are overrepresented as people who perpetrate violent crime—and this is made especially clear when news coverage is compared with arrest rates—but are underrepresented in portrayals and coverage of crime victims, despite the extraordinary rates at which they survive harm.[32] Although young men of all races from ages sixteen to twenty-four experience higher rates of violence than any other age group, including assault and robbery, data from the Bureau of Justice Statistics at the U.S. Department of Justice consistently show that young black men are among the most likely to be victimized by violence overall.[33] For young men of color, this violence is also more likely to include homicide.[34] According to the Centers for Disease Control and Prevention, homicide is the leading cause of death for young black males ages ten to twenty-four.[35] The impact of this disparity can be especially acute in urban settings, where homicide is more common.[36] In New York City, for instance, in the first half of 2012, 96 percent of shooting victims (fatal and nonfatal) were black or Latino.[37]

The exaggeration in our culture's narrative about the harm caused by men of color is a central element in normalizing this violence, as black men's overstated criminality becomes justification for sanctioning police violence against them, blaming them for their own victimization, not investing in victim services to tend to their pain, and presuming that their childhood exposure to violence was part of a socialization process that just made them harder and more violent, rather than understanding that process as something that might have harmed or hurt them.[38] Even stories that are explicitly about the victimization of young men of color reinforce the narrative about their presumed criminality. "Montgomery's Latest Homicide Victim Had a History of Narcotics Abuse, Tangles with the Law." And "Trayvon Martin Was Suspended Three Times from School." And "Police: Slain Lakeland Teen Had Been Shot Before; Death Possibly Drug-Related." And "Shooting Victim Had Many Run-ins with Law." And "Police: Warren Shooting Victim Was Gang Member." Or this: after Otis Byrd was found hanging from a tree in Mississippi in what many feared was a lynching, CNN noted that he'd been convicted of murder thirty-five years previously. His death later was ruled a suicide.[39] It is difficult, for instance, to find a single news piece about a young man of color who is killed that does not also include information about his criminal record, whether "he had been arrested seven times" or "he had never been arrested."[40] The former is supposed to tell us that this person in some way had it coming, as if having been arrested is justification for having been murdered. The latter is supposed to signal that the person we lost is an outlier, "one of the good ones," and is meant to animate our empathy—empathy we would not be called on to access were that person less "innocent." Reporting on the criminal history (or lack thereof) of young men of color has become so normalized that a story is considered incomplete until that last piece of information is shared: it is the conclusion, really, and is the central content that is meant to guide the meaning we make of the news. But of course this reporting is not normalized for everyone. If I, a white woman, were killed, it is nearly unthinkable that the report about my death would end with "she had no criminal record." People would regard that line as irrelevant at best, callous and disrespectful at worst. And they would be right. The problem is, it is just as outrageous and just as wrong in a story about a young man of color. Our attachment to innocence—as measured incoherently by a person's lack of criminal history—interferes with our ability to uphold basic values as a culture, most simply, that violence is wrong, and that it matters, every single time.

If a police officer tells a young man "He didn't shoot you for nothing," how are we to ask this survivor to believe that the violence against him is not normal when the officers do not ask him how he is, do not tell him what happened to him was wrong, do not promise him protection and care, and instead say directly that he must have had it coming? How can we ask him to place his trust in the same police to secure his safety going forward? And how dare we tell a story about that young man's diminished sense of the seriousness of violence without including the larger structural context as a core cause?

Just as the larger narratives shaped the police's response to this young man, so, too, do they shape the young man's response to what the officer said. People of color, as the Opportunity Agenda describes, "draw on far more experience than others to form images of themselves and their peers . . . but they are also members of the public, and they are not immune to the influence of the media, which they consume just as other Americans do."[41] It is one thing to persuade white people that violence against people of color is normal and justified. It is a harder and arguably more insidious thing to persuade people of color of the same thing. In that sense, the fact that black people can also underestimate black people's capacity to feel pain is also the direct result of structural racism. The audiences for the white historical message that violence against black people is normal includes not only white people, but black people, too, so the fact that some black people have internalized any or all of that message is not evidence of its race neutrality, but to the contrary of its far-reaching and heart-wrenching impact.

I think all the time about Victor, a survivor of a serious assault. He was beaten terribly, stripped of all his clothes down to his boxers, and left in the middle of the street in the heart of winter lying in his own blood. When he told me the story, he concluded it by saying, "I was almost a victim."

What he meant, of course, is that he almost died that night—that a victim isn't someone who was hurt, a victim is a dead body, a chalk outline on the cold street. That anything short of death was just more or less a normal part of life. That the only time a young man like him could get the "victim" label—for better or worse—was if he had died on the ground that day instead of eventually regaining consciousness and standing back up.

Victor didn't invent that story about the insignificance of his pain. His country did, and the story he is carrying is as old as this country. Like all of our narratives, when they are retold often enough in enough ways, we internalize them to the point that they overcome even our most elemental experiences of excruciating physical pain. The classic experiment in which young children were given a choice between a black doll and a white one—which ends, as we know to expect, with most children, including most black children, choosing the white one as more beautiful—is but one of countless examples of how early we are taught to value certain lives over others.[42] It is on top of that belief system that we overlay our stories of violence and healing.

The old framework about who can and can't be hurt in America is in our bones, and it constrains not just our understanding and decision-making, but even our own ability to experience and make sense of our pain.

Of course Victor was not an outlier. When I asked a group of ten young men of color coming home from Rikers Island, "How many of you have been victims of crime?" no hands went up. Not one. When I asked, "How many of you have had something taken from you by force?" eight hands went up. "How many of you have had something stolen from your home?" Ten hands. "How many of you have ever lost a fight and been hurt or been jumped?" Nine of the ten young men raised their hand. Yet none had been the "victim of crime." The distinction in their answers is not just about language—it is also about history, and the way we have defined not merely whose victimization matters, but whose victimization exists in the first place.

For these young men, the racialized denial of black people's susceptibility to pain is compounded by widespread cultural norms about masculinity. All too often, manhood is equated with toughness and toughness is equated with invulnerability and imperviousness to pain. We raise men in particular to be fearless and unfazed by what they endure; indeed, we consider many of these qualities to be benchmarks of boys reaching manhood. These norms shape a man's sense of himself and constrict what forms of feeling and expression are available to him. Men are known to be less likely to acknowledge being in emotional or physical pain, less likely to use certain subjective language (words like "hurt" or "sad") in describing how they feel, and less likely to seek help when they are hurt.

It becomes too easy as a society to believe that those things are okay, because these men often seem—as they say they are—"fine." When limited notions of masculinity unite with a racist and racialized narrative stressing that some victims feel pain less profoundly than others, the combination is toxic—and results in a near complete erasure of what would otherwise be our societal obligation to regard, care for, and help heal those wounds. Similarly, the same narrow conceptions of masculinity fuel homophobia and amplify the harm—including assault and sexual violence—done to gay, bisexual, transgender, queer, and gender nonconforming men of color, who live at the intersection of these biases.

Finally, when men of color are denied access to healing, their roles as healers and caretakers are often compromised. When their unhealed pain manifests as isolation, addiction, or violence, men who have survived violence are often less able to see and tend to the pain of the men and women and children who love them. When that happens, the people who love them also lose what they need and deserve to heal and be safe.

Two distinct things are simultaneously true: violence and mass incarceration disproportionately impact people of color, and violence and mass incarceration devastate the lives of white people. Having talked about the first reality, it is important to talk about the second, noting definitively that nothing about acknowledging the pain white people endure diminishes the reality of the racial inequities at hand or alleviates our obligation to correct them.

A full exploration of white culture and its relationship to violence and punishment is a necessary project but beyond the scope of this book. Still, we cannot talk about violence without talking explicitly about white people and our connections to violence.

We do not typically have this conversation. As a nation, when we talk about violence, we talk a great deal about harm that people of color commit against each other, talk disproportionately about the far rarer occasions when people of color commit violence against white people, and sometimes even talk about violence white people commit against people of color, but we rarely talk about the daily violence within white communities. This exclusion is problematic because it feeds the notion that violence is a "black problem," but also because it obscures the way many white communities across the country suffer from the traumatic interplay of violence and poverty. By downplaying or ignoring pain in white communities, we block pathways to advance equity and to develop strategies that can reduce and tend to that pain.

Similarly, our conversations about incarceration rarely include discussion of its impact on white people. The extraordinary disproportionality of people of color who are imprisoned has to be central to our understanding of mass incarceration in our culture and what it will take to end it. But the fact that the criminal justice system is inequitable and has roots in a history of structural racism has never meant that white people are fully protected from its damaging effects. Although white people overall have a greater expectation of access to and fairness in the justice system, they are not insulated from its detrimental impacts, nor have they been immune to its exponential growth over the past four decades. In fact, white people make up 39 percent of those incarcerated—close to one million people on any given day.[43] In Ohio, for instance, white people represented the fastest growing group entering prisons in 2013; 80 percent of women entering the state's prisons that year were white.[44] A recent report by the Vera Institute of Justice found that while the use of jail and prison is declining in many urban centers, rural jails in largely white communities have the highest rates of growth in pretrial detention in the country: pretrial detention rates in those counties increased a full 436 percent from 1970 to 2013.[45]

White people are not insulated from other forms of violence, either. Working-class and poor white communities in particular are beset with violence: intimate partner violence and domestic violence that are rampant in many communities and exacerbated by high rates of unemployment; physical and sexual abuse of children (which data have always shown know no boundaries of race, gender, or class); disputes over property, relationships, and honor that escalate to violence; violence related to illegal drug markets; and bar fights, street fights, assaults, and murder.[46] In white communities with neither wealth nor a strong social safety net, this violence does just what it does in communities of color: it initiates or perpetuates cycles of retaliatory violence, engenders or intensifies unhealthy substance use, tears families apart, and, when unhealed, results in lasting trauma that is passed down over generations.

Just as violence in communities of color intersects with our culture's stories about whose lives are valued and whose are not, so, too, does violence in white communities reflect a bigger story about power. Interpersonal violence is always shaped by the larger context in which it happens. And the larger context in America has always been both a story that all white people are better than people of color, especially black people, and a story that some white people are the least valuable of their kind.

We see these interlocked and competing stories in the ways white people behave in our own families and communities, in the painful and often harmful ways we attempt to resolve the tensions between the notion that we are better than everyone else and the constant evidence that we are imperfect, flawed, and sometimes terribly wrong. Because culture is persistent, the same characteristics of white culture that manifest in our historical and continued destructive treatment of people of color are also visible in the ways white people treat one another in our own communities, our own relationships, and our own homes. White culture is characterized by behavior meant to control, punish, exile, and exterminate. It is useful to say aloud that these patterns are real, and that they have become part of who and how we white people are in the world—it is only then that we will stand a chance at changing them.

White people control people. We want people to behave a certain way and we use power to try to ensure that they do so. In our own families and relationships and communities, we police behavior we regard as aberrant, as embarrassing, as strange, as improper, as rebellious, as imperfect, as somehow inconsistent with our supposed superiority, and we try to stop that behavior. To do so, we use incentives, we give or withhold money, we give or withhold love, we call on notions of loyalty and family and belonging, we embarrass people, we talk about people, we deceive people, we imply threats, and we issue overt threats—threats of exclusion, of deprivation, of violence, and of shame.

When we do not succeed in controlling people, we punish people. We withdraw support, withdraw love, withdraw resources, withdraw access. We discipline, we insult, we demean, we humiliate, we beat, we burn, we injure, we violate, we abuse, we wound, we shame.

And when punishment does not work, we exile. We throw people away. Our very own "white trash." We disown people, kick them out of our homes, our families, our communities. We deny our ties to them, deny our history with them, deny our part in them and who they are and what they do. We refuse their calls, block their access, block their numbers, block their names from our lips and our memory. We change the passwords, change the story, change the locks.

And when even exile fails to remedy the perceived threat to who we think we are, we exterminate. We kill. We kill and kill and kill.

This way of being is a recipe for mass incarceration. It is no coincidence that the criminal justice system white people built has four main functions: control (in the form of policing), punishment (in forms ranging from fines to imprisonment), exile (in the form of incarceration), and extermination (in the form of executions). But this way of being is also a recipe for violence.

It assumes that behavior is shaped by power and control rather than connection and responsibility. And all the way through, it is anchored in shame—by the avoidance, threat, and experience of shame, the most reliable driver of violence around.

Many white people, particularly those who are poor and working-class, have experienced the cruelty and inhumanity of these functions of white culture, even as they have benefited from the advantages that accompany it. They have been punished or exiled from their families, their churches, and their communities for their behavior or the behavior of their loved ones, their criminal convictions, their addictions, their mental illness, their violence, and their mistakes. Most people in working-class and poor white communities have experienced harms that are connected to this culture, precisely because of how damaging the current socioeconomic structure is for them. Plenty of middle-class and even wealthy white people have also endured these harms, which include addiction, physical and sexual abuse, domestic violence, other forms of violence, and loss. Trauma like this can have an ossifying effect—it can solidify our beliefs beyond intervention, it can narrow the range of people we trust and listen to, and it can create an appetite for a channel for our anger that, when coupled with those other effects, can be disastrous. Combine that trauma with a story that we are superior, and, whether we are rich or poor or somewhere in between, the combination can make us behave in hateful ways to the people closest to us and in horrific ways to those we regard as "other" or less than us.

We could end this kind of violence in white communities (or at least render it no longer normal) if we wanted to, just as we could end the high levels of incarceration everywhere. One way for us to do so would be by using even a fraction of the resources we currently spend on incarcerating people of color. If we did not allocate spending as we do, we could—not just for white people, but for everyone, equitably—restore cuts to Medicaid and

Medicare, build functional schools, invest in economic development programs that gave people a pathway to a dignified living wage, close the gap in access to healthy affordable food, or fix our roads and bridges and community centers and hospitals in all communities.[47]

But none of that has been our priority. Prisons have been—especially, but not only, prisons for people of color. Some of that is because our culture has made the control of people of color such a central piece of who we are as Americans. That control is one way we enact the story that all white people are better than people of color, especially black people. This story is not just about overt racism. It is not just about the hate groups whose presence has endured through every phase of progress toward racial justice and whose visible resurgence we have witnessed in recent years. While it is in part about the overt belief in white people's superiority, it is not just a set of beliefs and it is not always overt. It is also—and most often—what those beliefs look like woven into our unconscious thinking, our behavior, and our institutions. It is the scaffolding around the culture we built; even when it is no longer visible, it remains part of how the thing was made.

But that racism alone is not enough to have driven our lifeless prioritization of incarceration over the larger social good: we have also had to enact the other, parallel story—the one that teaches that some white people are the least valuable of their kind—that some are no more than "trash." This notion of "white trash" is as least as old as our country, and it separates a portion of our nation's people from the rest, exaggerates their criminality, accuses them of laziness even as it exploits their labor, and asserts the disposability of their lives.[48] This story is not contradictory to the larger story of white superiority—it is a part of it. It is the soft, ugly underbelly that aims to explain a world where white people are allegedly, innately superior and yet so many of them have so little of what they need. It at once drives comparably less advantaged white people's investment in being superior to people of color and ensures their relative position in the hierarchy below wealthier white people. And it causes pain—because the desperate grasp for dominance and the experience of relative powerlessness are both catalysts of violence.

There is no pathway out of mass incarceration that does not require dismantling and displacing a structure like this. And we will not end violence—not just against and among people of color, but against and among white people, too—without addressing head-on these stories and their far-reaching manifestations in our culture. This work will prove to be a non-negotiable element of any road to repair.

How, then, do we reverse the normalization of violence? The disregard and distortion of the pain people of color experience is not just about a gap in empathy, nor will it be solved by an increase in empathy alone. It is most centrally about power. Like the individual healing process, such a societal effort requires regarding violence seriously and situating both the pain and the response to it in its social and historical context. And also like that individual process, it requires realigning power.

To do so, first we have to tell a different story. We have to insist that the pain of women and trans people of color is spoken and heard, resist the narratives that render them as superhuman to the point of being impervious to pain, and insist that their pain is our collective responsibility to help heal. We have to push back against the narrative that the pain young men of color experience is insignificant—that it is somehow more tolerable than the harm others experience, that they are all involved in gangs anyway, that they are accustomed to violence as a way of resolving disputes, that they do not feel pain quite in the way other people do, that they are untrustworthy narrators of their own experience—and insist on the simpler and clearer story that they are people, many of them children, and that they hurt when they are harmed.

We have to resist the old, deadly stories to make space for new ones. But shifting this narrative requires stories that are not just simply newer, but more complete—stories like the ones many people of color have been telling for centuries. It requires acknowledging the legacy of slavery when we talk about the record-setting homicide rates on the South Side of Chicago. It requires acknowledging the impact of redlining when we talk about gang-related violence in Detroit. It requires an immediate end to the mainstream journalism practice of always reporting about a young man of color's criminal record if he is shot. It requires recognizing the distortions our mass media perpetuate any time we talk about women of color—and correcting those distortions. It also requires not just talking about pain, but tending to it, mourning and grieving it, and working to end it.

In April of 2018, under the leadership of Bryan Stevenson, the Equal Justice Initiative (EJI) in Alabama opened the nation's first National Memorial for Peace and Justice, "dedicated to the legacy of enslaved black people, people terrorized by lynching, African Americans humiliated by racial segregation and Jim Crow, and people of color burdened with contemporary presumptions of guilt and police violence."[49] This memorial grew out of EJI's work documenting incidents of lynching in America, an undertaking that always aimed to create and correct the historical record and understand "the terror and trauma this sanctioned violence against the black community created." In this work, EJI staff and volunteers have visited hundreds of lynching sites, where they have collected soil (which is then displayed at the memorial) and created public memorials that aim to displace our culture of denial with one of truth and repair. Set on top of a hill in Montgomery, with the hot Alabama sun blazing down on row after row after row of hanging markers raised to each person known to have been lynched in this country, the memorial is gut-wrenchingly solemn and its argument undeniable. It tells a whole truth. EJI understands the acknowledgment, recognition, and memory of mass atrocities and abuse as a prerequisite for a society's recovery from such violence.[50] This kind of sacred practice reflects the deep wisdom that the work of healing from our legacy of violence and fostering a future in which something else is possible must include, in part, the work of grief and mourning that such public acknowledgment not just allows but requires.

Erricka Bridgeford brings this work of sacred grief to present-day violence. Bridgeford lives in Baltimore, where she has emerged as a leader in her city's struggle against homicide. She works from the understanding that "Baltimore's violence not only produces pain but is the product of it, and the only way out is through healing."[51] Bridgeford began visiting the scene of every homicide in the city to grieve, to honor those lost, and to reclaim the space. She speaks of the imprint violence leaves on a place and the power of transforming that through acknowledgment and love. Her work combats the disregard that lies at the heart of the normalization of violence, and in making this healing public, contributes to shifting what is and can be normal.

One lesser-known feature of the work of Cure Violence, a program with sites all over the country, embodies the kind of spirit Bridgeford teaches. Every time someone is shot in an area where Cure Violence works, they hold a small street memorial and put up one of the makeshift altars with signs and candles and teddy bears that are all too familiar to people who live in neighborhoods where killings are common. They do this if the person was a bystander killed in a drive-by shooting. But they also do this if the person was a known gang member with a history of violent crime. This practice mirrors practices in neighborhoods across the country, where community members expand the work of grief to include everyone.

Combatting the normalization of violence is not just about grieving the lives we are already culturally primed to grieve. It is about the harder work of grieving every life lost—of saying no matter who you are, no matter what you have done, no matter how angry or afraid we are, we will still say that what happened to you was wrong, we do not believe that you are deserving of violence, we believe your life remains sacred, and we will grieve you because you are one of us. That does not mean we excuse whatever harm the person may have committed. It just means that we do not excuse the harm committed against them.

These efforts all recognize the interplay between collective and individual healing. When we treat violence like an individual problem absent its larger context, the solutions we envision are individualistic. When we understand violence in the context of society and history, then healing takes a different form. It continues to include the intimate personal processes of coming through specific acts of harm. But it also requires fostering a context that acknowledges and transforms the realities that made that harm likely. HealingWorks, a national field- and movement-building project committed to securing healing equity, includes as one of its central tenets for individual healing "addressing racial trauma head on." In years of listening to practitioners across the country about what helps people move through pain, over and over again these and other organizations have learned that situating pain in its larger context is essential to its transformation. Trauma has no respect for boundaries. New pain does not behave as separate from old pain, however much we might like to measure and treat it as such. In that way, the work of collective mourning is the work of individual grieving and vice versa. And the work of grieving is always also the work of reopening the possibility of imagination.

If healing is in part the struggle to wrest a future from a painful past, then it also includes the work of resistance. This includes developing new ways of thinking that make internalized oppression visible for what it is and offer strategies to disentangle from its nets.[52] It includes movement anthems, affirmations, and, as some say them, prayers like "Black Is Beautiful" and "Black Lives Matter," which insist, over and over again, on the fundamental truths that racism denies. It includes jazz and blues and hip-hop and other forms of truth-telling in the larger culture war at hand. It includes comedy and the kind of laughter that brings us to the edge of weeping, to the place where joy and grief reconnect. It includes food and stories and the reclamation of rituals that were never supposed to survive and whose survival includes the promise of other survivals, including one's own.

And it includes building power through organizing. Dr. Anna Ortega-Williams's groundbreaking 2018 dissertation asks in its title, "Is Organizing a Pathway for Wellbeing and Post-Traumatic Growth for Black Youth in New York City?" and traces the ways in which the work of building power can support young people in recovering from historical trauma and systemic violence.[53] Ortega-Williams's research finds that the act of resistance, of working to address harm and create change, can help young people transform traumatic experiences into ones that foster healing, growth, and power. As she implores people investing in supporting black youth's healing:

> Emphasize trauma recovery practices that take into account mass group trauma, intergenerational trauma responses, post-traumatic growth through action as well as an acknowledgment of their inheritance of historical resistance. Inquire into the narratives that fuel them, that shape their identities. Recognize ancestors that strengthen them and explore what a healed Black future means to them. Support them in alchemic translation of their lived experiences so they can use it as an indictment for systemic accountability and healing through working for social justice.

This almost surely holds true not only for black youth, but for so many people of color and other survivors who take on the nearly—yes, only nearly—impossible task of transforming pain.

And it is worth it. Healing is, as one survivor described it to me, "no joke." When people heal, the options foreclosed by trauma begin to reopen. Healed people have the experience of change—of going from pain to some measure of relief. Healed people are nimble. Healed people are often suspicious of belief systems that deny change, because the fact that they are still alive is because they were capable of change. Healed people are less susceptible to manipulation and less in need of toxic forms of protection. Healed people have a harder time being indifferent to other people's pain and often see themselves in others who have come through loss. Healed people cannot be persuaded that violence is normal. Healed people heal people.

In the context of the larger work of addressing this nation's historical and racialized trauma, these outcomes of healing will manifest in their own way for white people, too, for whom the combination of white supremacy and our own pain can harden into patterns of great harm to ourselves and others. Healing, then, is one of the ways white people will become capable of supporting a humane and rational response to harm—including the harm people of color endure, as well as the harm we ourselves endure—and of contributing to the disruption of our current deadening narratives that lock cycles of violence in place.

What would it mean to envision and build not just a set of services, but an entire healing infrastructure in America? How can we create an interlocking system of institutions, resources, people, and practices that together support survivors to initiate, engage in, and secure healing over the long term and to prevent future harm?

While building this infrastructure will require a realignment of priorities, funding, and cultural attitudes toward violence and recovery, it does not mean starting from scratch. To begin with, communities of color in this country would not still be here if they did not have within them measures to heal pain: the devastation across generations would be too vast. Rather, throughout the country, in these communities and elsewhere, people are already doing the work of healing harm. They are the GED teachers who grew up in the same neighborhood where they stay late to talk to their students who have suffered losses; they are the local barbershop owners who create a space where people can unload their pain and pick up strategies to cope with it; they are the school counselors who understand trauma and ask, "What happened to you?" before asking, "What's wrong with you?" when someone misbehaves in class; they are the violence interrupters who circle back around after an incident to talk to someone about his underlying pain; they are the women people call when someone is shot—women who can talk people out of retaliation, accompany grieving mothers to the morgue, plan a vigil, and keep an eye on the kids who witnessed it. They are the mourners, the grievers, the caretakers, and the imaginers. These healing resources exist, but they tend to be vastly under-resourced, devalued relative to more traditional nonprofits, disregarded as providing legitimate victim services, and disconnected from one another in ways that create barriers to improving practice, commanding resources, and building movement. Because these practices and leaders exist, developing a healing infrastructure does not require inventing some new evidence-based practice and exporting it to cities across the country. To the contrary, it requires investing in these local, steadfast healing supports so that they can achieve the scale of change and relief they are poised to deliver with adequate resources; supporting people engaged in healing work (professionals and others) to develop and expand strategies that work; honoring culture, geography, and history, and embracing a wide range of healing strategies, including those that depart from standard white and/or Western and/or middle-class and/or professional modalities; nurturing the development of strategies that address racial trauma head-on and work to heal through inter-generational trauma; integrating healing as a core objective of major policy platforms; and ensuring that people who have survived harm and are healing through it shape the development and implementation of a healing agenda.

The wide availability of these services will not just provide something, it will say something. It will convey that we believe what happened to those who are harmed is wrong, that their pain matters, and that they are deserving of support and capable of healing. Institutions like these not only reflect social norms and values but generate them—the existence of support conveys that violence is wrong and significant, that access to support is important, that people can and deserve to seek help, and that when people are harmed we will hold them closer rather than isolate them in their pain. Those are the norms and values of a society that no longer regards violence as normal. Those are not yet norms we hold equally for all people. But expanding that type of infrastructure equitably is within our reach if we choose to do it.

We also need to integrate a commitment to healing in other places where people make connections and access support, including schools, community programs, public housing, churches and mosques and other cultural hubs, job development programs, child care centers, and nursing homes. It requires viewing other social services within a framework of healing and adapting practices so as to support safety and recovery from harm. In our hospitals, it will mean not handcuffing people to their beds when they have been shot because we suspect them of having provoked their own near assassinations. In our schools, it will mean addressing students' trauma individually and teaching collectively about the history that has produced our current systems and conditions. In our jails and prisons, it will mean that violence carried out against incarcerated people—whether

by other incarcerated people or by staff—will no longer be toler-
ated, and that those responsible will be held accountable.

Critically, the best healing strategies reflect a lesson that survivors have been sounding for decades: that healing is both
broader and more varied than the criminal justice system and
even most mainstream victim service programs presume. Survivors want to live in safer neighborhoods, not just to be kept
safe from specific people. They want the resources to rebuild
their lives. They want safe housing and the opportunity to meet
their economic needs. They want to be able to protect and care
for their families. They want for others what they want for
themselves: to be safer, happier, and more whole. They want
justice, but they do not always want justice in the forms that
exist now.[54] This means that our responses cannot be confined
to addressing individual trauma, however broadly and creative-
ly we might do so. We will also have to shift toward a broad
prioritization of ending violence—in our justice systems, in our
distribution of resources, and in our culture. This will require
reversing the structural drivers of violence—from denial to
divestment to disempowerment—and in their place building
living promises that reflect a belief that violence is wrong and
always has been.

In our economic policy, it will mean creating pathways to a
living wage and upward mobility for everyone. In our housing
policy, it will mean ensuring access to safe, stable, decent homes
for everyone and reversing the inequities established by redlining
and amplified by the mortgage crises. In our civic policy, it will
require taking a stand against impunity and holding institutions
and government actors responsible for harm when they cause it.
In our budgets, it will mean that healing will take priority over
enforcement and equity over profit. It will require a substantial
and long-standing corrective redistribution of resources and the
power to direct them. And in our criminal justice policy, it will

mean using incarceration as the option of last resort that it always should have been.

Ultimately, the development of a healing infrastructure will require building power to demand, create, and protect the kind of structures that truly produce well-being. Survivors—including those who are angry, those who are forgiving, those who are in pain, those who have begun to heal, those who want systemic change, those who have caused harm, and those whose voices we have not yet heard and elevated—can and will define the direction and priorities of any principled healing agenda. This will not be about charity. Because trauma distills down to powerlessness, the opposite of trauma is not help; the opposite of trauma is power. It will therefore be essential that any reallocation of resources is not top-down, but grounded in an ever-increasing accountability on the part of government systems and community leaders to the political power built by those whose lives are at stake in violence and its elimination.

That power will secure the services and resources necessary for healing, but it will also help people heal. This is where the process becomes iterative, because healed people are formidable. People who have come through pain are more capable of participating in an ongoing way in their communities, of organizing with one another, developing strategic policy agendas, and doing the work to ensure that those agendas are implemented. In that way, supporting survivors is not only of benefit to them. It is of benefit to our democracy, which will be strengthened by the full and robust participation by more of its members. In the end, it is only that changed democracy that will deliver the policy and practice we need.

When we dig down through the dirt that is the normalization of violence in America, down to the roots, we find it grows from inequity. The story that violence is normal depends on the story that some of us are more deserving of safety than others, and some are more deserving of pain. It depends on the story that some of us should just expect to be hurt and that the rest of us bear no responsibility for that hurt. It depends on the story that some of us no longer even feel pain—if we ever did. It depends on a history awash with erasure—not just of violence, but of resistance to and healing from violence as well. It depends on stories of unworthiness, of numbness, of monstrosity, and of forgetting. And it depends on institutions that embody and enforce those stories.

There is no way out of the normalization and institutionalization of violence without a massive cultural reorientation. In thinking about imagining our way to a culture that has inverted the normalization of violence, I asked a number of people I respect deeply how they would complete the sentence: "The opposite of violence is _____." The answers included compassion, harmony, patience (this one from the historian in the group), dignity, safety, freedom, respect, mercy, honor, connection, and love.[55] I think they are all right.

The future healing promises is always related to the past in which it begins. Any road to a world in which violence is no longer normal, in which compassion and dignity and love define us instead, will therefore require steering head-on into the damage wrought by racism and the violence from which it originates, on which it relies, and which it protects. Whether or not we are up to that challenge may well be the central question of our generation. I am persuaded that it is, at the minimum, the question on which our ability to end both mass incarceration and violence depends.

Facing the past raises another question. If the answers above describe the opposite of violence in the present tense, what, then, is the opposite of violence that has already occurred? What is a corrective force equal and opposite to the violence we have done? In that sense, we might say the opposite of violence is healing. It is recovery. It is repair. But I would argue that it is something more than that, something that has the grace and weight of accountability in it as well. I would say that in the face of what we in this country have done, the opposite of violence is reckoning.

7

Our Reckoning

So what do we do with what we have done?

The scale of harm—both individual and structural—that we as a nation have committed is immense. Knowingly and unknowingly, honestly and dishonestly, we have crafted a story about violence and brought that story brutally to life in a new form. In incarceration, we have protected and exacerbated the core dimensions of slavery, woven and rewoven them into what could have been a changing story for our nation, entrenched them ever more deeply into our economy, and built our politics in service, rather than in opposition, to the core myths, values, and practices that define structural racism. We have locked up our own people at a rate and scale unprecedented in human history and have generated unfathomable pain—some now beyond all healing, and some that will take generations to heal.

We have built a culture of incarceration in a way that has devastated communities of color so disproportionately as to make the lineage from slavery through Jim Crow to our current jails and prisons undeniable. And yet even with that extraordinary inequity, we have still not built it in a way that has protected white people—at least not all white people. We have sent millions upon millions of white people to jail and prison, too, and we have failed to protect many white people—particularly poor white people—from the violence that incarceration is supposed to resolve. We have made clear that controlling and punishing people of color is more important than meeting the basic needs for food, housing, or medical care, not just for them, but for anyone. Our federal, state, and local budgets make it plain: if we look at cuts to Medicaid alongside our expanding investments in law enforcement and prisons, it is quite literally true that we will let poor people die so long as we can continue to finance our warped attachment to incarceration. At the same time that we have continually renewed our commitment to racism, we have simultaneously doubled down on the ethos of disposability at the heart of the term "white trash," have capitalized on the unhealed pain in poor white communities, and have fostered racial division through propaganda, intimidation, and policy to ensure that the shared portion of this experience of oppression does not become the basis for collaborative interracial resistance and struggle. Communities of color suffer immensely as a result. Poorer white communities do, too. And while many middle-class and wealthy white people will profit from such division, the price poorer white people will pay for their racial loyalty will be greater in the end than the near-term benefits they are given for adherence. Being just one rung up from the bottom of the ladder of power is little security when the floodwaters rise.

There is no way out of this without dealing with the past. We will have to face what we have done. We will have to face the people who have spent years of their lives in six- by nine-foot boxes with virtually no human contact. We will have to face the millions of children who spent their mornings, bedtimes, birthdays, holidays, and childhoods with their parents separated from them in prison. We will have to face the hundreds of thousands of people who survived sexual violence in the jails and prisons where we sent them. We will have to face people's pain and night terrors and flashbacks and hypervigilance. And, crucially, we will have to face all of the survivors in communities throughout this country to whom we promised safety as the reward for this devastation—and who did not become—and still are not—safe as a result. Their pain is our national harvest.

We have championed incarceration with full knowledge of its unquestionable brutality. And we have expanded it in the face of clear and rising evidence of its failure to produce the results it promises. Since incarceration does not merely fail to reduce violence but *generates* violence, our investment in incarceration has been an investment in violence. We are on the hook as a society for answering for the pain this investment has produced—not only to those people who suffer its harms directly, but to those communities that have suffered at the losing end of the policy failure it represents. We can continue to put off correcting our course and answering for it, but the scale of harm is growing and so, too, is what will be required of us to repair it. If by some small chance we have not already crossed the line into the terrain of the irreparable, we would be best off steering into our process of accounting for it now, while some transformation may still be within our reach.

Acts of individual and structural harm are meaningfully different, but the key elements of accountability—acknowledging responsibility for one's actions, acknowledging the impact of one's actions on others, expressing genuine remorse, taking actions to repair the harm to the degree possible, and no longer committing similar harm—apply to both. Just as we ask people who cause interpersonal violence to reckon with their actions, so should we as a society call on ourselves to reckon, too. Until we do, no different future will be possible.

The first element of accountability begins with truth-telling. By acknowledging responsibility for our actions, we own our individual and collective roles and power in generating, supporting, or being complicit in the harm that has been caused both by mass incarceration and by our failure to develop effective solutions for violence. It means saying, "We chose this. We had options, and this is what we did."

The second element, acknowledging the impact of our actions on others, means saying, "Not only did we choose this, but these are the results of our choices." It means saying, even if we want to claim that we did not know the effects mass incarceration would have (either individually as citizens, voters, lawmakers, or system actors—or more globally, as an entire society), that we could have known, it was our responsibility to know, and we know now. It means giving up the protection of certain myths and lies deployed to make the choices we have made feel morally sound when they were anything but. It means giving up the security of feigned ignorance. It means truth-seeking, and it means being honest about what we find when we look at our present and our history. "This is the crime of which I accuse my country and my countrymen," James Baldwin wrote, "and for which neither I nor time nor history will ever forgive them, that they have destroyed and are destroying hundreds of thousands of lives and do not know it and do not want to know it." It is this crime for which we must repent first.

The third element, expressing genuine remorse, requires apologizing. It means everyone who has contributed to or benefited from this harm—even those of us who were also harmed, even if less so than others were—should admit our role in it and say that we are sorry. This includes individuals addressing each other in our communities and our families in both private and public conversation. It includes leaders of and major investors in businesses that have profited from incarceration. It includes government actors who contributed to building incarceration as we know it. And it includes people currently positioned to speak on behalf of the government (such as elected officials, prosecutors, and judges) speaking publicly about what is right. It is important not to underestimate the importance and potential impact of acknowledgment and apology. They have been demonstrated to have the capacity to transform relationships on both the individual and community level. It is equally important not to overestimate the importance and potential impact of acknowledgment and apology, as their real and lasting force takes hold only when coupled with acts of repair: saying we are sorry calls for then "doing sorry"—the fourth element of accountability.

When we come to this point of making repair concrete, people often get caught up in logistical concerns about how we might calculate what is owed and how the mechanisms for distribution of those resources would operate. I think these concerns largely miss the point. First, they dodge the fundamental moral issue of whether that repair is owed or not. If it is, then the question is not whether we know how to do it, but how we can figure it out. Second, these concerns tend to vastly overestimate the difficulty of redistributing resources. America has a long history of creating mechanisms to redistribute wealth. The violent takeover of colonization, in which we turned land into profit, and slavery, in which we turned human beings into profit, come to mind as some larger-scale versions of transferring wealth from one group of people to another.

In the other direction, though rarely (if ever) in ways that have been racially equitable, we have the New Deal and the Works Progress Administration, the G.I. bill, and really, virtually all government expenditure, which through taxation distributes individually held resources to public goods upon which everyone depends and to which everyone is entitled. In the international context, the Marshall Plan, which Eddie Ellis, the visionary founder of the Center for NuLeadership on Urban Solutions, and, more recently, notable attorney and justice reform advocate Daryl Atkinson have invoked as a model for reparations, offers an example of a package investment following harm. Some of these mechanisms follow periods of wartime and reflect a recognition

that concentrated loss requires concentrated repair. Others are
the ongoing ways in which a society generates the level of basic
living standards and equity necessary to ensure not only justice, but social order and peace. I am not an economist, and it is
beyond the scope of this book to deliberate on the precise cal-
culations or mechanisms for redistributing resources, but we are
being dishonest if we pretend that this is not something we have
the intellectual and practical capacity to do. America knows how
to make money move.

Crucially, repair does not have to happen at a single time or in
a single way. The scope of harm we are repairing certainly did
not. We might therefore envision countless municipal strategies
to address housing discrimination across the country; local and
regional strategies to address lynching and racial terror; regional
and national strategies to address the legacy of slavery; and local,
regional, and national strategies to address the harms of mass
incarceration and of the violence it failed to prevent. These strategies, like the harms they address, could unfold on different and
sometimes overlapping timelines and places, with some people
participating in only one facet, some in several, and some in all.
This debt is owed and keeps accruing. As author and journalist
Ta-Nehisi Coates has written:

> Having been enslaved for 250 years, black people
> were not left to their own devices. They were terror-
> ized. In the Deep South, a second slavery ruled. In the
> North, legislatures, mayors, civic associations, banks,
> and citizens all colluded to pin black people into
> ghettos, where they were overcrowded, overcharged,
> and undereducated. Businesses discriminated against
> them, awarding them the worst jobs and the worst
> wages. Police brutalized them in the streets. And the
> notion that black lives, black bodies, and black wealth

were rightful targets remained deeply rooted in the broader society. Now we have half-stepped away from our long centuries of despoilment, promising, "Never again." But still we are haunted. It is as though we have run up a credit-card bill and, having pledged to charge no more, remain befuddled that the balance does not disappear. The effects of that balance, interest accruing daily, are all around us.[1]

Critically, the debt is not just financial. Coates describes reparations not just as some "hush money" or payout, but as "the full acceptance of our collective biography and its consequences."[2] It is not just a monetary debt that is owed. It is a moral one, too.

If we believe in the full humanity and belonging of every person in our nation, and if we know we have caused great harm to many of our own, then the only thing left to do is it try to make things as right as possible. I have long been persuaded that black people are entitled to reparations for slavery. I believe that workers should be paid for labor and compensated for the intergenerational impacts of mass-scale wage theft. I believe that people who have been violently injured deserve compensation for their pain. I believe that psychological damage is as important as physical injury and as deserving of repair. I believe that failing to address a set of wrongs of such a great scale as slavery effectively justifies those wrongs, normalizes them, excuses them, carries them into our present, and guarantees a future in which versions of them will persist. As Fania Davis has written, "This is urgent. Continued failure to deal with our country's race-based historical traumas dooms us to perpetually re-enact them."[3]

There is no new way forward without reconciling the debts of the past. I believe there is no expiration on the entitlement to repair, that it perseveres through generations just like the pain at its basis, and that time does not heal all wounds. Only healing heals all wounds. And as Sonya Shah, a leader in the restorative justice movement, reminds us, "accountability and healing are inextricably linked."[4]

It will be hard, if not impossible, to fully disentangle the different dimensions of harm from one another. Ultimately, we are obligated to deal with all of it as the massive totality that it is. But we are equally obligated to acknowledge every last wound in every last sector of our lives in which pain has been inflicted and borne. I do not know how the sequencing and interplay of the various dimensions of reckoning should work. I do not know how we will hold the complex positions of non-black people of color in America—America, a country so centrally defined by the black/white binary and so filled with people who do not belong at either end. These questions will be ours to answer collectively. What I do know is that the pain we must address is at once so particular to individual people and specific systems—and at the same time so interconnected, so overlapping, and so intergenerational that we will have to be ready for some nonlinear mess to unfold along the way—or perhaps more accurately, *as the way*—forward.

However the process might unfold, a core dimension of the project of repair must include accounting for the harms of mass incarceration and for the violence it generates and fails to reduce. Some of this repair will be particular and individual; I think of this subset of what is owed almost as restitution rather than reparations. In the criminal justice context, we could see individualized financial restitution used as a means to address wrongful convictions, the lasting financial impact of unjust and outdated bail policies, the indefensible collection of fines and fees in such a way as to debilitate the poor, and much more. These amounts are particular and calculable. As Amanda Alexander of the Detroit Justice Project puts it, "We have the receipts." It is not hard to imagine comparable forms of restitution for the results of housing discrimination and displacement, for the damage wrought by inequitable health care, for the wages stolen through "convict leasing," and more.

Alongside these various forms of individual restitution, some of this project of repair for mass incarceration will be collective and structural, because so much of the harm has been just that. This is the part I would call reparations. As we seek a pathway forward, we have the great benefit of the wisdom, advocacy, and organizing of many of the people who have paid the heaviest price for prison's failure and have already mapped out notions of what repair might look like. As with charting the course to repair the harms of slavery, many of these leaders are black Americans. But because mass incarceration has disproportionately harmed a wide range of people of color, not only black people, these leaders include people of other races, including leaders in Latino and Native American communities that have been devastated by incarceration and its associated pain.

If we are to rise to the vision they have put forward for us, we will demand an end to both mass incarceration and violence. We will make a commitment to real accountability for violence in a way that is more meaningful and more effective than incarceration. We will develop new strategies to address harm in communities without relying on police. We will expand restorative and transformative justice practices both within and beyond the criminal justice system. We will forge pathways to accountability rooted in the culture and beliefs of the people holding and being held accountable. We will demand healing opportunities as vast and accessible as our current policing infrastructure. We will change policy and we will realign power. We will do this with crime survivors, formerly incarcerated people, and a fundamental commitment to human dignity at the center of all we do. We will experiment, we will imagine, and we will work. The new forms of responding to violence that we develop will be imperfect methods—perhaps forever, but certainly at first. But they will grow in practice; they will develop the solidity that arises from time and experience; and they will become the very institutions that will anchor the culture we are now finally poised to build.

In practice, some of these changes will include the expansion of alternatives to incarceration, as well as policy shifts and the development of a robust healing infrastructure. But because part of the problem at hand is an overreliance on the criminal justice system to address broad social ills, repair will also require changes in practices entirely outside the criminal justice arena, including a realignment of policy and resources in education, housing, health care, wage equity, and the social service infrastructure as a whole. It will require raising our national standard for meeting everyone's basic needs and creating a context in which everyone can thrive. It will require changing the socioeconomic and structural conditions that make violence likely in the first place and that ensure its persistence.

Similarly, when we recognize the ways in which our dependence on incarceration has fostered violence—whether by nurturing it directly through the criminogenic features of prison or indirectly through the divestment in social services that funding incarceration at this scale has required—we know the people to whom we owe repair include currently and formerly incarcerated people and their families, but also the crime survivors we have failed to keep safe or to help heal. They will also be included as we create spaces for truth-telling and recognition; publicly acknowledge harm that has occurred and the people who have survived it; name policy changes as acts of repair; and compensate people who have been harmed with resources and opportunities that help them rebuild their lives and their communities.

We have available to us models for addressing systemic harm. The truth and reconciliation process in South Africa offers a large-scale reference point for contending with and seeking to transform the intergenerational impacts of structural racism. In Rwanda, the Truth Commission, or the National Unity and Reconciliation Commission, offers an example of how a nation might carve a path forward among people in the aftermath of genocide. As Fania Davis has observed, these efforts as a whole are limited in that they "strictly define and limit accountability to criminal prosecution and punishment for gross violation of human rights."[5] They do not, therefore, include the range of people harmed, the range of people responsible, or all the elements of accountability—including, perhaps most essentially, repair—that are outlined here. Still, they each hold unquestionably useful lessons for what we choose to undertake.

There are also narrower and nearer examples that provide critical insights. In Greensboro, North Carolina, a truth and reconciliation commission addressed a 1979 Ku Klux Klan and Nazi attack on a group of protesters that left five dead and ten injured.[6] Central to the commission's exploration—and to the harm caused—was the role of the police in sanctioning, or at least failing to prevent, the violence. In Maine, Native people convened the Maine Wabanaki-State Child Welfare Truth & Reconciliation Commission to address the harms caused by the child welfare system.[7] The Black Women's Truth and Reconciliation Commission is addressing sexual violence as a human rights atrocity against women and girls of African descent past and present.[8] In Boston, a truth-seeking process is examining the violence associated with school desegregation.[9] The Chicago Torture Justice Memorials Project and others secured reparations from the City of Chicago for victims of police torture.[10] Leading reform advocates Dr. Alice Greene and Kassandra Frederique have called for reparative justice responses to the War on Drugs. And countless people across the country, including Fania Davis, have called for truth and reconciliation commissions to address the harm caused to black people in the United States—both by the police and more broadly.[11] In that realm, the visionary work of the Equal Justice Initiative has already undertaken so much of the practical and moral burden of documenting the history we will all have to repair. We are not without examples or guides.

The acts of truth-telling and repair that are at the heart of such processes are critical foundations for the fifth and final element of accountability—becoming people who will not cause harm again. That transformation requires both personal change and change in structures: to be most durable, people have to not want to *and* not be able to cause the same kind of harm again. Ensuring that the harm will not recur therefore requires a realignment of power, from those who have caused harm to those who have been harmed. With mass incarceration and violence, that realignment involves relocating the authority to define and secure safety so that it shifts from the systems that have held that power to the communities that are most impacted. It means not only shrinking systems but developing solutions that stand to displace them. And it means building political power to protect those changes from backsliding and backlash. The people whose lives are at stake will need to have the durable collective power to choose, implement, and sustain solutions.

Because the repair at hand is structural, everyone who has been impacted—as people who have experienced harm, caused harm, or both—will have a role in driving, defining, and implementing repair. Central among those who will have to support this shift— and if history and culture are a guide, will be most likely to resist it—are white people. I believe that white people should participate in this shift for the benefit of people of color. But that is not the whole of it. What I have come to understand more recently is why we as white people need to engage in repair not just for our own humanity, but for our own interests. The exercise we must undertake is not race-neutral. Just as mass incarceration's impact has not been evenly distributed, so, too, must the repair be proportionate to the harm caused. That will mean a concentration of resources in communities of color. The repair must go to where the damage—and therefore the debt incurred—has been greatest, and we white people will need to be prepared for a substantial redistribution of resources toward communities of color throughout the country.

This obligation is straightforward if perhaps quite challenging for white people, particularly middle-class and wealthy white people whose families have not been affected by incarceration. This obligation is clear for white people who, even if they are relatively poor, have worked in jails or prisons or the industries connected to them and so have profited directly from what we have done as a society. But our debt and obligation may seem complicated for white people who have benefited from their racial privilege but at the same time have been on the losing side of class-based oppression that has led to incarcerating poor and working-class white people at rates vastly higher than their rich counterparts. What does this mean for poor and working-class white people who have been locked up and survived violence? What if people both owe and are owed for this collective pain?

However central racial equity will be to structural change, addressing the harms of mass incarceration will also mean repair to the families of white people who have been devastated by prison and its lasting aftermath in people's lives. When it comes to broad-scale realignment of resources, the beneficiaries must include all people of color, but others, too. Although the realignment of resources recommended here will begin to take from white people their relative advantage vis-à-vis people of color, for low-income white people, the changes proposed here will be overwhelmingly in their favor. The reinvestment of resources in schools, jobs, roads, treatment, hospitals, and healing will benefit white people whose communities have been under-resourced, partially as the result of our overinvestment in law enforcement, jails, and prisons. If our current system has pitted poor people of different races against each other in a way that is ultimately to the detriment of us all, then this realignment at its best will invert that pattern and create opportunities for shared struggle and well-being.

White people, even when we are disadvantaged in the system, are still always better positioned than similarly situated people of

color, so white people—even those of us who have been harmed
by mass incarceration—cannot merely wait to become recipients
of the benefits of this repair. We are, as we would say in a restorative justice context, both harmed and responsible parties. And
so we have to be active agents in bringing about that repair. We
have to tell the truth about our pain, about what we have lost,
about how mass incarceration has ravaged our lives and families.
At the same time, we have to tell the truth about the ways in
which we still got lighter sentences and better treatment than
many people of color who committed the same crimes that we
did. We have to name what was taken from us by this inhumane
system; and we have to acknowledge what we were given, even
in the belly of that beast, that folks of color never received. We
have to fight for more sensible sentencing, fair policing, humane
distribution of resources, accessible healing, durable change, fix-
ing what is broken, and building what we want in its place. We
have to advocate for these things for ourselves—and, to fulfill our
role in the larger repair, we have to ensure that our demands are
not met at the expense of others, as they have been for so long,
but rather we must insist on a rising tide that raises all ships. As
my incisive friend and colleague Lorenzo Jones put it, "Poor and
formerly incarcerated white people have to fight for what they're
due; and they have to make sure everyone gets it." And for white
people who have been fully insulated from the ravages of mass
incarceration—well, we just have to be ready to make thorough,
vast, and overdue amends. We have to steer into our reckoning.

That is, admittedly, a lot to ask. Most people don't take the
opportunity to choose a reckoning. Most wait for it to come to
them, though it is always worse when it does. It is like the choice
between going to the doctor when we feel a faint but troubling
pain in our chest or waiting until we collapse in the street to
address it; it is always better to go by choice, but that does not
always mean we go, nor does it almost ever mean the doctor's
news for us is good. Being honest about what we have done will

not be easy, nor should we expect to be greeted with an open, forgiving embrace from those whose lives we have destroyed brutally for generations. The grace on the other side of reckoning is matched only by the rage and pain and messiness of the road there. I do believe, based on history and analysis, that choosing such a reckoning is both logical and practical. I also believe it is an act of faith.

In cases of interpersonal wrongdoing, accountability is to those responsible for harm what grief is to those harmed. It is an unparalleled tool for responsible parties to transform their shame, and in so doing, to recuperate a sense of dignity, self-worth, connectedness, and hope—the things they lost when they caused harm. Accountability is as essential as any grieving process to restoring us to our best selves.

I think that holds true in the context of large-scale social harm as well. If it is true that when we hurt people we feel shame, that shame drives violence, and that the only pathway out of shame is through accountability, then the pathway out of mass incarceration and the violence that comes with it must include accountability—not just because those harmed deserve it, but because those of us who have contributed to or benefited from that harm deserve it, too—in the toughest and kindest senses of the word "deserve."

I believe that white people know, on some level, what we have done. I believe that because we are human and because human beings are fundamentally good, we feel ashamed of those choices and their impact. I believe that shame is compounded when people we love are caught up in the systems we have condoned. And I believe, because we are human, that until that shame is resolved, we will do what ashamed humans do: we will act it out as violence. We will do that interpersonally in our own families and communities. And because we have more access to structural power, we will do it through institutions—including, most centrally for the challenge explored here, through the criminal justice system. We will justify our inhumanity toward other people by making claims that they are inhuman—because only then will we feel any insulation from our shame for hurting them so terribly. We will punish more and more harshly, as if to prove that we were not wrong about who "those people" are—because if we *were* wrong, if we *are* wrong, then we have done an unimaginably terrible—even an irreparable?—thing. If we do not resolve our shame, we will do what Dr. James Gilligan saw countless people do: we will seek to eradicate the witnesses of our wrongdoing. We will do so through violence— our own violence and the violence of the state that acts in our names. We will do so through exclusion—including one of the largest-scale mass exclusion experiments in human history, in which we literally send people somewhere we refer to only as "away": mass incarceration. And we will do so through attempts at erasure—by retelling history in a way that excludes the bases for our responsibility or the evidence of its effects on others.

None of this will work. All of the harm we do to escape that reckoning will only add to the toll for which we ultimately have to answer. Because while shame compels us to violence, violence does not resolve our shame. Only accountability does.

And so white folks in America have—terrifyingly, urgently, blessedly—a choice. We can continue to act out of shame, stuck in its clutches, diminished by its force, constrained by its power over us. Or we can rise out of it through accountability. We can say that what we did was wrong. We can say that we know it hurt people. We can say we are sorry. We can do sorry, taking actions to make the harms of the past as right as possible. And we can begin to become a people who will never do it again.

When we do that, I believe we will reap benefits that are unimaginable to us from this side of that reckoning. I believe not only will we regain our dignity, self-worth, connectedness, and hope, I believe we will be able to give and receive love more and better than we've ever known. I believe we will be able to feel proud—not because we are superior to other people, but because we are superior to our own former selves. We will become people who are better—not better than others, but better than we once were. We will become people who have earned our dignity. And for those of us who are poor, we will become people who can finally align with people of color who share our conditions and fight to get the wages, housing, health care, and protection we have always deserved.

In all of this, many of us—not just white people—will be tempted to look only forward because what is behind us is so hard to face. We will want to do it once (at most) and say we are done. But only the discipline of anchoring our future in our past—not in a way that is constrained by it, but in a way that grows from it—will honor everyone who has been harmed and will strengthen those of us who have caused harm in our ongoing accountable rise out of shame. And for those we have hurt, like for most survivors of violence, what will happen on the other side of such a process, what healing or rage or transformation may arise from it, is unknowable on this side; but the fact that it is unknowable does not make it any less urgent or any less deserved.

One thing all this collective labor to address the harms of mass incarceration and violence will buy America is the chance to build something new in the place of what we are working to end. Our aim cannot only be less use of broken strategies. It has to be the development and expansion of better, more effective, more humane strategies. Of the key facets of sound responses to violence—survivor-centered, accountability-based, safety-driven, and racially equitable—the first three sound so familiar. Victims, accountability, and safety. These three have been deployed to advance draconian criminal justice policy for decades. But these principles belong to those of us who are fighting for a more just system. They are ours. And when we do the work of building alternatives to the system as it is, it turns out that not only do we believe them more deeply, we are better at

them, too. In the end, we do not have to just push back against
the system as we know it. We have to render that system obsolete.

One day we will tell the history of how these new ways of
being came to be, and that history will include the fact that we
told the truth, that we who were responsible said we were sorry,
and that we all did something different from what we had done.
If (and I believe, only if) we do that, "we can," as James Baldwin
foretold, "make America what America must become."

When I think about that road to repair, I do not believe that those
of us who have had the fortune to participate in accountability
processes, including restorative justice circles, have everything
that is needed to displace mass incarceration. But I do believe
we have something essential to offer. We know a thing about
reckoning.

I have had the huge privilege of spending the past decade of
my life with people who are in the process of reckoning with
what they have done. And what I know is that virtually no one
wants to choose it. It is unappealing at best, terrifying at worst.
Very few of our responsible parties at Common Justice go into
their circles with great enthusiasm. Most go in trembling or
dragging themselves along. Many of our harmed parties, while
always there voluntarily, go in with similar ambivalence and fear.
It never quite seems like a good idea right before it begins. And
then—every single time—it turns out to have been the right
thing to do. People typically get the things they hoped for going
in—closure, recognition, answers, connection, clarity, a path to
repair. But people almost always get something more. There is a
level of dignity and of pride available to our responsible parties
that most could not even imagine for themselves on their way in
to the circle. There is a level of resolution and well-being for our
harmed parties that most believed could never be theirs. There is
a way of being in the world and with what happened that becomes
clear only on the other side of reckoning. It is more—bigger, bet-

ter, more complete—than we knew to ask for. And it is almost always there.

I believe America has advanced as far as we can toward equity without facing the truth about our history. I believe we got every drop of change we could out of our current story, and that the next step requires telling some greater truths. I believe we are due for a reckoning. I understand our collective desire and the wild contortions of our culture that we are going through to avoid it. But I also believe it is time. And I believe that on the other side of that reckoning is an America we never even dared to imagine— not really, not in our bones, not yet. I believe it is an America that can, for the first time, hold us all. It is an America that is ours to choose, ours to create, and ours to earn.

Acknowledgments

Sometimes, in a restorative justice process, we will invite people to call their ancestors or teachers into the room. People will either go around in a circle or just shout out the names of the people who should be recognized before the process moves forward. It seems right, then, to start by saying the names of some of the visionaries in the restorative justice movement who live this work every day.

For those of us who come to this work from other struggles for justice, often driven by outrage and fury, Fania Davis has taught us that we can still be warriors even if our central tools are based in love. I have been lucky to have her as a mentor for more than a decade. Anyone who thinks restorative justice is "soft" should meet Mariame Kaba: She is among the most rigorous, incisive thinkers and practitioners I have known in any movement of which I have been a part. Her simultaneous generosity of spirit and her utter and unequivocal intolerance for nonsense may well be what justice looks like in practice. Cheryl Graves and Ora Schub (may she rest in power) are unfaltering in their belief that people are capable of mending the harm that occurs between them, and that those with a stake in the outcome will always find better pathways to justice than any system ever can. I am honored to be answerable to Dr. Morris Jenkins, who has steered us into honest conversations about race and held us accountable to being our best selves in a way that has been catalytic in the movement. Sonya Shah knows how to sit: to sit with the worst kinds of harm people cause, the worst kinds of pain people endure, and the difficulties of surviving and witnessing such pain. To my great fortune, she also sits with me, and I am always better for it. While sujatha baliga's widely recognized work has mostly been in the juvenile justice system, for many of us, her greatest teaching is the way she pushes us to think beyond where restorative justice has gone thus far and to move into the territory of the pain and intergenerational harm that persists in our families; in this and countless other ways, she challenges us to extend the reach of our capacity for forgiveness. Lauren Abramson in Baltimore models the unfaltering belief that those impacted by harm are capable of resolving it and the persistence that this movement requires of us all. Howard Zehr's teachings on restorative justice are as far-reaching as anyone's, and still he teaches us daily about humility.

I am indebted to the Vera Institute of Justice, which took a chance on me when I had nothing but a vision, and which supported me in bringing that vision to life, sometimes clumsily, often through great challenges, for a decade; and to the board of directors of Common Justice, people who double down on that bet every day and push me to, of all things, dream bigger.

I cannot possibly list everyone who informed whatever wisdom is contained in this book, but I can at least name the people who helped in its writing. Ruth Parlin's unsurpassed research assistance provided this book with the stable ground it needed to stand on. Jalon Arthur, Todd Clear, Fania Davis, Richard Dudley, Norris Henderson, Mariame Kaba, Fatimah Muhammad, Khalil Muhammad, Anna Ortega-Williams, gabriel sayegh, Vincent Schiraldi, Christopher Stone, and Bruce Western each took valuable time, provided critical insights, and stood in my blind spots so that I could see more clearly. Michelle Alexander did more than she will accept credit for in persuading me that this book would be useful and that I could write it. My family, both biological and chosen, loves me in a way that makes me better and braver—and it turns out, far more than I expected, that it requires quite a bit of bravery to write a book.

Diane Wachtell at The New Press persuaded me to undertake this project and, midwife that she is, always expressed exactly the right balance of compassion and indifference to my discomfort necessary to move the project forward. She is incisive, adept at her craft, and kind. The rest of the team at The New Press contributed immeasurably, and it was an honor to benefit from their care, skill, and patience all along the way. I cannot imagine the book without Jules Verdone, copy editor extraordinaire, who can distinguish unlike anyone I know between when something sings and when it is off-key, and who edited every last line of this book, including this one.

The movement to end mass incarceration in the United States is powerful and growing, and I am lucky to have been raised by it and to have gotten to know personally some of the prophets of our time. My hope is really that this book will be a good step stool—that it will be solid enough to bear our weight and will give us enough height to reach whatever it is we need next. I am honored to have a place in this relay race and hope this leg of it does right by the people who have brought the baton this far and the ones who will carry it from here.

I am deeply indebted to the extraordinary people I have worked with at Common Justice over the past decade. The survivors I have known and the people who have caused serious harm have taught me what accountability is, what healing is, what transforming really requires, and what is possible when we do. And finally, the incomparable Common Justice team has shaped me daily and irrevocably, and their deep wisdom is woven permanently into the fabric of what Common Justice is and what it stands to become. They are the smartest, fiercest, most compassionate, and most courageous group of people I know, and it is my honor to try to move the world alongside them. The best of what is contained here is a credit to them; the mistakes are all my own.

Notes

Introduction

1. James Baldwin, "The Negro Child—His Self-Image," *Saturday Review*, December 21, 1963, 60, reprinted as "A Talk to Teachers" in *The Price of the Ticket: Collected Nonfiction, 1948–1985* (New York: Macmillan, 1985), 332.

2. Albert Reiss and Jeffrey Roth, eds., "Patterns of Violence in American Society," in *Understanding and Preventing Violence: Panel on the Understanding and Control of Violent Behavior*, vol. 1 (Washington, DC: National Academy Press, 1993), 70, nap.edu/catalog/1861/understanding-and-preventing-violence-volume-1.

3. Bruce Kennedy, Ichiro Kawachi, Deborah Prothrow-Stith, Kimberly Lochner, and Vanita Gupta, "Social Capital, Income Inequality, and Firearm Violent Crime," *Social Science and Medicine* 47, no. 1 (1998): 7–17; Cleopatra H. Caldwell, Laura P. Kohn-Wood, Karen H. Schmeelk-Cone, Tabbye M. Chavous, and Marc A. Zimmerman, "Racial Discrimination and Racial Identity as Risk or Protective Factors for Violent Behaviors in African American Young Adults," *American Journal of Community Psychology* 33 (2004): 91–105.

4. Reiss and Roth, "Perspectives on Violence," in *Understanding and Preventing Violence*, 1993, 145.

5. James Gilligan, *Violence: Our Deadly Epidemic and Its Causes* (New York: Putnam Publishing Group, 1996).

6. Li-yu Song, Mark Singer, and Trina Anglin, "Violence Exposure and Emotional Trauma as Contributors to Adolescents' Violent Behaviors," *Archives of Pediatric and Adolescent Medicine* 152 (1998): 531–6.

7. Kara Williams, Lourdes Rivera, Robert Neighbours, and Vivian Reznik, "Youth Violence Prevention Comes of Age: Research, Training and Future Directions," *The Annual Review of Public Health* 28 (2007): 195–211.

8. U.S. Department of Education, Policy and Program Studies Service, "State and Local Expenditures on Corrections and Education," 2016, 1, www2.ed.gov/rschstat/eval/other/expenditures-corrections-education /brief.pdf; Christian Henrichson and Ruth Delaney, "The Price of Prisons: What Incarceration Costs Taxpayers," Vera Institute of Justice, 2012, 2, archive.vera.org/sites/default/files/resources/downloads/price -of-prisons-updated-version-021914.pdf; and Justice Policy Institute, "Rethinking the Blues: How We Police in the U.S. and at What Cost," 2012, 11, justicepolicy.org/uploads/justicepolicy/documents/rethinking theblues_final.pdf.

9. Charlotte Garden and Nancy Leong, "'So Closely Intertwined': Labor Interests and Racial Solidarity," *George Washington Law Review* 81 (2013), 1170–4, digitalcommons.law.seattleu.edu/faculty/121; Elizabeth A. Baker, Mario Schootman, Ellen Barnidge, and Cheryl Kelly, "The Role of Race and Poverty in Access to Foods That Enable Individuals to Adhere to Dietary Guidelines," *Preventing Chronic Disease* 3, no. 3 (2006), cdc.gov/pcd/issues/2006/jul/05_0217.htm; and Jacob S. Rugh and Douglas S. Massey. "Racial Segregation and the American Foreclosure Crisis," *American Sociological Review* 75, no. 5 (2010): 629–51, ncbi.nlm.nih.gov /pmc/articles/PMC4193596.

10. See Eric S. Mankowski and Kenneth I. Maton, "A Community Psychology of Men and Masculinity: Historical and Conceptual Review," *American Journal of Community Psychology* 45 (2010): 73–86; Kathryn Reid-Quinones, Wendy Kliewer, Brian J. Shields, Kimberly Goodman, Margaret H. Ray, and Emily Wheat, "Cognitive, Affective, and Behavioral Responses to Witnessed Versus Experienced Violence," *American Journal of Orthopsychiatry* 81, no. 1 (2011): 51–60; Raewyn W. Connell, *Masculinities*, 2nd ed. (Berkeley: University of California Press, 1995); Sonia Schwarts, Joel Hoyte, Thea James, Lauren Conoscenti, Renee Johnson, and Jane Liebschutz, "Challenges to Engaging Black Male Victims of Community Violence in Healthcare Research: Lessons Learned from Two Studies," *Psychological Trauma: Theory, Research, Practice and Policy* 2, no. 1 (2010): 54–62; and Veronika Burcar and Malin Akerström, "Negotiating a Victim Identity: Young Men as Victims of Violence," *Journal of Scandinavian Studies in Criminology and Crime Prevention* 10 (2009): 37–54.

11. "The Challenges of Prisoner Reentry: Facts and Figures," The Urban Institute, 2008, urban.org/sites/default/files/alfresco/publication-pdfs /411683-The-Challenges-of-Prisoner-Reentry-Facts-and-Figures.PDF.

12. Michelle Alexander, *The New Jim Crow: Mass Incarceration in the Age of Colorblindness* (New York: The New Press, rev. ed. 2012), 20–6; Douglas A. Blackmon, *Slavery by Another Name: The Re-Enslavement of Black*

Americans from the Civil War to World War II (New York: Anchor Books, 2009); Ta-Nehisi Coates, "The Case for Reparations," *The Atlantic*, June 2014; and Alex F. Schwartz, *Housing Policy in the United States* (New York: Routledge, 2010), 332.

13. "Lynching in America: Confronting the Legacy of Racial Terror, Second Edition," Equal Justice Initiative, 2015, eji.org/reports/lynching -in-america.

14. Christopher Hartney and Linh Vuong, "Created Equal: Racial and Ethnic Disparities in the US Criminal Justice System," National Council on Crime and Delinquency, 2009, 3, nccdglobal.org/sites/default /files/publication_pdf/created-equal.pdf.

15. Randy Borum, "Assessing Violence Risk Among Youth," *Journal of Clinical Psychology* 56, no. 10 (2000), 1263–88; and Jennifer N. Shaffer and R. Barry Ruback, "Violent Victimization as a Risk Factor for Violent Offending Among Juveniles," *Juvenile Justice Bulletin* (Washington, DC: U.S. Department of Justice, Office of Justice Programs, Office of Juvenile Justice and Delinquency Prevention, 2002), 6, 8, citeseerx.ist. psu.edu/viewdoc/download?rep=rep1&type=pdf&doi=10.1.1.218.5315; Kenneth V. Hardy and Tracey A. Laszloffy, *Teens Who Hurt: Clinical Interventions to Break the Cycle of Adolescent Violence* (New York: The Guilford Press, 2005); John A. Rich and Courtney M. Grey, "Pathways to Recurrent Trauma Among Young Black Men: Traumatic Stress, Substance Use, and the 'Code of the Street,'" *The American Journal of Public Health* 95, no. 5 (2005), 816–24; Erika Harrell, "Black Victims of Violent Crime," special report, U.S. Department of Justice, Office of Justice Programs, Bureau of Justice Statistics, 2007, NCJ 214258, 8, bjs.gov/content/pub/pdf /bvvc.pdf.

16. "Beyond Innocence: Toward a Framework for Serving All Survivors of Crime," Vera Institute of Justice, Common Justice, 2015, 1–9, storage.googleapis.com/vera-web-assets/downloads/Publications/beyond -innocence-toward-a-framework-for-serving-all-survivors-of-crime /legacy_downloads/beyond-innocence-blog-digest.pdf.

17. "California Proposition 57, Parole for Non-Violent Criminals and Juvenile Court Trial Requirements (2016)," Ballotpedia, ballotpedia.org/California_Proposition_57,_Parole_for_Non-Violent_Criminals and_Juvenile_Court_Trial_Requirements_(2016); and "Oklahoma Reclassification of Some Drug and Property Crimes as Misdemeanors, State Question 780 (2016)," Ballotpedia, ballotpedia.org/Oklahoma_Reclassification _of_Some_Drug_and_Property_Crimes_as_Misdemeanors_State _Question_780_(2016).

18. See Hal Dardick and Matthew Walberg, "Kim Foxx Declares Win in Cook County State's Attorney's Race," *Chicago Tribune*, November 8, 2016;

Elyssa Cherney, "Aramis Ayala Upsets Jeff Ashton for State Attorney," *Orlando Sentinel*, August 31, 2016; Brian Rogers, Margaret Kadifa, and Emily Foxhall, "Anderson Defeated in Harris County DA Race," *Houston Chronicle*, November 8, 2016; and Fernanda Santos, "Sheriff Joe Arpaio Loses Bid for 7th Term in Arizona," *New York Times*, November 9, 2016.

19. E. Ann Carson, "Prisoners in 2016," Department of Justice, Bureau of Justice Statistics, January 2018, rev. August 7, 2018, 1, 18, bjs.gov /content/pub/pdf/p16.pdf.

20. Ryan King, Bryce Peterson, Brian Elderbroom, and Elizabeth Pelletier, "Reducing Mass Incarceration Requires Far-Reaching Reforms," The Urban Institute, 2015, webapp.urban.org/reducing-mass-incarceration.

21. "Defining Violence: Reducing Incarceration by Rethinking America's Approach to Violence," Justice Policy Institute, 2016, 4, justicepolicy.org /uploads/justicepolicy/documents/jpi_definingviolence_final_report_9 .7.2016.pdf.

22. "Expanded Homicide Data Table 2: Murder Victims by Age, Sex, Race, and Ethnicity, 2016," in *Crime in the United States* (Washington, DC: U.S. Department of Justice, Federal Bureau of Investigation, 2016), ucr.fbi.gov/crime-in-the-u.s/2016/crime-in-the-u.s.-2016/tables /expanded-homicide-data-table-2.xls; "Table 3-10, Maltreatment Types of Victims, 2015," *Child Maltreatment 2015* (Washington, DC: U.S. Department of Health and Human Services, Administration for Children and Families, Administration on Children, Youth and Families, Children's Bureau, 2015), 45, acf.hhs.gov/cb/resource/child-maltreatment-2015; "Number of Aggravated Assaults, and Simple Assaults by Sex and Victim-Offender Relationship, 2016" (Washington, DC: U.S. Department of Justice, Bureau of Justice Statistics, 2016), generated using the NCVS Victimization Analysis Tool at bjs.gov; "Number of Aggravated Assaults, and Simple Assaults by Sex, 2016" (Washington, DC: U.S. Department of Justice, Bureau of Justice Statistics, 2016), generated using the NCVS Victimization Analysis Tool; and "Number of Robberies by Sex, 2016" (Washington, DC: U.S. Department of Justice, Bureau of Justice Statistics, 2016), generated using the NCVS Victimization Analysis Tool); "Violence Against the Transgender Community in 2017," Human Rights Campaign, 2017, hrc.org/resources/violence-against -the-transgender-community-in-2017; and Katherine A. Fowler, Linda L. Dahlberg, Tadesse Haileyesus, et al. "Childhood Firearm Injuries in the United States," *Pediatrics* 140, no. 1 (June 2017), doi.org/10.1542/peds.2016-3486.

23. Jeremy Travis, Bruce Western, and Steve Redburn, eds., *The Growth of Incarceration in the United States: Exploring Causes and Consequences* (Washington, DC: National Academies Press, National Research Council, 2014), 33–7, nap.edu/18613.

24. According to the World Prison Brief, the U.S. has 4.4 percent of the world's population and 21.4 percent of the world's incarcerated population.

Roy Walmsley, *World Prison Population List*, 11th ed. (London: Birkbeck University of London, Institute for Criminal Policy Research, 2016), 5, 14, prisonstudies.org/sites/default/files/resources/downloads/world_prison _population_list_11th_edition_0.pdf.

25. Alexander, *The New Jim Crow*, 180.

26. Thomas Bonczar, "Prevalence of Imprisonment in the U.S. Population, 1974–2001," U.S. Department of Justice, Bureau of Justice Statistics, August 17, 2003, 1, 8, bjs.gov/index.cfm?ty=pbdetail&iid=836.

27. Allen J. Beck and Ramona R. Rantala, "Sexual Victimization Reported by Adult Correctional Authorities, 2009–11," U.S. Department of Justice, Bureau of Justice Statistics, January 2014, 1, 3, bjs.gov /content/pub/pdf/svraca0911.pdf. In 2011 alone, correctional administrators reported 8,763 allegations of sexual victimization in jails and prisons— and this in a context of widespread underreporting; Nancy Wolff and Jing Shi, "Contextualization of Physical and Sexual Assault in Male Prisons: Incidents and Their Aftermath," *Journal of Correctional Health Care* 15, no. 1 (January 2009), 58–77, doi.org/10.1177/10783)45808326622; Review Panel on Prison Rape, "Report on Sexual Victimization in Prisons, Jails, and Juvenile Correctional Facilities," U.S. Department of Justice, Office of Justice Programs, April 2016, vi–vii, 2–4, ojp.gov/reviewpanel/pdfs/panel _report_prea_apr2016.pdf.

28. Paul Boxer, Keesha Middlemass, and Tahlia Delorenzo, "Exposure to Violent Crime During Incarceration: Effects on Psychological Adjustment Following Release," *Criminal Justice and Behavior* 36, no. 8 (2009): 793–807, doi.org/10.1177/0093854809336453; Jason Schnittker and Andrea John, "Enduring Stigma: The Long-Term Effects of Incarceration on Health," *Journal of Health and Social Behavior* 48: 115–30 (June 2007); Craig Haney, "Prison Effects in the Era of Mass Incarceration," *Prison Journal* (July 25, 2012): 1–24, doi.org/10.1177/0032885512448604.

29. Susan Turner, "Reentry," in *Reforming Criminal Justice: Volume 4: Punishment, Incarceration, and Release*, Eric Luna, ed. (Phoenix: Arizona State University, Sandra Day O'Connor School of Law, 2017): 342, academyforjustice.org/volume4; Haney, "Prison Effects in the Era of Mass Incarceration."

30. Lauren E. Glaze and Laura M. Maruschak, "Parents in Prison and Their Minor Children," U.S. Department of Justice, Bureau of Justice Statistics, August 2008, 3–5, bjs.gov/content/pub/pdf/pptmc.pdf; Christopher J. Mumola, "Incarcerated Parents and Their Children," U.S. Department of Justice, Bureau of Justice Statistics, August 2000, 1–2, 4, bjs.gov/content/pub/pdf/iptc.pdf.

31. Eric Martin, "Hidden Consequences: The Impact of Incarceration on Dependent Children," *National Institute of Justice Journal* 278 (May 2017): 2, ncjrs.gov/pdffiles1/nij/250349.pdf; Albert M. Kopak and Dorothy

Smith-Ruiz, "Criminal Justice Involvement, Drug Use, and Depression Among African American Children of Incarcerated Parents," *Race and Justice* 6, no. 2: (2016): 89–116; Leila Morsy and Richard Rothstein, "Mass Incarceration and Children's Outcomes: Criminal Justice Policy Is Education Policy," Economic Policy Institute, December 15, 2016, 8–12, epi.org/publication/mass-incarceration-and-childrens-outcomes.

32. Christian Henrichson and Ruth Delaney, "The Price of Prisons: What Incarceration Costs Taxpayers," Vera Institute of Justice, February 2012, vera .org/publications/price-of-prisons-what-incarceration-costs-taxpayers.

33. "State and Local Expenditures on Corrections and Education: A Brief from the U.S. Department of Education, Policy and Program Studies Service," U.S. Department of Education, July 2016, 1, www2.ed.gov /rschstat/eval/other/expenditures-corrections-education/brief.pdf; Tracey Kyckelhahn and Tara Martin, "Justice Expenditures and Employment Extracts, 2012—Preliminary," U.S. Department of Justice, Bureau of Justice Statistics, 2013, Table 1, bjs.gov/index.cfm?ty=pbdetail&iid=5239; Melissa S. Kearney and Benjamin H. Harris, "Ten Economic Facts About Crime and Incarceration in the United States," Brookings Institution, May 2014, brookings.edu/research/ten-economic-facts-about-crime-and -incarceration-in-the-united-states.

34. According to the National Priorities Project, the United States' military budget in 2016 was $618.8 billion. "The Militarized Budget 2017," National Priorities Project, April 23, 2017, nationalpriorities.org/ analysis/2017/militarized-budget-2017. War spending (on "Overseas Contingency Operations") in 2015 was $598 billion. "Overseas Contingency Operations: The Pentagon Slush Fund," National Priorities Project, 2015, nationalpriorities.org/campaigns/overseas-contingency-operations.

35. Alexander, *The New Jim Crow*, 234.

36. Alexander, 234.

37. "Willie Horton," *Gale Biography in Context*, Gale Group, 1999.

38. John DiIulio, "The Coming of the Super-Predators," *Weekly Standard*, November 27, 1995; Clyde Haberman, "When Youth Violence Spurred 'Superpredator' Fear," *New York Times*, April 6, 2014; James C. Howell, *Preventing and Reducing Juvenile Delinquency: A Comprehensive Framework*, 2nd ed. (Thousand Oaks, CA: SAGE, 2009), 4.

39. Doris J. James and Lauren E. Glaze, "Mental Health Problems of Prison and Jail Inmates," Bureau of Justice Statistics Special Report, U.S. Department of Justice, Office of Justice Programs, Bureau of Justice Statistics, 2006, NCJ 213600, 1–2 and 7–8, bjs.gov/content/pub/pdf /mhppji.pdf; Edward P. Mulvey, "Assessing the Evidence of a Link Between Mental Illness and Violence," *Psychiatric Services* 45, no. 7 (1994): 663–8, dx.doi.org/10.1176/ps.45.7.663.

40. Deborah Prothrow-Stith and Michael Weissman, *Deadly Conse-quences: How Violence Is Destroying Our Teenage Population and a Plan to Begin Solving the Problem* (New York: HarperCollins, 1991); James Collins and Pamela Messerschmidt, "Epidemiology of Alcohol-Related Violence," *Alcohol Health and Research World* 17, no. 2 (1993): 93–100; Paul J. Goldstein, "Drugs and Violent Crime" in *Pathways to Criminal Violence*, Neil A. Weiner and Marvin E. Wolfgang, eds. (Thousand Oaks, CA: Sage Publications, 1989, NCJ 118926): 16–48; Helene White, "Alcohol, Illicit Drugs, and Violence" in *Handbook of Antisocial Behavior*, David M. Stoff, James Breiling, and Jack D. Maser, eds. (New York: John Wiley and Sons, 1997), 511–23.

41. Danielle Sered, "Accounting for Violence: How to Increase Safety and Break Our Failed Reliance on Mass Incarceration," Vera Institute of Justice, 2017, 8, storage.googleapis.com/vera-web-assets/downloads/Publications/accounting-for-violence/legacy_downloads/accounting-for-violence.pdf.

1: Across the River of Fire

1. Joseph A. Boscarino, "Posttraumatic Stress Disorder and Physical Illness: Results from Clinical and Epidemiologic Studies," *Annals of the New York Academy of Sciences* 1032 (2004), 141–53; Wendy D'Andrea, Ritu Sharma, Amanda D. Zelechoski, and Joseph Spinazzola, "Physical Health Problems After Single Trauma Exposure: When Stress Takes Root in the Body," *Journal of the American Psychiatric Nurses Association* 17, no. 6 (2011): 378–92; Dean G. Kilpatrick and Ron Acierno, "Mental Health Needs of Crime Victims: Epidemiology and Outcomes," *Journal of Traumatic Stress* 16, no. 2 (2003): 119–132, doi.org/10.1023/A:1022891005388; "Post-Traumatic Stress Disorder," National Institute of Mental Health, nimh.nih.gov/health/topics/post-traumatic-stress-disorder-ptsd/index.shtml; "PTSD in Children and Adolescents," U.S. Department of Veterans Affairs, National Center for PTSD, 2004; and American Psychiatric Association, "Trauma- and Stressor-Related Disorders: Posttraumatic Stress Disorder" in *Diagnostic and Statistical Manual of Mental Disorders*, 5th ed. *(DSM-5)* (Arlington, VA: APA, 2013), Section II.

2. Crime victims show much higher incidences of PTSD than people not victimized by crime. Research shows that 25 percent of crime victims experienced lifetime PTSD and 9.7 percent had current PTSD (PTSD within six months of being surveyed), whereas 9.4 percent of people who had not been victims of crime had lifetime PTSD and 3.4 percent had current PTSD. See Kilpatrick and Acierno, "Mental Health Needs of Crime Victims," 126: "Studies of children at risk of violence show high rates of PTSD. As many as 100 percent of children who witness a parental homicide or sexual assault, 90 percent of sexually abused children, 77 percent of children exposed to school shootings, and 35 percent of

children exposed to community violence develop PTSD." See "PTSD in Children and Adolescents," National Center for Post Traumatic Stress Disorder, Department of Veteran Affairs, 2004; see also "Post Traumatic Stress Disorder Fact Sheet," PTSD Alliance, Sidran Institute, 2004, sidran.org/resources/for-survivors-and-loved-ones/post-traumatic-stress -disorder-fact-sheet-2; "DSM-5 Fact Sheets: Posttraumatic Stress Disorder," American Psychiatric Association, 2013, 1, psychiatry.org/File%20 Library/Psychiatrists/Practice/DSM/APA_DSM-5-PTSD.pdf. As the fact sheet describes it: "Re-experiencing covers spontaneous memories of the traumatic event, recurrent dreams related to it, flashbacks or other intense or prolonged psychological distress. Avoidance refers to distressing memories, thoughts, feelings or external reminders of the event. Negative cognitions and mood represent myriad feelings, from a persistent and distorted sense of blame of self or others, to estrangement from others or markedly diminished interest in activities, to an inability to remember key aspects of the event. Finally, arousal is marked by aggressive, reckless or self-destructive behavior, sleep disturbances, hypervigilance or related problems."

3. This is both figurative and literal. See California Department of Corrections and Rehabilitation, "Victim's Bill of Rights: Marsy's Law," cdcr.ca.gov/victim_services/Marsys_Law.html; New York State Office of Mental Health, "Kendra's Law," omh.ny.gov/omhweb/Kendra_web/ KHome.htm; and U.S. Department of Justice, Office of Justice Programs, "AMBER Alert," www.amberalert.gov.

4. Matt Schiavenza, "Hatred and Forgiveness in Charleston," *The Atlantic*, June 20, 2015; Rachel Kaadzi Ghansah, "A Most American Terrorist: The Making of Dylann Roof," *GQ*, August 21, 2017.

5. Paul Tullis, "Can Forgiveness Play a Role in Criminal Justice?," *New York Times Magazine*, January 4, 2013.

6. Audra Smith Haney, *Forgiving Your Son's Killer* (video and transcript), Christian Broadcasting Network, www1.cbn.com/700club/forgiving -your-sons-killer.

7. Alan Blinder, "Death Penalty Is Sought for Dylann Roof in Charleston Church Killings," *New York Times*, May 24, 2016.

8. Mary Achilles and Howard Zehr, "Restorative Justice for Crime Victims: The Promise, the Challenge," in *Restorative Community Justice: Repairing Harm and Transforming Communities*, Gordon Bazemore and Mara Schiff, eds. (New York: Routledge, 2001), 89–90.

9. Achilles and Zehr, "Restorative Justice for Crime Victims," 90.

10. Howard Zehr, *The Little Book of Restorative Justice, Revised and Expanded* (New York: Good Books, 2015).

11. Bruce J. Winick, "Foreword: Therapeutic Jurisprudence Perspectives on Dealing with Victims of Crime," *Nova Law Review* 33, no. 3 (Summer 2009): 540; Yvette G. Flores, "Sexual Abuse," in *Oxford Encyclopedia of Latinos and Latinas in the United States*, Suzanne Oboler and Deena J. Gonzalez, eds. (New York: Oxford University Press, 2005); Achilles and Zehr, "Restorative Justice for Crime Victims," 88.

12. Linda G. Mills. "The Justice of Recovery: How the State Can Heal the Violence of Crime," *Hastings Law Journal* 57 (2005–2006): 457.

13. Antony Pemberton, Frans Willem Winkel, and Marc Groenhuijsen, "Evaluating Victims Experiences in Restorative Justice," *British Journal of Community Justice* 6, no. 2 (Summer 2008): 100.

14. Ulrich Orth, "Does Perpetrator Punishment Satisfy Victims' Feelings of Revenge?," *Aggressive Behavior* 30, no. 1 (February 2004): 63, doi.org/10.1002/ab.20003.

15. Danielle Sered, "Accounting for Violence: How to Increase Safety and Break Our Failed Reliance on Mass Incarceration," Vera Institute of Justice, February 2017, 13; Heather Strang and Lawrence W. Sherman, "Repairing the Harm: Victims and Restorative Justice," *Utah Law Review* 2003, no. 1 (2003): 21.

16. Stacy Hoskins Haynes, Alison C. Cares, and R. Barry Ruback, "Reducing the Harm of Criminal Victimization: The Role of Restitution," *Violence and Victims* 30, no. 3 (2015): 450.

17. Tina Vasquez, "#MeToo: Addressing Sexual Assault and Abuse in Social Justice Movements," *Rewire*, November 3, 2017; Marcia Chatelain and Kaavya Asoka, "Women and Black Lives Matter: An Interview with Marcia Chatelain," *Dissent*, Summer 2015; Sarah Stillman, "Black Wounds Matter," *New Yorker*, October 15, 2015.

18. Tara Mathews, Margaret Dempsey, and Stacy Overstreet, "Effects of Exposure to Community Violence on School Functioning: The Mediating Role of Posttraumatic Stress Symptoms," *Behaviour Research and Therapy* 47, no. 7 (2009): 586–91; and Sheryl Kataoka, Audra Langley, Marleen Wong, Shilpa Baweja, and Bradley Stein, "Responding to Students with PTSD in Schools," *Child and Adolescent Psychiatric Clinics of North America* 21, no. 1 (2012), 119–33.

19. Mark W. Smith, Paula P. Schnurr and Robert A. Rosenheck, "Employment Outcomes and PTSD Symptom Severity," *Mental Health Services Research* 7, no. 2 (2005): 89–101.

20. Randy Borum, "Assessing Violence Risk Among Youth," *Journal of Clinical Psychology* 56, no. 10 (2000), 1263–88, 1268; and Jennifer N. Shaffer and R. Barry Ruback, "Violent Victimization as a Risk Factor for Violent Offending Among Juveniles," *Juvenile Justice Bulletin* (Washington, DC: U.S.

Department of Justice, Office of Justice Programs, Office of Juvenile Justice and Delinquency Prevention, December 2002), 6, 8, citeseerx.ist.psu.edu /viewdoc/download?rep=rep1&type=pdf&doi=10.1.1.218.5315.

21. According to the Cost-Benefit Knowledge Bank for Criminal Justice of the Vera Institute of Justice, a 2010 study by McCollister et al. offers the most current estimate of victim costs, using the cost-of-illness and jury-compensation approaches. According to the study, the estimated costs related to *victimization* for aggravated assault are $96,254; $24,211 for robbery; and $1,653 for burglary. See Cost-Benefit Knowledge Bank for Criminal Justice, "Victim Costs," cbkb.org/toolkit/victim-costs.

22. "Vision 21: Transforming Victim Services: Final Report," Office for Victims of Crime, 2013, 17–23, ovc.ncjrs.gov/vision21/pdfs/Vision21 _Report.pdf.

23. *Victims Compensation and Assistance Act of 1984, Pub. L. 98-473, Title II, Chapter XIV, as amended*, navaa.org/misc/Statute.html.

24. Sered, "Accounting for Violence," 13.

25. Sered, 13; Judith L. Herman, "Recovery from Psychological Trauma," *Psychiatry and Clinical Neurosciences* 52 (October 1998 Supp.): S98–S103, S146, doi.org/10.1046/j.1440-1819.1998.0520s5S145.x; Uli Orth, "Secondary Victimization of Crime Victims by Criminal Proceedings," *Social Justice Research* 15, no. 4 (December 2002): 315, doi.org/10.1023 /a:1021210323461.

26. Sered, "Accounting for Violence," 13.

27. "Crime Survivors Speak: The First-Ever National Survey of Victims' Views on Safety and Justice," Alliance for Safety and Justice, 2016, 5, allianceforsafetyandjustice.org/wp-content/uploads/documents/Crime %20Survivors%20Speak%20Report.pdf.

28. Christopher Bromson, Erin Eastwood, Michael Polenberg, Kimberly Sanchez, Danielle Sered, and Susan Xenarios, "A New Vision for Crime Victims," *Huffington Post*, November 4, 2016.

29. Alliance for Safety and Justice, "Crime Survivors Speak," 14.

30. Alliance for Safety and Justice, 14.

31. Bromson et al., "A New Vision for Crime Victims."

32. Orth, "Does Perpetrator Punishment Satisfy Victims' Feelings of Revenge?," 62–70.

33. Judith L. Herman, *Trauma and Recovery: The Aftermath of Violence—From Domestic Abuse to Political Terror*, 2015 ed. (New York: Basic Books, 2015).

34. "Clearances," 2015 Crime in the United States, U.S. Department of Justice, Federal Bureau of Investigation, 2016, ucr.fbi.gov/crime-in-the-u.s

/2015/crime-in-the-u.s.-2015/offenses-known-to-law-enforcement /clearances; "Criminal Cases," U.S. Department of Justice, Bureau of Justice Statistics, bjs.gov/index.cfm?ty=tp&tid=23; and Judith L. Herman, "The Mental Health of Crime Victims: Impact of Legal Intervention, *Journal of Traumatic Stress* 16, no. 2 (2003): 159–66, doi.org/10.1023 /A:1022847223135.

35. See U.S. Department of Justice, Office of Justice Programs, Bureau of Justice Statistics, *Sourcebook of Criminal Justice Statistics*, 31st ed. 2003 (Washington, DC: Government Printing Office, 2005), 418, Table 5.17, and 450, Table 5.46; Lindsey Devers, "Plea and Charge Bargaining: Research Summary," U.S. Department of Justice, Bureau of Justice Assistance, 2011, 2–3, bja.gov/Publications/PleaBargainingResearchSummary.pdf; John L. Kane, "Plea Bargaining and the Innocent," The Marshall Project, December 26, 2014, themarshallproject.org/2014/12/26/plea-bargaining-and-the-innocent.

36. Edna Erez and Pamela Tontodonato, "The Effect of Victim Participation in Sentencing on Sentence Outcome," *Criminology* 28, no. 3 (1990): 451–74.

37. See Mary P. Koss, "Restoring Rape Survivors, *Annals of the New York Academy of Sciences* 1087, no. 1 (2006): 206–34; Herman, "The Mental Health of Crime Victims," 159–66, doi.org/10.1023/A:102284722313 5; "Responses from the Field: Sexual Assault, Domestic Violence, and Policing," American Civil Liberties Union, 2015, 11–23 and 29–31, aclu .org/feature/responses-field; Rhissa Briones-Robinson, Ràchael A. Powers, and Kelly M. Socia, "Sexual Orientation Bias Crimes: Examination of Reporting, Perception of Police Bias, and Differential Police Response," *Criminal Justice and Behavior* 43, no. 12 (2016), 1688–709; and Edna Erez and Nawal Ammar, "Violence Against Immigrant Women and Systemic Responses: An Exploratory Study," 2003, ncjrs.gov/pdffiles1/nij /grants/202561.pdf.

38. Jim Parsons and Tiffany Bergin, "The Impact of Criminal Justice Involvement on Victims' Mental Health," *Journal of Traumatic Stress* 23, no. 2 (2010): 182–8, doi.org/10.1002/jts.20505; Uli Orth, "Secondary Victimization of Crime Victims by Criminal Proceedings," *Social Justice Research* 15, no. 4 (December 2002): 313–25, doi.org/10.1023/a:1021210323461; the quote is from Judith Lewis Herman, "Justice from the Victim's Perspective," *Violence Against Women* 11, no. 5 (May 2005): 574, doi.org/10.1177 /1077801205274450.

39. Parsons and Bergin, "The Impact of Criminal Justice Involvement," 184; Patricia A. Resick, "Psychological Effects of Victimization: Implications for the Criminal Justice System," *Crime & Delinquency* 33, no. 4 (1987): 475.

40. Orth, "Secondary Victimization," 315.

41. Herman, *Trauma and Recovery*, 72–3.

42. "Persons Arrested," 2016 Crime in the United States, U.S. Department of Justice, Federal Bureau of Investigation, 2017, ucr.fbi.gov/crime-in-the-u.s/2016/crime-in-the-u.s.-2016/topic-pages/persons-arrested; "Clearances," 2016 Crime in the United States, U.S. Department of Justice, Federal Bureau of Investigation, 2017, ucr.fbi.gov/crime-in-the-u.s/2016/crime-in-the-u.s.-2016/topic-pages/clearances; "Table 5.44 2006: Felony Convictions in State Courts by Offense," *Sourcebook of Criminal Justice Statistics Online* (Albany, NY: University at Albany, School of Criminal Justice), www.albany.edu/sourcebook/pdf/t5442006.pdf; "Table 5.24 2006: Defendants Disposed in U.S. District Courts," *Sourcebook of Criminal Justice Statistics Online* (Albany, NY: University at Albany, School of Criminal Justice), www.albany.edu/sourcebook/pdf/t5242006.pdf.

43. Lynn Langton et al., "Victimizations Not Reported to the Police, 2006–2010," U.S. Department of Justice, Bureau of Justice Statistics, August 2012, 1, www.bjs.gov/content/pub/pdf/vnrp0610.pdf.

44. Langton et al., "Victimizations Not Reported to the Police," 5.

45. Langton et al., 5.

46. Langton et al., 7, 8.

47. Robert J. Sampson and Janet L. Lauritsen, "Racial and Ethnic Disparities in Crime and Criminal Justice in the United States," *Crime and Justice* 21 (1997): 311–74, doi.org/10.1086/449253; and Harrell, *Black Victims of Violent Crime*, 7–8, 11.

48. Langton et al., 3.

49. Uli Orth, "Punishment Goals of Crime Victims," *Law and Human Behavior* 27, no. 2 (April 2003): 173–86, doi.org/10.1023/a:1022547213760 ("Through offender punishment, victims presumably expect reduction of aversive emotions like revenge and fear of repeated victimization. . . . In the subjective view of observers, harder punishment ensures security better," 182; security, not well-being or healing); Orth, "Does Perpetrator Punishment Satisfy Victims' Feelings of Revenge?," 62–70 ("The results of the two studies taken together suggest that perpetrator punishment only partially, and moreover only transitorily, satisfies feelings of revenge among victims of violent crimes, and that in the long run feelings of revenge are not influenced by severity of perpetrator punishment," 68; revenge, not well-being or healing); Edna Erez and Pamela Tontodonato, "Victim Participation in Sentencing and Satisfaction with Justice," *Justice Quarterly* 9, no. 3 (September 1992): 393–417 ("The findings regarding the impact of victim participation on satisfaction with the sentence support the hypothesis concerning the unintended effect of victims' heightened expectations on satisfaction. Previous research using these data revealed that the VIS had a measurable impact on sentence outcome (probation versus incarceration). . . . The present findings, however, show that for some victims, asking them to fill out

a VIS raises their expectations about their ability to influence the sentence. Therefore, when they feel that their input has had no effect on the outcome, their satisfaction with the sentence is decreased. These unfulfilled expectations may compound victims' pain and anger, and may increase the negative feelings that accompany the victimization and the criminal justice experience," 410); Linda G. Mills, "The Justice of Recovery: How the State Can Heal the Violence of Crime," *Hastings Law Journal* 57, no. 3 (2005–2006): 458 ("One of the assumptions of the criminal justice system is that victims benefit in some way from the prosecution and punishment of the person who caused them harm. . . . While such legal redress may indeed benefit some crime victims, it provides none with a meaningful opportunity to heal" [citation omitted], 458).

50. Strang and Sherman, "Repairing the Harm," 21; Erez and Tontodonato, "Victim Satisfaction," 395.

51. Erez and Tontodonato, 412; Malini Laxminarayan, "Procedural Justice and Psychological Effects of Criminal Proceedings: The Moderating Effect of Offense Type," *Social Justice Research* 25, no. 4 (2012): 391, doi.org/10.1007/s11211-012-0167-6.

52. Strang and Sherman, "Repairing the Harm," 21, 24.

53. Achilles and Zehr, "Restorative Justice for Crime Victims," 90; Strang and Sherman, "Repairing the Harm," 20–1.

54. Orth, "Punishment Goals of Crime Victims," 182; Orth, "Does Perpetrator Punishment Satisfy Victims' Feelings of Revenge?," 68; Erez and Tontodonato, "Victim Participation in Sentencing and Satisfaction with Justice," 410.

55. Beth Schwartzapfel, "How Parole Boards Keep Prisoners in the Dark and Behind Bars," *Washington Post*, July 11, 2015.

56. Julian V. Roberts, "Crime Victims, Sentencing, and Release from Prison," in *Oxford Handbook of Sentencing and Corrections*, Joan Petersilia and Kevin R. Reitz, eds. (New York: Oxford University Press, 2012), 114–20; Brent L. Smith, Erin Watkins, and Kathryn Morgan, "The Effect of Victim Participation on Parole Decisions: Results from a Southeastern State," *Criminal Justice Policy Review* 8, no. 1 (March 1997): 57–74; Joel M. Caplan, "Parole Release Decisions: Impact of Positive and Negative Victim and Nonvictim Input on a Representative Sample of Parole-Eligible Inmates," *Violence and Victims* 25, no. 2 (2010): 224–42.

57. This reflects Common Justice outreach data from February 2009–July 2018.

58. Sered, "Accounting for Violence," 13–14.

59. Alliance for Safety and Justice, "Crime Survivors Speak," 21.

60. Alliance for Safety and Justice, 21.

61. "Bridging the Divide: A New Paradigm for Addressing Safety, Crime, and Victimization," November 2014, ejusa.org/wp-content/uploads /Bridging-the-Divide-FINAL.pdf.

62. "California Crime Victims' Voices: Findings from the First-Ever Survey of California Crime Victims and Survivors" Californians for Safety and Justice, 2013, 16–18, safeandjust.org/wp-content/uploads/CA-Crime -Victims-Report-8_24_17.pdf.

63. Bromson et al., "A New Vision for Crime Victims."

64. Bromson et al.

65. Alysia Santo, "Kentucky's Protracted Struggle to Get Rid of Bail," The Marshall Project, November 12, 2015, themarshallproject.org/2015 /11/12/kentucky-s-protracted-struggle-to-get-rid-of-bail.

2: Prison's Broken Promise

1. "Perspectives on Punishment: An Interdisciplinary Roundtable on Punitiveness in America," John Jay College of Criminal Justice, 2015, johnjay.jjay.cuny.edu/punitivenessinamerica/roundtable.asp.

2. U.S. Department of Education, Office for Civil Rights, "Civil Rights Data Collection: Data Snapshot: Early Childhood Education," U.S. Department of Education, March 2014, 1, 3–4, www2.ed.gov/about /offices/list/ocr/docs/crdc-early-learning-snapshot.pdf.

3. Nancy Gertner, "Undoing the Damage of Mass Incarceration," Boston Globe, November 4, 2015.

4. Brandon K. Applegate, et al., "Assessing Public Support for Three-Strikes -and-You're-Out Laws: Global Versus Specific Attitudes," Crime & Delinquency 42, no. 4 (1996): 517–18, doi.org/10.1177/0011128796042004002.

5. Nicole Shoener, "Three Strikes Laws in Different States," LegalMatch, February 14, 2018, legalmatch.com/law-library/article/three-strikes-laws -in-different-states.html.

6. Matt Taibbi, "Cruel and Unusual Punishment: The Shame of Three Strikes Laws," Rolling Stone, March 27, 2013.

7. Andrew Karch and Matthew Cravens, "Rapid Diffusion and Policy Reform: The Adoption and Modification of Three Strikes Laws," State Politics & Policy Quarterly 14, no. 4 (2014): 461–91.

8. Jeremy Travis, Bruce Western, and Steve Redburn, eds., The Growth of Incarceration in the United States: Exploring Causes and Consequences (Washington, DC: National Academies Press, National Research Council, 2014), 44; Jessica Eaglin, "California Quietly Continues to Reduce Mass Incarceration," Brennan Center for Justice, February 17, 2015, brennancenter.org /blog/california-quietly-continues-reduce-mass-incarceration.

9. Timothy A. Hughes, Doris James Wilson, and Allen J. Beck, "Trends in State Parole, 1990–2000," U.S. Department of Justice, Bureau of Justice Statistics, October 2001, 1–3; Citizens Alliance on Prisons and Public Spending, "The High Cost of Denying Parole: An Analysis of Prisoners Eligible for Release," November 2003, 5, static.prisonpolicy.org/scans/cappsmi/fulldatareport.pdf; Ilyana Kuziemko, "Going off Parole: How the Elimination of Discretionary Prison Release Affects the Social Costs of Crime," Working Paper 13380, National Bureau of Economic Research, September 2007, 2–5, nber.org/papers/w13380.pdf.

10. Alfred Blumstein, "The Notorious 100:1 Crack: Powder Disparity— The Data Tell Us That It Is Time to Restore the Balance," *Federal Sentencing Reporter* 16 (October 2003): 87–92.

11. Khalil Muhammad, *The Condemnation of Blackness* (Cambridge, MA: Harvard University Press, 2011), 6.

12. Douglas A. Blackmon, *Slavery by Another Name: The Re-Enslavement of Black Americans from the Civil War to World War II* (New York: Anchor Books, 2009), 61–9.

13. U.S. Constitution, Amendment 13.

14. Michelle Alexander, *The New Jim Crow*, rev. ed. (New York: New Press, 2012), 20–2.

15. Alexander, *The New Jim Crow*, 13.

16. Alexander, 164.

17. James Forman Jr., *Locking Up Our Own: Crime and Punishment in Black America* (New York: Farrar, Strauss and Giroux, 2017), 10–11.

18. Forman, *Locking Up Our Own*, 12–13.

19. Bernadette Rabuy and Daniel Kopf, "Prisons of Poverty: Uncovering the Pre-incarceration Incomes of the Imprisoned," Prison Policy Initiative, July 9, 2015, prisonpolicy.org/reports/income.html; Matt Taibbi, *The Divide: American Injustice in the Age of the Wealth Gap* (New York: Spiegel & Grau, 2014), 4–9; Gregg Barak, Paul Leighton, and Allison Cotton, *Class, Race, Gender, and Crime: The Social Realities of Justice in America*, 5th ed. (Lanham, MD: Rowman & Littlefield, 2018), 67–89; Jeffrey H. Reiman and Paul Leighton, *The Rich Get Richer and the Poor Get Prison*, 11th ed. (New York: Routledge, 2016), 83–9; Bruce Western and Becky Pettit, "Incarceration and Social Inequality," *Daedalus* V, no. 1 (Summer 2010): 8–19; Sean Maddan, et al., "Sympathy for the Devil: An Exploration of Federal Judicial Discretion in the Processing of White-Collar Offenders," *American Journal of Criminal Justice* 37, no. 1 (March 2012): 4–18.

20. Rape, Abuse, and Incest National Network (RAINN), "The Criminal Justice System: Statistics," rainn.org/statistics/criminal-justice-system, citing Department of Justice, Office of Justice Programs, Bureau of Justice Statistics,

274   Notes

"National Crime Victimization Survey, 2010–2014," 2015; ii; Federal Bureau of Investigation, "National Incident-Based Reporting System, 2012–2014," 2015; iii; Federal Bureau of Investigation, "National Incident-Based Reporting System, 2012–2014," 2015, iv; and "Department of Justice, Office of Justice Programs, Bureau of Justice Statistics, Felony Defendants in Large Urban Counties, 2009," 2013; Patricia Tjaden and Nancy Thoennes, "Extent, Nature, and Consequences of Intimate Partner Violence," U.S. Department of Justice, July 2000, 52; *but see* Erica L. Smith, Matthew R. Durose, and Patrick A. Langan, "State Court Processing of Domestic Violence Cases," U.S. Department of Justice, Bureau of Justice Statistics, February 2008, 1–4.

21. M. Marit Rehavi and Sonja B. Starr, "Racial Disparity in Federal Criminal Charging and Its Sentencing Consequences," Empirical Legal Studies Center Paper No. 12-002, University of Michigan, Empirical Legal Studies Center, May 7, 2012, 2–4.

22. "Studies: Death Penalty Overwhelmingly Used for White-Victim Cases," Death Penalty Information Center, deathpenaltyinfo. org/node/6036, citing Frank R. Baumgartner, Amanda J. Grigg, and Aliso Mastro, "#BlackLivesDon'tMatter: Race-of-Victim Effects in US Executions, 1976–2013," *Politics, Groups, and Identities* 3, no. 2 (2015): 209–21, doi.org/10.1080/21565503.2015.1024262.

23. Rebecca C. Hetey and Jennifer L. Eberhardt, "Racial Disparities in Incarceration Increase Acceptance of Punitive Policies," *Psychological Science* 25 (10): 1949–54 (October 2014), doi.org/10.1177/0956797614540307.

24. Philip Cook, "The Deterrent Effects of California's Proposition 8," *Criminology and Public Policy* 5, no. 3 (2006): 415; A. McClelland and Geoffrey P. Alpert, "Factor Analysis Applied to Magnitude Estimates of Punishment Seriousness: Patterns of Individual Differences," *Journal of Quantitative Criminology* 1, no 3 (1985): 307–18; Eleni Apospori and Geoffrey Alpert "Research Note: The Role of Differential Experience with the Criminal Justice System in Changes in Perceptions of Severity of Legal Sanctions Over Time," *Crime and Delinquency* 39, no. 2 (1993): 189; Anthony N. Doob and Cheryl Marie Webster, "Sentence Severity and Crime: Accepting the Null Hypothesis," in *Crime and Justice: A Review of Research*, 30, Michael Tonry, ed. (Chicago: University of Chicago Press, 2003): 143–95; Tamasak Wicharaya, *Simple Theory, Hard Reality: The Impact of Sentencing Reforms on Courts, Prisons, and Crime* (Albany, NY: State University of New York Press, 1995), discussed in Doob and Webster, *Sentence and Severity*, 22; and Michael Tonry and David P. Farrington, *Strategic Approaches to Crime Prevention* (Minneapolis: University of Minnesota Law School, 1995), 6.

25. David M. Kennedy, *Deterrence and Crime Prevention: Reconsidering the Prospect of Sanction* (Abingdon, Oxon: Routledge, 2009); Harold

G. Grasmick and George J. Bryjak, "The Deterrent Effect of Perceived Severity of Punishment," *Social Forces* 59 (1980): 471–91; Wouter Buikhuisen, "General Deterrence: Research and Theory," in *General Deterrence* (Stockholm: National Swedish Council for Crime Prevention, 1974): 82, cited in Grasmick and Bryjack, "The Deterrent Effect of Perceived Severity of Punishment," 476; Richard T. Wright and Scott H. Decker, *Armed Robbers in Action: Stickups and Street Culture* (Boston: Northeastern University Press, 1997), 123; Anne M. Piehl, *From Cell to Street: A Plan to Supervise Inmates After Release* (Boston: Massachusetts Institute for a New Commonwealth, 2002), 8; Ben M. Crouch, "Is Incarceration Really Worse? Analysis of Offenders' Preferences for Prison Over Probation," *Justice Quarterly* 10, no. 1 (1993): 67–88; Joan Petersilia and Elizabeth Deschenes, "Perceptions of Punishment: Inmates and Staff Rank the Severity of Prison Versus Intermediate Sanctions," *Prison Journal* 74, no. 3 (1994): 306–28; William Spelman, "The Severity of Intermediate Sanctions," *Journal of Research in Crime and Delinquency* 32, no. 2 (1995): 107–35; and David C. May, Peter B. Wood, Jennifer L. Mooney, and Kevin I. Minor, "Predicting Offender-Generated Exchange Rates: Implications for a Theory of Sentence Severity," *Crime and Delinquency* 51, no. 3 (2005): 373–99.

26. Travis, Western, and Redburn, *The Growth of Incarceration*, 326.

27. David Garland, *Punishment and Modern Society: A Study in Social Theory* (Chicago: University of Chicago Press, 2012); Andrew Ashworth and Andrew Von Hirsch, *Principled Sentencing: Readings on Theory and Policy*, 2nd ed. (Oxford: Hart Publishing, 2000).

28. Eric Luna, "Punishment Theory, Holism, and the Procedural Conception of Restorative Justice," *Utah Law Review* 2003, no. 1 (2003): 205–302; *Reforming Criminal Justice: Volume 4: Punishment, Incarceration, and Release*, Eric Luna, ed. (Phoenix: Arizona State University, Sandra Day O'Connor College of Law, 2017), 7.

29. Paul H. Robinson, "Hybrid Principles for the Distribution of Criminal Sanctions," *Northwestern University Law Review* 82, no. 1: 19–42 (1987); Travis, Western, and Redburn, *The Growth of Incarceration*, 72, 78; Michael Tonry, "Explanations of American Punishment Policies: A National History," *Punishment and Society* 11, no. 3 (2009): 377–94; Douglas A. Berman, "Sentencing Guidelines," in *Reforming Criminal Justice: Volume 4: Punishment, Incarceration, and Release*, Eric Luna, ed. (Phoenix: Arizona State University, Sandra Day O'Connor College of Law, 2017), 95–115.

30. Kathleen Stassen Berger, *The Developing Person Through Childhood and Adolescence* (New York: Macmillan, 2008), 444; *but see* Jess Shatkin, *Born to Be Wild: Why Teens Take Risks, and How We Can Help Keep Them Safe* (New York: Penguin, 2017), 9.

31. Raymond R. Swisher and Tara D. Warner, "If They Grow Up: Exploring the Neighborhood Context of Adolescent and Young Adult Survival Expectations," *Journal of Research on Adolescence* 23, no. 4 (December 2013): 679, doi.org/10.1111/jora.12027.

32. Valerie Wright, "Deterrence in Criminal Justice: Evaluating Certainty vs. Severity of Punishment," Sentencing Project, November 2010, 9, sentencingproject.org/publications/deterrence-in-criminal-justice-evaluating -certainty-vs-severity-of-punishment; Daniel S. Nagin, "Deterrence," *Reforming Criminal Justice* 4, no. 35 (2017).

33. Nagin, "Deterrence," 33–5; Daniel S. Nagin, "Deterrence in the Twenty-First Century," *Crime & Justice* 42, no. 1 (2013): 203, doi.org /10.1086/670398.

34. Marc Mauer and Nazgol Ghandnoosh, "Fewer Prisoners, Less Crime: A Tale of Three States," The Sentencing Project, July 23, 2014, 1, 4, sentencingproject.org/publications/fewer-prisoners-less-crime -a-tale-of-three-states; Don Stemen, "The Prison Paradox: More Incarceration Will Not Make Us Safer," Vera Institute of Justice, July 2017, 4–5. storage.googleapis.com/vera-web-assets/downloads/Publications/for -the-record-prison-paradox-incarceration-not-safer/legacy_downloads /for-the-record-prison-paradox_02.pdf; Judith A. Greene and Vincent Schiraldi, "Better by Half: The New York City Story of Winning Large-Scale Decarceration While Increasing Public Safety," *Federal Sentencing Reporter* 29, no. 1 (2016): 22, justicestrategies.org /Better_by_Half.

35. Todd Clear, "In Their Own Voices: People in High Incarceration Communities Talk About the Impact of Incarceration," in *Imprisoning Communities: How Mass Incarceration Makes Disadvantaged Neighborhoods Worse* (Oxford: Oxford University Press, 2007), 121–48.

36. E. Ann Carson, "Prisoners in 2015," U.S. Department of Justice, Bureau of Justice Statistics, December 2016, 16–27, bjs.gov/content /pub/pdf/p15.pdf; Human Rights Watch, "Ill-Equipped: U.S. Prisons and Offenders with Mental Illness," 2003, 30–44, hrw.org/reports/2003/ usa1003/usa1003.pdf; Dean Aufderheide, "Mental Illness in America's Jails and Prisons: Toward a Public Safety/Public Health Model," *Health Affairs Blog*, April 1, 2014, doi.org/10.1377/hblog20140401.038180; National Criminal Justice Association and Vera Institute of Justice, "The Impact of Federal Budget Cuts from FY10–FY13 on State and Local Public Safety: Results from a Survey of Criminal Justice Practitioners," 2014, 7–8, vera.org/publications/the-impact-of-federal-budget-cuts-from-fy10-fy13-on -state-and-local-public-safety; Lois M. Davis et al., "How Effective Is Correctional Education, and Where Do We Go from Here?," Rand Institute, 2014, 61–70, doi.org/10.7249/RR564.

37. Carson, "Prisoners in 2015," 16–27, bjs.gov/content/pub/pdf/p15 .pdf; Massachusetts Department of Correction, "Quarterly Report on the Status of Prison Capacity, Fourth Quarter 2017," January 2018, 7, mass.gov /files/documents/2018/02/23/2017-4thQtr-PrisonCapacity-Report.pdf.

38. U.S. Government Accountability Office, "Bureau of Prisons: Growing Inmate Crowding Negatively Affects Inmates, Staff, and Infrastructure," September 2012, 18; Commission on Safety and Abuse in America's Prisons, "Confronting Confinement," Vera Institute of Justice, June 2006, 12; Ross Homel and Carleen Thompson, "Causes and Prevention of Violence in Prisons," Griffith University, 2005, 4, 8.

39. Francis T. Cullen, Cheryl Lero Jonson, and Daniel S. Nagin, "Prisons Do Not Reduce Recidivism: The High Cost of Ignoring Science," *Prison Journal* 91, no. 3 supplement (2011): 48S–65S, tpj.sagepub.com/content /91/3_suppl/48S.abstract; Paul Gendreau, Claire Goggin, Francis T. Cullen, and Donald A. Andrews, *Forum on Corrections Research* 12, no. 2 (2000): 10–13; Paula Smith, Claire Goggin, and Paul Gendreau, "The Effects of Prison Sentences and Intermediate Sanctions on Recidivism: General Effects and Individual Differences," Public Works and Government Services Canada, 2002, JS42-103/2002, 20–1; Patrice Villettaz, Martin Killias, and Isabelle Zoder, "The Effects of Custodial vs. Noncustodial Sentences on Re-Offending: A Systematic Review of the State of Knowledge," Campbell Collaboration Crime and Justice Group, 2006, 40–2, campbellcollaboration.org/media/k2/attachments/Killias _Sentencing_review_corrected.pdf; Daniel S. Nagin, Francis T. Cullen, and Cheryl Lero Jonson, "Imprisonment and Reoffending," *Crime and Justice*, 38, no. 1 (2009): 115–200; Cheryl Lero Jonson, "The Impact of Imprisonment on Reoffending: A Meta-Analysis" (PhD diss., University of Cincinnati, 2010), 45–65; Anthony Petrosino, Carolyn Turpin-Petrosino, and Sarah Guckenburg, "Formal System Processing of Juveniles: Effects on Delinquency," Campbell Collaboration, 2010, 9; Ted Chiricos, Kelle Barrick, William Bales, and Stephanie Bontrager, "The Labeling of Convicted Felons and Its Consequences for Recidivism," *Criminology* 45, no. 3 (2007): 547–81; and Michael Mueller-Smith, "Criminal and Labor Market Impacts of Incarceration," 2015, 57–8. irp .wisc.edu/newsevents/workshops/2015/participants/papers/10-Mueller -Smith-IRP-draft.pdf.

40. Francis T. Cullen, Cheryl Lero Jonson, and Daniel S. Nagin, "Prisons Do Not Reduce Recidivism," *Prison Journal* 91, no. 3 supp. (September 2011): 48S, 50S.

41. Cullen et al., "Prisons Do Not Reduce Recidivism," 51S.

42. Cullen et al., 53S.

43. Chiricos et al., "The Labeling of Convicted Felons," 547–81.

44. Robert J. Sampson and John H. Laub, *Crime in the Making: Pathways and Turning Points Through Life* (Cambridge, MA: Harvard University Press, 1993), 168, 255; Cassia Spohn and David Holleran, "The Effect of Imprisonment on Recidivism Rates of Felony Offenders: A Focus on Drug Offenders," *Criminology* 40 (2002): 329–47.

45. Paul Gendreau, Claire Goggin, Francis T. Cullen, and Donald A. Andrews, "The Effects of Community Sanctions and Incarceration on Recidivism," *Forum on Corrections Research* 12 (May 2000): 10–13; Paula Smith, Claire Goggin, and Paul Gendreau, *The Effects of Prison Sentences and Intermediate Sanctions on Recidivism: General Effects and Individual Differences* (Ottawa: Solicitor General of Canada, 2002), 18–22, publicsafety.gc.ca/cnt/rsrcs/pblctns/ffcts-prsn-sntncs/ffcts-prsn-sntncs-eng.pdf; Villettaz et al., *Effects of Custodial vs. Noncustodial Sentences, on Re-Offending: A Systematic Review of the State of Knowledge*, 40–43.

46. James Gilligan, *Violence: Our Deadly Epidemic and Its Causes* (New York: Putnam Publishing Group, 1996).

47. John A. Rich and Courtney M. Grey, "Pathways to Recurrent Trauma Among Young Black Men: Traumatic Stress, Substance Use, and the 'Code of the Street,'" *American Journal of Public Health* 95, no. 5 (May 2005): 816–24, doi.org/10.2105/AJPH.2004.044560.

48. "Key Concepts: Resilience," Harvard University, Center on the Developing Child, developingchild.harvard.edu/science/key-concepts/resilience; Mark A. Bellis, Katie Hardcastle, Kat Ford, Karen Hughes, Kathryn Ashton, Zara Quigg, and Nadia Butler, "Does Continuous Trusted Adult Support in Childhood Impart Life-Course Resilience Against Adverse Childhood Experiences—A Retrospective Study on Adult Health-Harming Behaviours and Mental Well-Being," *BMC Psychiatry* 17 (2017): 110, doi.org/10.1186/s12888-017-1260-z.

49. Timothy Williams, "The High Cost of Calling the Imprisoned," *New York Times*, March 30, 2015, A12; "The Price to Call Home: State-Sanctioned Monopolization in the Prison Phone Industry," Prison Policy Initiative, September 11, 2012, prisonpolicy.org/phones/report.html; "Legal Issues Pertaining to Inmate Telephone Use," *AELE Monthly Law Journal* 2008, no 2 (February 2008): 301; Jane McGrath, "How Prison Telecommunications Work," May 27, 2008, HowStuffWorks, people.howstuffworks.com/prison-telecommunication.htm.

50. "Solitary Confinement Facts," American Friends Service Committee, afsc.org/resource/solitary-confinement-facts; Deborah M. Golden, "The Federal Bureau of Prison's Abuses of Solitary Confinement," written testimony submitted to the Senate Judiciary Subcommittee on the Constitution, Civil Rights, and Human Rights hearing, *Reassessing Solitary Confinement II:*

The Human Rights, Fiscal, and Public Safety Consequences (Washington, DC: Washington Lawyers' Committee for Civil Rights and Urban Affairs, February 25, 2014), 3.

51. Jack Denton, "Massachusetts Prisoners Sent to Solitary After Meeting with State Legislators About Prison Reform," Solitary Watch, May 24, 2016, solitarywatch.com/2016/05/24/massachusetts-prisoners-sent-to-solitary-after-meeting-with-state-legislators-about-prison-reform; "Worse Than Second-Class: Solitary Confinement of Women in the United States," ACLU Foundation, April 2014, 7; "CMUs: The Federal Prison System's Experiment in Social Isolation," Center for Constitutional Rights, March 31, 2010,crjustice.org/home/get-involved/tools-resources/fact-sheets-and-faqs/cmus-federal-prison-system-s-experiment.

52. United Nations General Assembly, "Interim Report of the Special Rapporteur of the Human Rights Council on Torture and Other Cruel, Inhuman or Degrading Treatment or Punishment," A/66/268, 21–15, August 5, 2011, daccess-ods.un.org/access.nsf/Get?Open&DS=A/66/268&Lang=E.

53. Craig Haney, "Mental Health Issues in Long-Term Solitary and 'Supermax' Confinement," *Crime & Delinquency* 49, no. 1 (January 2003): 124–56, doi.org/10.1177/0011128702239239; Fatos Kaba, Andrea Lewis, Sarah Glowa-Kollisch, James Hadler, David Lee, Howard Alper, Daniel Selling, Ross MacDonald, Angela Solimo, Amanda Parsons, and Homer Venters, "Solitary Confinement and Risk of Self-Harm Among Jail Inmates," *American Journal of Public Health* 104 no. 3 (March 2014): 442–7, doi.org/10.2105/AJPH.2013.301742; Bruce A. Arrigo and Jennifer Leslie Bullock, "The Psychological Effects of Solitary Confinement on Prisoners in Supermax Units: Reviewing What We Know and Recommending What Should Change," *International Journal of Offender Therapy and Comparative Criminology* 52 no. 6 (November 2007): 622–40, doi.org/10.1177/0306624X07309720; David H. Cloud, et al., "Public Health and Solitary Confinement in the United States," *American Journal of Public Health* 105, no. 1 (January 2015): 18–26, doi.org/10.2105/AJPH.2014.302205.

54. "Voices from Solitary: A Second-by-Second Attack on Your Soul," Solitary Watch, August 4, 2015, solitarywatch.com/2015/08/04/voices-from-solitary-a-second-by-second-attack-on-your-soul. Excerpts are from an interview with Johnny Perez.

55. Li-yu Song, Mark Singer, and Trina Anglin, "Violence Exposure and Emotional Trauma as Contributors to Adolescents' Violent Behaviors," *Archives of Pediatric and Adolescent Medicine* 152 (1998): 531–6; Jennifer N. Shaffer and R. Barry Ruback, "Violent Victimization as a Risk Factor for Violent Offending Among Juveniles," *Juvenile Justice Bulletin*

(Washington, DC: U.S. Department of Justice, Office of Juvenile Justice and Delinquency Prevention, December 2002), 3–8, ncjrs.gov/pdffiles1 /ojjdp/195737.pdf; Randy Borum, "Assessing Violence Risk Among Youth," *Journal of Clinical Psychology* 56, no. 10 (October 2000): 1263–88, doi.org/10.1002/1097-4679(200010)56:10<1263::AID-JCLP3>3.0 .CO;2-D.

56. Shannon M. Lynch, Dana D. DeHart, Joanne Belknap, and Bonnie L. Green, "Women's Pathways to Jail: The Roles and Intersections of Serious Mental Illness and Trauma," U.S. Department of Justice, Bureau of Justice Assistance, September 2012, 20, bja.gov/Publications/Women_Pathways_to_Jail .pdf; Elizabeth Swavola, Kristine Riley, and Ram Subramanian, "Overlooked: Women and Jails in an Era of Reform," Vera Institute of Justice, August 2016, 11; Caroline Wolf Harlow, "Prior Abuse Reported by Inmates and Probationers," U.S. Department of Justice, Bureau of Justice Statistics, April 1999, 1–2; Mary E. Gilfus, "Women's Experiences of Abuse as a Risk Factor for Incarceration," National Resource Center on Domestic Violence, VAWNet, December 2002, 1–3, ncdsv.org/images/At_risk_for_jail.pdf; "Factsheet: Women in Prison," The Sentencing Project, May 2003.

57. Nancy Wolff and Jing Shi, "Contextualization of Physical and Sexual Assault in Male Prisons: Incidents and Their Aftermath," *Journal of Correctional Health Care* 15, no. 1 (January 2009): 58–82, cited by Dave Gilson, "What We Know About Violence in America's Prisons," *Mother Jones*, July/August 2016; Allen J. Beck, Marcus Berzofsky, Rachel Caspar, Christopher Krebs, "Sexual Victimization in Prisons and Jails Reported by Inmates, 2011–12-Update," U.S. Department of Justice, Bureau of Justice Statistics, December 9, 2014, 13, 17, 27–8.

58. Donna Hylton, personal correspondence, February 26, 2018.

59. Kevin R. Corlew, "Congress Attempts to Shine a Light on a Dark Problem: An In-Depth Look at the Prison Rape Elimination Act of 2003," *American Journal of Criminal Law* 33, no. 2 (Spring 2006): 161; Allison Rogne, "U.S. Institutionalized Torture with Impunity: Examining Rape and Sexual Abuse in Custody Through the ICTY Jurisprudence," *Revista De Direito Internacional/Brazilian Journal of International Law* 10, no. 2 (2013): 131, doi.org/10.5102/rdi.v10i2.2447.

60. "National Prison Rape Elimination Commission Report," National Prison Rape Elimination Commission, June 2009, www.ncjrs.gov/ pdffiles1/226680.pdf, 37–44; and Prison Rape Elimination Act National Standards—Prisons and Jails, 28 C.F.R. Part 115 (2007).

61. Allen J. Beck and Paige M. Harrison, "Sexual Victimization in State and Federal Prisons Reported by Inmates, 2007," U.S. Department of Justice, Bureau of Justice Statistics, December 2007, 1, www.bjs.gov/content /pub/pdf/svsfpri07.pdf.

62. Joanne Mariner, "Continuing Sexual Abuse," in *No Escape: Male Rape in U.S. Prisons* (New York: Human Rights Watch, April 2001), 69–71; Corlew, "Congress Attempts to Shine a Light," 160nlvi; Rogne, "U.S. Institutionalized Torture with Impunity," 131nlvi.

63. Corlew, 160nlvi; Rogne, 130nlvi.

64. Albert Reiss and Jeffrey Roth, eds., "Patterns of Violence in American Society," in *Understanding and Preventing Violence: Panel on the Understanding and Control of Violent Behavior*, vol. 1 (Washington, DC: National Academy Press, 1993), 70, www.nap.edu/catalog/1861/understanding-and-preventing-violence-volume-1.

65. Reiss and Roth, "Perspectives on Violence," 145.

66. Sarah Shemkus, "Beyond Cheap Labor: Can Prison Work Programs Benefit Inmates?," *The Guardian*, December 9, 2015; Wendy Sawyer, "How Much Do Incarcerated People Earn in Each State?," *Prison Policy Initiative*, April 10, 2017, www.prisonpolicy.org/blog /2017/04/10/wages; Beth Schwartzapfel, "Modern-Day Slavery in America's Prison Workforce," *Prison Legal News*, September 19, 2014, www.prisonlegalnews.org/news/2014/sep/19/modern-day-slavery -americas-prison-workforce; James J. Stephan, "Census of State and Federal Correctional Facilities, 2005," U.S Department of Justice, Bureau of Justice Statistics, October 2008, 2, 6.

67. Sawyer, "How Much Do Incarcerated People Earn"; Kanyakrit Vongkiatkajorn, "Why Prisoners Across the Country Have Gone on Strike," *Mother Jones*, September 19, 2016, citing Rebekah Diller, Alicia Bannon, and Mitali Nagrecha, "Criminal Justice Debt: A Barrier to Reentry," Brennan Center for Justice, October 4, 2010; Katherine Beckett and Alexes Harris, "Monetary Sanctions as Misguided Policy," *Criminology & Public Policy* 10, no. 3 (2011): 516, doi.org/10.1111/j.1745-9133.2011.00726.x; "Targeted Fines and Fees Against Low-Income Communities of Color: Civil Rights and Constitutional Implications," U.S. Commission on Civil Rights, 2017, 90.

68. Rebecca Vallas and Sharon Dietrich, "One Strike and You're Out: How We Can Eliminate Barriers to Economic Security and Mobility for People with Criminal Records," Center for American Progress, December 2014, 9; "Research on Reentry and Employment," U.S. Department of Justice, National Institute of Justice, April 3, 2013, nij.gov/topics/corrections /reentry/pages/employment.aspx, citing Davah Pager and Bruce Western, "Investigating Prisoner Reentry: The Impact of Conviction Status on the Employment Prospects of Young Men," U.S. Department of Justice, National Institute of Justice, October 2009.

69. John Rakis, "Improving the Employment Rates of Ex-Prisoners Under Parole," *Federal Probation* 69, no. 1 (June 2005): 7; and Dorsey Nunn,

"Taking 'Ban the Box' to the Next Level," Open Society Foundations, November 13, 2015, opensocietyfoundations.org/voices/taking-ban-box -next-level.

70. Rakis, "Improving the Employment Rates," 7–8; and Nunn, "Taking 'Ban the Box' to the Next Level."

71. U.S. Department of Justice, U.S. Attorney for the Southern District of Alabama, "Project H.O.P.E. Re-Entry Initiative," March 6, 2018, justice.gov /usao-sdal/programs/ex-offender-re-entry-initiative.

72. Cathryn A. Chappell, "Post-Secondary Correctional Education and Recidivism: A Meta-Analysis of Research Conducted 1990–1999," *Journal of Correctional Education* 55, no. 2 (2004): 162; Mary Ellen Batiuk, Karen F. Lahm, Matthew McKeever, Norma Wilcox, and Pamela Wilcox, "Disentangling the Effects of Correctional Education: Are Current Policies Misguided? An Event History Analysis," *Criminology & Criminal Justice* 6, no. 1 (February 2005): 60, 61, 67–8; Grant Duwe and Valerie Clark, "The Effects of Prison-Based Educational Programming on Recidivism and Employment," *Prison Journal* 94, no. 4 (December 2014): 469, 476.

73. "Building Effective Partnerships for High-Quality Postsecondary Education in Correctional Facilities: Fact Sheet," Vera Institute of Justice, January 2016; Wendy Erisman and Jeanne Bayer Contardo, "Learning to Reduce Recidivism: A 50-State Analysis of Postsecondary Correctional Education Policy," Institute for Higher Education Policy, November 2005, 27–35, ihep.org/sites/default/files/uploads/docs/pubs /learningreducerecidivism.pdf.

74. Michelle Chen, "Prison Education Reduces Recidivism by Over 40 Percent. Why Aren't We Funding More of It?," *The Nation*, August 17, 2015; "Why Prison Education?," Harvard University, Prison Studies Project, prisonstudiesproject.org/why-prison-education-pro grams/#home-3, citing Erisman and Contardo, "Learning to Reduce Recidivism," 2005; Bobby D. Rampey, Shelley Keiper, Leyla Mohadjer, Tom Krenzke, Jianzhu Li, Nina Thornton, Jacquie Hogan, Holly Xie, and Stephen Provasnik, "Highlights from the U.S. PIAAC Survey of Incarcerated Adults: Their Skills, Work Experience, Education, and Training," U.S. Department of Education, National Center for Education Statistics, November 2016, "Table 3.1: Percentage of Incarcerated Adults by the Highest Level of Education Completed During their Current Incarceration: 2014," 24, and "Table 3.5: Percentage Distribution of Incarcerated Adults Who Wanted to Enroll in an Academic Class, by the Degree or Certificate Program They Would Like to Enroll in: 2014," 27, nces.ed.gov/pubs2016/2016040.pdf.

75. Names have been changed to protect confidentiality.

76. David Seifman, "NYPD Cop Count Sinking to 34,000," *New York Post*, March 19, 2011.

77. Eric Martin, "Hidden Consequences: The Impact of Incarceration on Dependent Children," *National Institute of Justice Journal* 278 (May 2017): 10–16, nij.gov/journals/278/Pages/impact-of-incarceration-on-dependent-children.aspx; Megan Cox, "The Relationships Between Episodes of Parental Incarceration and Students' Psycho-Social and Educational Outcomes: An Analysis of Risk Factors" (PhD diss., Philadelphia: Temple University, 2009), 4–6; Albert M. Kopak and Dorothy Smith-Ruiz, "Criminal Justice Involvement, Drug Use, and Depression Among African American Children of Incarcerated Parents," *Race and Justice* 6, no. 2 (2016): 89–116, doi.org/10.1177/2153368715586633; Leila Morsy and Richard Rothstein, "Mass Incarceration and Children's Outcomes: Criminal Justice Policy Is Education Policy," Economic Policy Institute, December 15, 2016, 8–12, epi.org/files/pdf/118615.pdf.

78. Ebony Underwood, "My One Wish for Father's Day," *Huffington Post*, June 19, 2015.

79. "Essie Justice Group: Our Mission," essiejusticegroup.org/mission.

80. "Releases from State Prison," in *Reentry Trends in the United States* (Washington, DC: U.S. Department of Justice, Bureau of Justice Statistics, 2002, rev. 2004), bjs.gov/content/reentry/releases.cfm; "Prisoners and Prisoner Re-Entry," U.S. Department of Justice, Faith-Based and Community Initiatives, justice.gov/archive/fbci/progmenu_reentry.html.

81. Jose A. Canela-Cacho, Alfred Blumstein, and Jacqueline Cohen, "Relationship Between the Offending Frequency (Gamma) of Imprisoned and Free Offenders," *Criminology* 35, no. 1 (1997): 133–75.

82. Ram Subramanian and Alison Shames, "Sentencing and Prison Practices in Germany and the Netherlands: Implications for the United States," Vera Institute of Justice, 2013, 11–14, storage.googleapis.com/vera-web-assets/downloads/Publications/sentencing-and-prison-practices-in-germany-and-the-nethe rlands-implications-for-the-united-states/legacy_downloads/european -american-prison-report-v3.pdf.

83. Joel Feinberg, "The Expressive Function of Punishment," *The Monist* 49, no. 3 (1965): 400; Albert Alschuler, "The Changing Purposes of Criminal Punishment: A Retrospective on the Past Century and Some Thoughts About the Next," *University of Chicago Law Review* 70, no. 1 (2003): 17.

84. Neil Vidmar, "Retribution and Revenge," in *Handbook of Justice Research in Law*, Joseph Sanders and V. Lee Hamilton, eds. (New York: Springer, 2011), 31–63.

85. Ulrich Orth, "Does Perpetrator Punishment Satisfy Victims' Feelings of Revenge?," *Aggressive Behavior* 30, no. 1 (February 2004): 62–70, doi.org/10.1002/ab.20003; Kevin M. Carlsmith, Timothy D. Wilson, and Daniel T. Gilbert, "The Paradoxical Consequences of Revenge," *Journal of Personality and Social Psychology* 95, no. 6 (December 2008): 1316–24, doi.org/10.1037/a0012165; Margaret U. Walker, "The Cycle of Violence,"

Journal of Human Rights 5, no. 1 (January 2006): 81–105, doi.org/10.1080 /14754830500485890.

86. Bruce Western, "Lifetimes of Violence," *Homeward: Life in the Year After Prison* (New York: Russell Sage Foundation, 2018).

3: In Praise of Accountability

1. U.S. Department of Justice, *Sourcebook of Criminal Justice Statistics*, 31st ed. 2003, 418, Table 5.17, and 450, Table 5.46; Lindsey Devers, "Plea and Charge Bargaining: Research Summary," 2–3; John L. Kane, "Plea Bargaining and the Innocent."

2. Merriam-Webster, "mercy (n.)," merriam-webster.com/dictionary /mercy.

3. Bryan Stevenson, *Just Mercy: A Story of Justice and Redemption* (New York: Random House, 2014), 290.

4. Michael E. McCullough and Carlotte van Oyen Witvliet, "The Psychology of Forgiveness," in *Handbook of Positive Psychology*, C.R. Snyder and Shane J. Lopez, eds. (New York: Oxford University Press, 2001), 446, citing Steven Reiss and Susan M. Havercamp, "Toward a Comprehensive Assessment of Fundamental Motivation: Factor Structure of the Reiss Profiles," *Psychological Assessment* 10, no. 2 (June 1998): 97–106.

5. "Pumla Gobodo-Madikizela: Forgiveness Is Possible" (interview transcript), Faith & Leadership, Duke Divinity School, July 30, 2012, faithandleadership.com/pumla-gobodo-madikizela-forgiveness-possible.

6. "Pumla Gobodo-Madikizela."

7. Richard M. Ryan and Edward L. Deci, "Intrinsic and Extrinsic Motivations: Classic Definitions and New Directions," *Contemporary Educational Psychology* 25 (2000): 60–1, doi.org/10.1006/ceps.1999.1020; Tom R. Tyler, "Restorative Justice and Procedural Justice: Dealing with Rule Breaking," *Journal of Social Issues* 62, no. 2 (2006): 311, 313, doi.org/10.1111/j.1540-4560.2006.00452.x.

8. Fredo Villasenor, "Pranis: How Can Driftwood Solve Conflict?," *Chautauquan Daily*, August 1, 2013, chqdaily.wordpress.com/2013/08/01 /pranis-how-can-driftwood-solve-conflict.

9. Shameeka Mattis and Danielle Sered, "Goals for the Common Justice Preparatory Process," 2009.

10. Simon I. Singer, "Homogeneous Victim-Offender Populations: A Review and Some Research Implications," *Journal of Criminal Law and Criminology* 72, no. 2 (Summer 1981): 782; Wesley G. Jennings, Alex R. Piquero, and Jennifer M. Reingle, "On the Overlap Between Victimization and Offending: A Review of the Literature," *Aggression and Violent*

Behavior 17, no. 1 (January–February 2012): 16–26, doi.org/10.1016/j. avb.2011.09.003; Robert J. Sampson and Janet L. Lauritsen, "Violent Victimization and Offending: Individual-, Situational-, and Community-Level Risk Factors," in *Understanding and Preventing Violence, Volume 3: Social Influences*, Albert J. Reiss, Jr., and Jeffrey A. Roth, eds. (Washington, DC: National Academies Press, 1994), 34.

11. Danielle Sered, "Young Men of Color and the Other Side of Harm: Addressing Disparities in Our Responses to Violence," Vera Institute of Justice, December 2014, 7.

12. Elisabeth Kubler-Ross, *On Death and Dying* (New York: Macmillan, 1969). Ninety-two percent of all victims of robbery and 91 percent of victims of assault received no known assistance after being the victim of crime.

13. James Gilligan, "Shame, Guilt, and Violence," *Social Research* 70, no. 4 (Winter 2003): 1155.

4: Displacing Incarceration

1. "About Circles: The Indigenous Origins of Circles," Living Justice Press, www.livingjusticepress.org; and Morris Jenkins, "Gullah Island Dispute Resolution: An Example of Afrocentric Restorative Justice," *Journal of Black Studies* 37, no. 2 (2006): 299–319, doi.org/10.1177 /0021934705277497.

2. Mark S. Umbreit, Robert B. Coates, and Betty Vos, "The Impact of Victim-Offender Mediation: Two Decades of Research," *Federal Probation* 65, no. 3 (December 2001); "Scaling Restorative Community Conferencing Through a Pay for Success Model: A Feasibility Assessment Report," National Council on Crime & Delinquency, 2015, 9; and sujatha baliga, Sia Henry, and George Valentine, "Restorative Community Conferencing: A Study of Community Works West's Restorative Justice Youth Diversion Program in Alameda County," Community Works Web, 2017, 6–9, impactjustice.org/wp -content/uploads/2017/07/CWW-Report_Final_6.14.17_electronic.pdf.

3. Howard Zehr, *The Little Book of Restorative Justice, Revised and Expanded* (New York: Good Books, 2015).

4. Fania E. Davis, "What's Love Got to Do With It?," *Tikkun* 27, no. 1 (2012): 30–3, doi.org/10.1215/08879982-2012-1014.

5. Mark S. Umbreit, Robert B. Coates, and Betty Vos, "The Impact of Victim-Offender Mediation: Two Decades of Research," *Federal Probation* 65, no. 3 (2001): 29–35; Mark S. Umbreit, Robert B. Coates,and Betty Vos, "Victim-Offender Mediation: Three Decades of Practice and Research," *Conflict Resolution Quarterly*, 22, nos. 1–2 (2004): 279–303, onlinelibrary. wiley.com/doi/10.1002/crq.102/abstractwww.nccdglobal.org/sites/default /files/publication_pdf/rj-pfs-feasibility-report.pdf.

6. Caroline M. Angel, "Crime Victims Meet Their Offenders: Testing the Impact of Restorative Justice Conferences on Victim's Post-Traumatic Stress Symptoms" (PhD diss., University of Pennsylvania, 2005), repository.upenn.edu/dissertations/AAI3165634.

7. Accounting for Violence forum, April 11, 2017, vera.org/events/accounting-for-violence.

5: Policy and Power

1. Steven N. Durlauf and Daniel S. Nagin, "Imprisonment and Crime: Can Both Be Reduced?," *Criminological and Public Policy* 10, no. 1, (2011): 13–54; Durlauf and Nagin, "The Deterrent Effect of Imprisonment," in *Controlling Crime: Strategies and Tradeoffs*, edited by Philip J. Cook, Jens Ludwig, and Justin McCrary (Chicago: University of Chicago Press, 2012), 43–94, nber.org/chapters/c12078.pdf.

2. Judith A. Greene and Vincent Schiraldi, "Better by Half: The New York City Story of Winning Large-Scale Decarceration While Increasing Public Safety," *Federal Sentencing Reporter* 29, no. 1 (2016), 23–5, justicestrategies.org/Better_by_Half.

3. Marc Mauer and Nazgol Ghandnoosh, "Fewer Prisoners, Less Crime: A Tale of Three States," The Sentencing Project, 2014, 2–6, sentencingproject.org/publications/fewer-prisoners-less-crime-a-tale-of-three-states.

4. Mauer and Ghandnoosh, "Fewer Prisoners, Less Crime," 2–5.

5. Death Penalty Information Center, "Executed but Possibly Innocent," deathpenaltyinfo.org/executed-possibly-innocent. The Death Penalty Information Center lists 161 death-row inmates who have been exonerated from 1973 to 2017; DPIC also lists fourteen people executed despite strong evidence of their innocence. Death Penalty Information Center, "Innocence: List of Those Freed from Death Row," deathpenaltyinfo.org/innocence-list-those-freed-death-row.

6. Henry Gass, "Juvenile Incarceration Rate Has Dropped in Half. Is Trend Sustainable?," *Christian Science Monitor*, November 10, 2015; Patrick McCarthy, Vincent Schiraldi, and Miriam Shark, "The Future of Youth Justice: A Community-Based Alternative to the Youth Prison Model," *New Thinking in Community Corrections Bulletin* (Washington, DC: U.S. Department of Justice, National Institute of Justice, 2016), 18–19, ncjrs.gov/pdffiles1/nij/250142.pdf; James Austin, Kelly Dedel Johnson, and Ronald Weitzer, "Alternatives to Secure Detention and Confinement of Juvenile Offenders," *Juvenile Justice Bulletin* (September 2005), 12–21, ncjrs.gov/pdffiles1/ojjdp/208804.pdf; "Beyond Bars: Keeping Young People Safe at Home and Out of Youth Prisons," National Collaboration for Youth, 2016, 27–31,

nationalassembly.org/resources/beyond-bars-keeping-young-people-safe
-at-home-and-out-of-youth-prisons.

7. The National Center on Addiction and Substance Abuse, "Crossing
the Bridge: An Evaluation of the Drug Treatment Alternative-to-Prison
(DTAP) Program," Columbia University, National Center on Addiction
and Substance Abuse, 2003, 6–7, centeronaddiction.org/addiction-research
/reports/crossing-bridge-evaluation-drug-treatment-alternative-prison
-dtap-program.

8. Rachel Porter, Sophia Lee, and Mary Lutz, "Balancing Punishment
and Treatment: Alternatives to Incarceration in New York City," Vera Institute of Justice, 2002, 62–5, vera.org/publications/balancing-punishment
-and-treatment-alternatives-to-incarceration-in-new-york-city.

9. James B. Jacobs, "Gang Databases Context and Questions," *Crim-
inology & Public Policy* 8, no. 4 (2009): 706; Joshua D. Wright, "The
Constitutional Failure of Gang Databases," *Stanford Journal of Civil Rights &
Civil Liberties* 2 (2005): 115.

10. Wayne A. Logan and Andrew Guthrie, "Policing Criminal Justice Data," *Minnesota Law Review* 101, no. 2 (2016): 554; "The CalGang
Criminal Intelligence System, Report 2015–130," California State Audi-
tor, August 2016, bsa.ca.gov/pdfs/factsheets/2015-130.pdf.

11. "More on the Discretionary Power of Prosecutors," in *The Human
Toll of Jail* (New York: Vera Institute of Justice, 2018), humantollofjail.vera.
org/the-discretionary-power-of-prosecutors.

12. U.S. Department of Justice, *Sourcebook of Criminal Justice Statistics*,
31st ed. 2003, 418, Table 5.17, and 450, Table 5.46; Lindsey Devers, "Plea
and Charge Bargaining: Research Summary," 2–3; John L. Kane, "Plea
Bargaining and the Innocent."

13. Devers, "Plea and Charge Bargaining," 2.

14. Lauren-Brooke Eisen, Nicole Fortier, and Inimai Chettiar, "Federal Prosecution for the 21st Century," Brennan Center for Justice, 2014,
brennancenter.org/publication/federal-prosecution-21st-century.

15. See Law Enforcement Leaders to Reduce Crime & Incarceration
homepage, lawenforcementleaders.org.

16. "Promising Practices in Prosecutor-Led Diversion," Fair and Just
Prosecution, 2017, 3–18, fairandjustprosecution.org/wp-content/uploads
/2017/09/FJPBrief.Diversion.9.26.pdf.

17. Hal Dardick and Matthew Walberg, "Kim Foxx Declares Win in
Cook County State's Attorney's Race," *Chicago Tribune*, November 8,
2016; Elyssa Cherney, "Aramis Ayala Upsets Jeff Ashton for State Attorney," *Orlando Sentinel*, August 31, 2016; Brian Rogers, Margaret Kadifa, and

Emily Foxhall, "Anderson Defeated in Harris County DA Race," *Houston Chronicle*, November 8, 2016; and Fernanda Santos, "Sheriff Joe Arpaio Loses Bid for 7th Term in Arizona," *New York Times*, November 9, 2016.

18. Noah Hurowitz, "Gonzalez Announces DA Bid with Pledge to Continue Ken Thompson's Legacy," DNAinfo, April 26, 2017, dnainfo.com/new-york/20170426/bed-stuy/eric-gonzales-da-campaign -ken-thompson.

19. Ronald F. Wright, "How Prosecutor Elections Fail Us," *Ohio State Journal of Criminal Law* 6 (November 2009): 593.

20. Lael Chester and Vincent Schiraldi, "Public Safety and Emerging Adults in Connecticut: Providing Effective and Developmentally Appropriate Responses for Youth Under Age 21," Harvard Kennedy School Malcolm Wiener Center for Social Policy, 2016, v, hks.harvard.edu/sites/default/files/centers/wiener/programs/pcj /files/public_safety_and_emerging_adults_in_connecticut.pdf; Howard N. Snyder, Alexia D. Cooper, and Joseph Mulako-Wangota, Bureau of Justice Statistics, "U.S. Arrest Estimates: Arrest Rates by Age for Violent Crime Index Offenses," generated January 14, 2018, using the Arrest Data Analysis Tool at bjs.gov/index.cfm?ty=datool&surl =/arrests/index.cfm; U.S. Census Bureau, "Age and Sex Composition: 2010 and Age and Sex Composition in the United States: 2014," U.S. Census Bureau, 2011, 2, census.gov/prod/cen2010/briefs/c2010br-03.pdf.

21. Howard N. Snyder, Alexia D. Cooper, and Joseph Mulako-Wangota, Bureau of Justice Statistics, "U.S. Arrest Estimates: Arrest Rates by Age for Violent Crime Index Offenses," generated January 14, 2018, using the Arrest Data Analysis Tool at bjs.gov/index.cfm?ty=datool&surl=/arrests/index.cfm.

22. Snyder et al, "U.S. Arrest Estimates."

23. Mary Beckman, "Crime, Culpability, and the Adolescent Brain," *Science* 305 (July 30, 2004), 596; "Reforming Juvenile Justice: A Developmental Approach," National Academies Press, National Research Council, 2013, 92, 95.

24. Vincent Schiraldi and Bruce Western, "Why 21 Year-Old Offenders Should Be Tried in Family Court," *Washington Post*, October 2, 2015.

25. Vincent Schiraldi, Bruce Western, and Kendra Bradner, "Community-Based Responses to Justice-Involved Young Adults," *New Thinking in Community Corrections* 1 (September 2015): 8–15, hks.harvard .edu/sites/default/files/centers/wiener/programs/pcj/files/ESCC-Com-munityBasedResponsesJusticeInvolvedYA.pdf.

26. Barry C. Feld, "Juvenile Justice," in *Reforming Criminal Justice*, vol. 1, Eric Luna, ed. (Phoenix: Arizona State University, Sandra Day O'Connor College of Law, 2017), 330.

27. Schiraldi, Western, and Bradner, "Community-Based Responses," 15.

28. Alex A. Stamm, "Young Adults Are Different, Too: Why and How We Can Create a Better Justice System for Young People Age 18 to 25," *Texas Law Review* 95 (2017): 80.

29. Vincent Schiraldi, "Thoughts on Creating a Developmentally Appropriate Justice System for Emerging Adults in Washington," written testimony, Washington State House of Representatives Committee on Public Safety, November 16, 2017.

30. Dana Goldstein, "Too Old to Commit Crime?," The Marshall Project, March 20, 2015, themarshallproject.org/2015/03/20/too-old-to -commit-crime#.qvKnV7O0I.

31. Patrick Langan and David Levin, "Recidivism of Prisoners Released in 1994," U.S. Department of Justice, Bureau of Justice Statistics, 2002, 1, bjs.gov/index.cfm?ty=pbdetail&iid=1134; Tracy Velazquez, "The Pursuit of Safety: Sex Offender Policy in the United States," Vera Institute of Justice, 2008, 6, storage.googleapis.com/vera-web-assets/downloads/Publications /the-pursuit-of-safety-sex-offender-policy-in-the-united-states/legacy _downloads/Sex_offender_policy_with_appendices_final.pdf; R. Karl Hanson and Monique T. Bussiere, "Predicting Relapse: A Meta-Analysis of Sexual Offender Recidivism Studies," *Journal of Consulting and Clinical Psychology* 66, no. 2 (1998): 357; Patrick Langan, Erica Schmitt and Matthew Durose, "Recidivism of Sex Offenders Released from Prison in 1994," U.S. Department of Justice, Office of Justice Programs, Bureau of Justice Statistics, 2003, 13–14, bjs.gov/index.cfm?ty=pbdetail&iid=1136.

32. Mariel Alper, "By the Numbers: Parole Release and Revocation Across 50 States," Minneapolis: University of Minnesota, 2016, i–iii, robinainstitute.umn.edu/publications/numbers-parole-release-and -revocation-across-50-states; Joan Petersilia, *When Prisoners Come Home: Parole and Prisoner Reentry* (New York: Oxford University Press, 2003), 55–65; American Probation and Parole Association, "Discretionary Parole," 2002, appa-net.org/eweb/DynamicPage.aspx?WebCode=IB_Position Statements&Site=APPA-3.

33. Alison Lawrence, "Cutting Corrections Costs: Earned Time Policies for State Prisoners," National Conference of State Legislatures, 2009, 1–4, ncsl.org/Portals/1/Documents/cj/Earned_time_report.pdf.

34. Sarah Lawrence, Daniel P. Mears, Glenn Dubin, and Jeremy Travis, "The Practice and Promise of Prison Programming," Urban Institute, May 2002, 20–2, urban.org/sites/default/files/publication/60431/410493-The -Practice-and-Promise-of-Prison-Programming.PDF.

35. Assembly Bill A2350A, 2017–2018 Legislative Session, New York State Senate, nysenate.gov/legislation/bills/2017/a2350/amendment/a.

36. Alliance for Safety and Justice, "Crime Survivors Speak: The First-Ever National Survey of Victims' Views on Safety and Justice," 2016, 5, allianceforsafetyandjustice.org/crimesurvivorsspeak; Diana L. Falco and Noelle C. Turner, "Examining Causal Attributions Towards Crime on Support for Offender Rehabilitation," *American Journal of Criminal Justice* 39, no. 3 (September 2014), 631–4, doi.org/10.1007/s12103-013-9231-5.

37. Rebecca Vallas and Sharon Dietrich, "One Strike and You're Out: How We Can Eliminate Barriers to Economic Security and Mobility for People with Criminal Records," Center for American Progress, December 2014, 1, americanprogress.org/issues/poverty/reports/2014/12/02/102308/one-strike-and-youre-out; Cherrie Bucknor and Alan Barber, "The Price We Pay: Economic Costs of Barriers to Employment for Former Prisoners and People Convicted of Felonies," Center for Economic and Policy Research, 2016, 6, cepr.net/images/stories/reports/employment-prisoners-felonies-2016-06.pdf?v=5. (Vallas and Dietrich are silent on the number of people with felony convictions; Bucknor and Barber write, "The approach used in this paper estimates that there were between 14.0 million and 15.8 million people with felony convictions in 2014. In their earlier report using the same methods, Schmitt and Warner [2010] estimated that there were between 12.3 million and 13.9 million people with felony convictions in 2008.")

38. Jeremy Travis, "Invisible Punishment: An Instrument of Social Exclusion," in *Invisible Punishment: The Collateral Consequences of Mass Imprisonment*, Marc Mauer and Meda Chesney-Lind, eds. (New York: New Press, 2002), 16; Sarah B. Berson, "Beyond the Sentence—Understanding Collateral Consequences," *National Institute of Justice Journal* no. 272 (September 2013): 25, ncjrs.gov/pdffiles1/nij/241924.pdf.

39. U.S. Code § 13661 (c): Screening of Applicants for Federally Assisted Housing; Rebecca Oyama, "Do Not Re(Enter): The Rise of Criminal Background Tenant Screening as a Violation of the Fair Housing Act," *Michigan Journal of Race & Law* 15, no. 1 (Winter 2010): 181–222.

40. *Adoption and Safe Families Act of 1997*, Public Law No. 105–89, 111 Stat. 2115 (1997) (codified in scattered sections of U.S. Code, vol. 42).

41. Michelle Natividad Rodriguez and Beth Avery, "Unlicensed and Untapped: Removing Barriers to State Occupational Licenses for People with Records," National Employment Law Project, April 2016, 1,ncsecondchance.org/wp-content/uploads/2018/03/Unlicensed-Untapped-Removing-Barriers-State-Occupational-Licenses.pdf; Adoption and Safe Families Act Section 106: Criminal Records Checks for Prospective Foster and Adoptive Parents, 111 Stat. 2120; Eli Hager, "Forgiving vs. Forgetting," The Marshall Project, March 17, 2015, themarshallproject.org/2015/03/17/forgiving-vs-forgetting.

42. U.S. Code § 1091(r)(1): "A student who is convicted of any offense under any Federal or State law involving the possession or sale of a controlled substance for conduct that occurred during a period of enrollment for which the student was receiving any grant, loan, or work assistance under this subchapter shall not be eligible to receive any grant, loan, or work assistance under this subchapter from the date of that conviction for the period of time specified in the following table."

43. "Text Table C: Suspension of Eligibility for Title IV Federal Student Financial Aid Due to a Drug-Related Conviction or Failure to Report Conviction Status on Aid Application Form: 2007–08 Through 2013–14," *Digest of Education Statistics 2015*, 51st ed. (Washington, DC: U.S. Department of Education, National Center for Education Statistics, December 2016): 441.

44. "Federal Statutes Imposing Collateral Consequences upon Conviction," U.S. Department of Justice, 2006, justice.gov/sites/default /files/pardon/legacy/2006/11/13/ collateral_consequences.pdf; the welfare reform law is the *Personal Responsibility and Work Opportunity Reconciliation Act of 1996*, Public Law No. 104–103, 110 Stat. 2105 (1996).

45. Marc Mauer and Virginia McCalmont, "A Lifetime of Punishment: The Impact of the Felony Drug Ban on Welfare Benefits," The Sentencing Project, November 2013, updated September 2015, 2.

46. Tracy Velázquez, "The Pursuit of Safety: Sex Offender Policy in the United States," Vera Institute of Justice, 2008, 3; Jill Levenson and Richard Tewksbury, "Collateral Damage: Family Members of Registered Sex Offenders," *American Journal of Criminal Justice* 34, nos. 1–2 (Spring 2009): 54; National Center for Missing and Exploited Children, "Map of Registered Sex Offenders in the United States," May 30, 2018; U.S. Department of Housing and Urban Development, "Mandatory Prohibition for Lifetime Sex Offenders" regulations, 24 CFR §§ 5.856, 960.204(a)(4), and 982.553(a)(2).

47. Saba Ahmed, Adina Appelbaum, and Rachel Jordan, "The Human Cost of IIRIRA—Stories from Individuals Impacted by the Immigration Detention System," *Journal on Migration and Human Security* 5, no. 1 (2017): 915; Katherine Beckett and Heather Evans, "Crimmigration at the Local Level: Criminal Justice Processes in the Shadow of Deportation," *Law & Society Review* 49, no. 1 (2015): 245; William A. Kandel, "Interior Immigration Enforcement: Criminal Alien Programs," U.S. Congress, Congressional Research Service, September 8, 2016, 4.

48. Jean Chung, "Felony Disenfranchisement: A Primer," The Sentencing Project, May 10, 2016, 1, sentencingproject.org/wp-content /uploads/2015/08/Felony-Disenfranchisement-Primer.pdf.

49. Chung, "Felony Disenfranchisement," 2.

50. Christopher Uggen, and Jeff Manza, "Voting and Subsequent Crime and Arrest: Evidence from a Community Sample," *Columbia Human Rights Law Review* 36, no. 1 (2004): 193–215.

51. Christopher Uggen and Jeff Manza, "Democratic Contraction? Political Consequences of Felon Disenfranchisement in the United States," *American Sociological Review* 67, no. 6, (2002): 777–803.

52. Jeff Manza, Clem Brooks, and Christopher Uggen, "Public Attitudes Toward Felon Disenfranchisement in the United States, *Public Opinion Quarterly* 68, no. 2 (2004): 275–86; Nicole D. Porter, "Expanding the Vote: State Felony Disenfranchisement Reform, 1997–2010" (The Sentencing Project, 2010), 2.

53. Jill Leovy, *Ghettoside* (New York: Random House, 2015); Ashley M. Mancik, Karen F. Parker, and Kirk R. Williams, "Neighborhood Context and Homicide Clearance: Estimating the Effects of Collective Efficacy," *Homicide Studies* 22, no. 2 (2018): 191; German Lopez, "Americans Are Supposed to Turn to Police After a Murder. In Black Communities, They Often Can't," *Vox*, August 26, 2016; Edwin Rios and Kai Wright, "Black Deaths Matter," *Mother Jones*, May/June 2015; Sarah Ryley, Barry Paddock, Rocco Parascandola, and Rich Schapiro, "Tale of Two Cities," *New York Daily News*, January 5, 2014; Tom Meagher, "Why Are American Cops So Bad at Catching Killers?," The Marshall Project, April 2, 2015, themarshallproject.org/2015 /04/02/why-are-american-cops-so-bad-at-catching-killers.

54. Sam Kuhn and Stephen Lurie, "Reconciliation Between Police and Communities: Case Studies and Lessons Learned," John Jay College National Network for Safe Communities, 2018, 5–11, nnscommunities.org /uploads/Reconciliation_Full_Report.pdf.

55. David A. Graham, "What Can the U.S. Do to Improve Police Accountability?," *The Atlantic*, March 6, 2016; Tim Lynch, "How Mayors, Police Unions and Cops Rig Civilian Review Boards," Cato Institute, October 24, 2016, cato.org/publications/commentary/how-mayors-police -unions-cops-rig-civilian-review-boards; Rachel Lu, "How Expecting Police to Be All Things to All People Can Fuel Violence," *The Federalist*, May 3, 2017; J.B. Wogan, "The New, More Powerful Wave of Civilian Oversight of Police," *Governing*, February 27, 2017; Joel Miller and Cybele Merrick, "Civilian Oversight of Policing: Lessons from the Literature," Vera Institute of Justice, 2002, 12.

56. "Community Control," The Movement for Black Lives, policy. m4bl.org/community-control.

57. Doris J. James and Lauren E. Glaze, "Mental Health Problems of Prison and Jail Inmates," Department of Justice, Bureau of Justice Statistics, September 2006, 1–7, bjs.gov/content/pub/pdf/mhppji.pdf; Jennifer Bronson and Marcus Berzofsky, "Indicators of Mental Health Problems; Reported by Prisoners and Jail Inmates, 2011–12," Department of Justice, Bureau of Justice Statistics, June 2017; "Behind Bars II: Substance Abuse and America's Prison Population," Columbia University, National Center on

Addiction and Substance Abuse, February 2010, 1–4, centeronaddiction.org /addiction-research/reports/behind-bars-ii-substance-abuse-and -america's-prison-population.pdf; Jennifer C. Karberg and Doris J. James, "Substance Dependence, Abuse, and Treatment of Jail Inmates, 2002," Department of Justice, Bureau of Justice Statistics, July 2005, 1–2, bjs.gov /content/pub/pdf/sdatji02.pdf.

58. Phillip Atiba Goff, Matthew Christian Jackson, Brooke Allison Lewis Di Leone, et al., "The Essence of Innocence: Consequences of Dehumanizing Black Children," *Journal of Personality and Social Psychology* 106, no. 4: 532, doi.org/10.1037/a0035663.

59. Goff, Jackson, Di Leone, et al., "The Essence of Innocence," 532; Robert M. Entman, "Young Men of Color in the Media: Images and Impacts," Joint Center for Political and Economic Studies, 2006, 5, 13, jointcenter.org/docs/pdfs/YMOC%20and%20the%20Media.pdf; Danielle Sered, "Young Men of Color and the Other Side of Harm: Addressing Disparities in Our Responses to Violence," Vera Institute of Justice, December 2014, 4, 9, vera.org/publications/young-men-of-color-and-the-other-side-of -harm-addressing-disparities-in-our-responses-to-violence (citing sources).

60. John A. Rich and David A. Stone, "The Experience of Violent Injury for Young African-American Men? The Meaning of Being a 'Sucker,'" *Journal of General Internal Medicine* 11, no. 2 (1996): 77–82, at 77, citing Deborah W. Sims, Brack A. Bivins, Farouck N. Obeid, H. Mathilda Horst, Victor J. Sorensen, and John J. Fath, "Urban Trauma: A Chronic Recurrent Disease," *Trauma* 29, no. 7 (1989): 940–7.

61. Danielle Sered and Bridgette Butler, "Expanding the Reach of Victim Services: Maximizing the Potential of VOCA Funder for Underserved Survivors," Vera Institute of Justice, 2016), 3, vera.org/publications /expanding-the-reach-of-victim-services.

62. Sered and Butler, "Expanding the Reach," 3.

63. Mim Kim, Donna Coker, sujatha baliga, and Alsia Bierria, "Plenary 3—Harms of Criminalization and Promising Alternatives (Transcript)," *University of Miami Race & Social Justice Law Review* 5, no. 2 (2015): 375, repository.law.miami.edu/umrsjlr/vol5/iss2/14.

64. Kim, Coker, baliga, and Bierria, "Plenary 3," 375–6.

65. Sered and Butler, "Expanding the Reach," 14–16.

66. See Mac Taylor, "The 2015–16 Budget: Implementation of Proposition 47," California Legislature, Legislative Analyst's Office, 2015, 8, lao.ca.gov /reports/2015/budget/prop47/implementation-prop47-021715.aspx.

67. "What You Can Do if You Are a Victim of Crime," U.S. Department of Justice, Office for Victims of Crime, April 2010, ovc.gov/publications /infores/whatyoucando_2010/WhatUCanDo_508.pdf.

68. "Eligibility Requirements," National Association of Crime Victim Compensation Boards, nacvcb.org/index.asp?bid=6.

69. "Eligibility Requirements," National Association of Crime Victim Compensation Boards.

70. Kenton Kirby, "'Guilty Victims,' Have Suffered Too, and Deserve Our Care," in *Beyond Innocence: Toward a Framework for Serving All Survivors of Harm* (New York: Vera Institute of Justice, 2015), 4, storage.googleapis. com/vera-web-assets/downloads/Publications/beyond-innocence -toward-a-framework-for-serving-all-survivors-of-crime/legacy_down- loads/beyond-innocence-blog-digest.pdf; Carla Murphy, "Crime Victim Compensation Policies Leave Too Many Behind," *Colorlines*, Janu- ary 9, 2014, colorlines.com/articles/crime-victim-compensation-policies -leave-too-many-behind; Lisa Newmark, Judy Bonderman, Barbara Smith, and E. Blaine Liner et al., "The National Evaluation of State Victims of Crime Act Assistance and Compensation Programs: Trends and Strate- gies for the Future," Urban Institute, April 2003, 80, urban.org/research /publication/national-evaluation-state-victims-crime-act-compensation -and-assistance-programs-trends-and-strategies-future-executive -summary.

71. Lynn Langton, Marcus Berzofsky, Christopher Krebs, and Hope Smiley-McDonald, "Victimizations Not Reported to the Police, 2006–2010," U.S. Department of Justice, Bureau of Justice Statistics, August 2012, 4–7, bjs.gov/content/pub/pdf/vnrp0610.pdf.

72. Emily Waters, Chai Jindasurat, and Cecilia Wolfe, "Lesbian, Gay, Bisexual, Transgender, Queer, and HIV-Affected Hate Violence in 2015," National Coalition of Anti-Violence Programs, 2016, 24, 31, avp.org/wp- content/uploads/2017/04/ncavp_hvreport_2015_final.pdf.

6: The Opposite of Violence

1. Sophie Trawalter, Kelly M. Hoffman, and Adam Waytz, "Racial Bias in Perceptions of Others' Pain," *PLOS ONE* 7, no. 1 (2012): e48546, doi.org/10.1371/journal.pone.0048546.

2. Carolyn Moxley Rouse, *Uncertain Suffering: Racial Health Care Dispari- ties and Sickle Cell Disease* (Berkeley, CA: University of California Press, 2009), 12, 72, 108, 246; Keith Wailoo, *Dying in the City of the Blues: Sickle Cell Ane- mia and the Politics of Race and Health* (Chapel Hill, NC: University of North Carolina Press, 2001); Carlton Haywood, Paul Tanabe, Rakhi Naik, Mary Catherine Beach, and Sophie Lanzkron, "The Impact of Race and Disease on Sickle Cell Patient Wait Times in the Emergency Department," *Ameri- can Journal of Emergency Medicine* 31, no. 4 (2013): 651–6, doi.org/10.1016/j. ajem.2012.11.005. In 1994, life expectancy for sickle cell patients was age 42

for men and 48 for women. Orah S. Platt, Donald J. Brambilla, Wendell F. Rosse, Paul F. Milner, Oswaldo Castro, Martin H. Steinberg, and Panpit P. Klug, "Mortality in Sickle Cell Disease—Life Expectancy and Risk Factors for Early Death," *New England Journal of Medicine* 330, no. 23 (1994): 1639–44, DOI: 10.1056/NEJM199406093302303. A 2013 study found that life expectancy had dipped to age 38 for men and 42 for women in 2005. Sophie Lanzkron, C. Patrick Carroll, and Carlton Haywood Jr., "Mortality Rates and Age at Death from Sickle Cell Disease: U.S., 1979–2005," *Public Health Reports* 128, no. 2 (2013): 110–16, doi.org/10.1177/003335491312800206.

3. R.L. Listenbee, Joe Torre, Gregory Boyle, et al., "Report of the Attorney General's National Task Force on Children Exposed to Violence," Office of Juvenile Justice and Delinquency Prevention, 2012, 5, justice.gov/defendingchildhood/cev-rpt-full.pdf.

4. Listenbee et al., "Report of the Attorney General's National Task Force," 5.

5. "What's Normal?," Common Justice Core Curriculum, 2018.

6. John A. Rich and Courtney M. Grey, "Pathways to Recurrent Trauma Among Young Black Men: Traumatic Stress, Substance Use, and the 'Code of the Street,'" *American Journal of Public Health* 95, no. 5 (2005): 816–24, doi:10.2105/ajph.2004.044560.

7. Kenneth V. Hardy and Tracy A. Laszloffy, *Teens Who Hurt: Clinical Interventions to Break the Cycle of Adolescent Violence* (New York: The Guilford Press, 2005); Rich and Grey, "Pathways to Recurrent Trauma," 821–3; Randy Borum, "Assessing Violence Risk Among Youth," *Journal of Clinical Psychology* 56, no. 10 (2000): 1263–88; and Jennifer N. Shaffer and R. Barry Ruback, "Violent Victimization as a Risk Factor for Violent Offending Among Juveniles," *Juvenile Justice Bulletin*, OJJDP, December 2002, 4–9, files.eric.ed.gov/fulltext/ED474391.pdf.

8. Nils Christie, "Conflicts as Property," *British Journal of Criminology* 17, no. 1 (1977): 1–15.

9. "Hyunhee's Story," Ever After, 2018, myeverafter.org/hyunhees_story.

10. Sharin N. Elkholy, "Feminism and Race in the United States," *Internet Encyclopedia of Philosophy*, iep.utm.edu/fem-race; Elizabeth R. Cole and Alyssa N. Zucker, "Black and White Women's Perspectives on Femininity," *Cultural Diversity and Ethnic Minority Psychology* 13, no. 1 (2007): 1, doi.org/10.1037/1099-9809.13.1.1; Mari Mikkola, "Feminist Perspectives on Sex and Gender," *Stanford Encyclopedia of Philosophy* (2008; revised 2017), plato.stanford.edu/entries/feminism-gender.

11. Judith Bonderman, "Working with Victims of Gun Violence," 2–3; Govindshenoy and Spencer, "Abuse of The Disabled Child," 556–7;

Hibbard, Desch, et al., "Maltreatment of Children with Disabilities," 1018; Kesner, Bingham, and Kwon, "Child Maltreatment in United States," 433–44; Baba and Murray, "Racial/Ethnic Differences Among Battered"; Wolf, Ly, Hobart, and Kernic, "Barriers to Seeking Police Help," 121–9; Zweig, Schlichter, and Burt, "Assisting Women Victims of Violence," 162–80; and Langton, "Use of Victim Service Agencies," 5; and Lynn Langton, "Use of Victim Service Agencies by Victims of Serious Violent Crime, 1993–2009," U.S. Department of Justice, Bureau of Justice Statistics, 2011, 5, bjs.gov/content/pub/pdf/uvsavsvc9309.pdf.

12. Violence Policy Center, "When Men Murder Women: An Analysis of 2015 Homicide Data," Violence Policy Center, September 2017, 4–7, vpc.org /studies/wmmw2017.pdf; Emiko Petrosky, Janet M. Blair, Carter J. Betz, et al., "Racial and Ethnic Differences in Homicides of Adult Women and the Role of Intimate Partner Violence—United States, 2003–2014," *Morbidity and Mortality Weekly Report* 66, no. 28 (July 21, 2017): 742, cdc.gov/mmwr /volumes/66/wr/mm6628a1.htm; the *Washington Post* Police Shootings Database, 2017, washingtonpost.com/graphics/national/police-shootings-2017.

13. Emily Waters, Larissa Pham, Chelsea Convery, and Sue Yack-Bible, "A Crisis of Hate: A Report on Lesbian, Gay, Bisexual, Transgender and Queer Hate Violence Homicides in 2017," National Coalition of Anti-Violence Programs, 2018, 7–8, avp.org/wp-content/uploads /2018/01/a-crisis-of-hate-january-release.pdf; "A Time to Act: Fatal Violence Against Transgender People in America 2017," Human Rights Campaign and Trans People of Color Coalition, November 2017, updated January 2018, 4, assets2.hrc.org/files/assets/resources/A_Time_To_Act _2017_REV3.pdf.

14. "Domestic Violence: Communities of Color," Women of Color Network, June 2006, 2–6, doj.state.or.us/wp-content/uploads/2017/08 /women_of_color_network_facts_domestic_violence_2006.pdf; Matthew J. Breiding, Sharon G. Smith, Kathleen C. Basile, et al., "Prevalence and Characteristics of Sexual Violence, Stalking, and Intimate Partner Violence Victimization—National Intimate Partner and Sexual Violence Survey, United States, 2011," *Morbidity and Mortality Weekly Report: Surveillance Summaries* 63, no. 8 (September 5, 2014), cdc.gov/mmwr/preview /mmwrhtml/ss6308a1.htm.

15. Patricia Tjaden and Nancy Thoennes, "Extent, Nature, and Consequences of Intimate Partner Violence: Findings from the National Violence Against Women Survey," U.S. Department of Justice, National Institute of Justice, 2000, 25–7, ncjrs.gov/pdffiles1/nij/181867.pdf; Feminist Majority Foundation's Choices Campus Campaign, "Women of Color and Reproductive Justice: African American Women," feministcampus.org/fmla /printable-+materials/WomenofColor/AfricanAmericanWomen.pdf.

16. "Statistics on Violence Against API Women," Asian Pacific Institute on Gender-Based Violence, api-gbv.org/about-gbv/statistics-violence -against-api-women; Tjaden and Thoennes, "Extent, Nature, and Consequences of Intimate Partner Violence," 25–7. According to the National Violence Against Women Survey, 23.4 percent of Hispanic/Latina females are victimized by intimate partner violence in a lifetime, defined by rape, physical assault, or stalking; and Caroline Wolf Harlow, "Prior Abuse Reported by Inmates and Probationers," U.S. Department of Justice, Bureau of Justice Statistics, April 1999, 1–2, bjs.gov/content/pub/pdf/parip.pdf.

17. "Violence Against Trans and Non-Binary People," National Resource on Domestic Violence, VAWNet, 2018, vawnet.org/sc/ser ving-trans-and-non-binary-survivors-domestic-and-sexual-violence /violence-against-trans-and; "HIV/AIDS: Transgender People," World Health Organization, 2018, who.int/hiv/topics/transgender/about/en; Sari L. Reisner, Tonia Poteat, JoAnne Keatley, et al., "Global Health Burden and Needs of Transgender Populations: A Review," *The Lancet* 388, no. 10042 (July 23, 2016): 427–8, doi.org/10.1016/S0140-6736(16)00684-X ; Taylor N.T. Brown and Jody L. Herman, "Intimate Partner Violence and Sexual Abuse Among LBGT People: A Review of Existing Research," UCLA School of Law, Williams Institute, November 2015, 2–4, williamsinstitute.law.ucla.edu/wp-content/uploads/Intimate-Partner -Violence-and-Sexual-Abuse-among-LGBT-People.pdf.

18. Timothy C. Hart and Callie Rennison, "Reporting Crime to the Police, 1992–2000," Department of Justice, Bureau of Justice Statistics, March 2003; the numbers are from Bureau of Justice Statistics, "Rates of Rape/Sexual Assaults by Race and Sex, 2012–2016," generated using the NCVS Victimization Analysis Tool at bjs.gov.

19. Michael L. Benson and Greer Litton Fox, "When Violence Hits Home: How Economics and Neighborhood Play a Role," *NIJ Research in Brief*, U.S. Department of Justice, National Institute of Justice, September 2004, ii; "Fact Sheet: Barriers to Safety for Women of Color," YWCA San Diego; Shebe McCants, "Breaking Down Barriers for Domestic Violence Victims of Color, *Madison Times*, February 27, 2015; "Understanding the Survivor: Communities of Color," in *Striving for Justice: A Toolkit for Judicial Resolution Officers on College Campuses*, University of Michigan Sexual Assault Prevention and Awareness Center, sapac.umich.edu/article/216.

20. Shondrah Tarrezz Nash, "Through Black Eyes: African American Women's Construction of Their Experiences with Intimate Male Partner Violence," *Violence Against Women* 11 (2005): 1427, ncbi.nlm.nih.gov /pubmed/16204732.

21. Carl C. Bell and Jacqueline Mattis, "The Importance of Cultural Competence in Ministering to African American Victims of Domestic

Violence," *Journal of Counseling and Development* 66 (2000): 266–71, doi.org /10.1177/10778010022182001; Patricia A. Washington, "Disclosure Patterns of Black Female Sexual Assault Survivors," *Violence Against Women* 7 (2001): 1254–83, doi.org/10.1177/10778010122183856. Cited in "Domestic Violence: Communities of Color," 2.

22. These include, but are no means limited to Audre Lorde, Ida B. Wells, Cherrie Moraga, Gloria Anzaldúa, Ella Baker, Alicia Garza, Patrice Cullors, Opal Tometi, Beth Ritchie, Angela Davis, Rosa Parks, Toni Cade Bambara, June Jordan, Toni Morrison, Anna Julia Cooper, Barbara Smith, Alice Walker, Grace Lee Boggs, Octavia Butler, bell hooks, Sonia Sanchez, Lala Zannelle, Lourdes Ashley Hunter, and Kimberlé Williams Crenshaw.

23. Zenobia Jeffries, "Why Police Violence Against Women of Color Stays Hidden," *Yes!*, August 10, 2017, yesmagazine.org/peace-justice/why -police-violence-against-women-of-color-stays-hidden-20170810.

24. African American Policy Forum, "#SayHerName: Resisting Police Brutality Against Black Women," press release, July 16, 2015, aapf.org/sayher -namereport.

25. "Dangerous Intersections," INCITE! Women of Color Against Violence, incite-national.org/page/dangerous-intersections.

26. Fatimah Muhammad, personal correspondence, June 1, 2018.

27. Linda G. Tucker, *Lockstep and Dance: Images of Black Men in Popular Culture* (Jackson, MS: University Press of Mississippi, 2007); Robert M. Entman and Andrew Rojecki, *The Black Image in the White Mind: Media and Race in America* (Chicago, IL: University of Chicago Press, 2000); Robert M. Entman and Kimberly A. Gross, "Race to Judgement: Stereotyping Media and Criminal Defendants," *Law and Contemporary Problems* 71 (2008), 98, citing Travis L. Dixon and Daniel Linz, Race and the Misrepresentation of Victimization on Local Television News, *Communication Research* 27, no. 5 (2000), scholarship.law.duke.edu/cgi/viewcontent. cgi?article=1495&context=lcp; M. Rich et al., "Aggressors or Victims: Gender and Race in Music Video Violence," *Pediatrics* 101 (1998), lionlamb .org/research_articles/Aggressors%20or%20Victims.pdf; and Robert M. Entman, "Young Men of Color in the Media: Images and Impacts," Joint Center for Political and Economic Studies, 2006, 2025bmb.org/pdf/justice /menofcolor_media.pdf.

28. The Opportunity Agenda, "Social Science Literature Review: Media Representations and Impact on the Lives of Black Men and Boys," The Opportunity Agenda, 2011, racialequitytools.org/resource-files/Media-Impact-onLives-of-Black-Men-and-Boys-OppAgenda.pdf.

29. Entman, "Young Men of Color in the Media: Images and Impacts," 13.

30. Entman and Rojecki, *The Black Image in the White Mind*, 81.

31. The Opportunity Agenda, "Social Science Literature Review: Media Representations and Impact on the Lives of Black Men and Boys," The Opportunity Agenda, 2011, 13, racialequitytools.org/resourcefiles/Media -Impact-onLives-of-Black-Men-and-Boys-OppAgenda.pdf.

32. Robert M. Entman and Kimberly A. Gross, "Race to Judgment: Stereotyping Media and Criminal Defendants," *Law and Contemporary Problems* 71, no. 4 (Autumn 2008): 98, citing Travis L. Dixon and Daniel Linz, "Overrepresentation and Underrepresentation of African Americans and Latinos as Lawbreakers on Television News," *Journal of Communication* 50, no. 2 (June 2000): 131–54.

33. "Table 10: Number of Victimizations and Victimization Rates for Persons Age 12 and Over, by Race, Gender, and Age of Victims and Type of Crime, 1996–2007," in "National Crime Victimization Survey," U.S. Department of Justice, Bureau of Justice Statistics, 1996–2007, bjs.gov /content/pub/sheets/cvsprshts.cfm. When these numbers are broken down by crime type, other groups are significantly more likely to be victims for certain types of crime, such as domestic violence.

34. Karen F. Parker, *Unequal Crime Decline: Theorizing Race, Urban Inequality, and Criminal Violence* (New York: New York University Press, 2008), 2.

35. "Youth Violence: Facts at a Glance," U.S. Department of Health and Humans Services, Centers for Disease Control, National Center for Injury Prevention and Control, 2016, cdc.gov/violenceprevention/pdf/yv-datasheet.pdf.

36. Mark S. Eberhardt and Elsie R. Pamuk, "The Importance of Place of Residence: Examining Health in Rural and Nonrural Areas," *American Journal of Public Health* 94, no. 10 (2004): 1682–6.

37. "Crime and Enforcement Activity in New York City (Jan 1–Dec 31, 2017)," New York City Police Department, 11, www1.nyc.gov/assets/nypd /downloads/pdf/analysis_and_planning/year-end-2017-enforcement -report.pdf.

38. "OVC FY 2011 National Field-Generated Training, Technical Assistance, and Demonstration Projects Request for Proposals," Office for Victims of Crime, 2013, 13: "The data on victimization of young male victims of color, including African Americans and Latinos, is especially troubling and is rarely an area of focus of many traditional victim service providers. There are few nonprofit victim-serving organizations that have the resources and expertise to provide comprehensive, accessible services to male victims of any race or ethnicity who are physically or sexually assaulted or otherwise victimized, nor are many of these victims likely to access victim services available through law enforcement or prosecutorial agencies."

39. Nikita Stewart and Luis Ferre-Sadurni, "Parents Mourn Their Son, a Quirky Crown Heights Fixture Shot by Police," *New York Times*, April 10, 2018, A23; Nick Wing, "When the Media Treats White Suspects and Killers Better Than Black Victims," *Huffington Post*, August 14, 2014; Adam H. Johnson, "How the Media Smears Black Victims," *Los Angeles Times*, March 30, 2017.

40. Johnson, "How the Media Smears Black Victims."

41. "Social Science Literature Review: Media Representations and Impact," 14.

42. Jenna Gant, "New Felony Sentencing Guidelines Take Effect," *Court News Ohio*, April 1, 2013, courtnewsohio.gov/happening/2013/sentencingGuidelines_040113.asp.

43. Leah Sakala, "Breaking Down Mass Incarceration in the 2020 Census: State-by-State Incarceration Rates by Race/Ethnicity," Prison Policy Initiative, May 28, 2014, prisonpolicy.org/reports/rates.html.

44. John Caniglia, "White Women Sent to Ohio Prisons in Record Numbers, Reports Say," *Plain Dealer*, August 15, 2013.

45. Jacob Kany-Brown and Ram Subramanian, "Out of Sight: The Growth of Jails in Rural America," Vera Institute of Justice, June 2017, 12, storage.googleapis.com/vera-web-assets/downloads/Publications/out-of-sight-growth-of-jails-rural-america/legacy_downloads/out-of-sight-growth-of-jails-rural-america.pdf.

46. Erika Harrell, Lynn Langton, Marcus Berzofsky, et al., "Household Poverty and Nonfatal Violent Victimization, 2008–2012," U.S. Department of Justice, Bureau of Justice Statistics, November 2014, 2–5; Claire M. Renzetti, "Economic Stress and Domestic Violence," National Resource Center on Domestic Violence, Vawnet, September 2009, 2–4, vawnet.org/sites/default/files/materials/files/2016-09/AR_EconomicStress.pdf; Lois Weis, Michelle Fine, Amira Proweller, Corrine Bertram, and Julia Marusza, "'I've Slept in Clothes Long Enough': Excavating the Sounds of Domestic Violence Among Women in the White Working Class," *Urban Review* 30, no. 1 (March 1998): 1–27; Chase Sackett, "Neighborhoods and Violent Crime," in *Evidence Matters: Transforming Knowledge into Housing and Community Development Policy*, U.S. Department of Housing and Urban Development, Office of Policy Development and Research, Summer 2016, 16–24, huduser.gov/portal/sites/default/files/pdf/EM-Newsletter-summer-2016.pdf; Melissa S. Kearney and Benjamin H. Harris, "The Unequal Burden of Crime and Incarceration on America's Poor," The Brookings Institution, Hamilton Project, April 28, 2014, 2, brookings.edu/wp-content/uploads/2016/06/Crime-blog-post_april28FINAL-v3.pdf.

47. U.S. Department of Education, "State and Local Expenditures on Corrections and Education," 2–3; Henrichson and Delaney, "The Price of Prisons," 7.

48. Nancy Isenberg, *White Trash: The 400-Year Untold History of Class in America* (New York: Viking, 2016), xiv–xv.

49. "The National Memorial for Peace and Justice," Equal Justice Initiative, 2017, eji.org/national-lynching-memorial.

50. "The National Memorial."

51. "Marylander of the Year: Erricka Bridgeford," *Baltimore Sun*, December 28, 2017.

52. Frantz Fanon, *The Wretched of the Earth* (New York: Grove Press, 2007), 181–3; Frantz Fanon, *Black Skin, White Masks* (New York: Grove Press, rev. ed. 2008), xiv–xv.

53. Anna Ortega-Williams, "Is Organizing a Pathway for Wellbeing and Post-Traumatic Growth for Black Youth in New York City? Exploring Recovery from Historical Trauma and Systemic Violence" (PhD diss., Fordham University, 2017), 27–32, fordham.bepress.com/dissertations/AAI10279034.

54. Downstate Coalition for Crime Victims, "A New Vision for Crime Victims," *Huffington Post*, November 4, 2016.

55. These are from Andre Ward, Norris Henderson, Khalil Muhammad, Bruce Western, Michael Rowe, Richard Smith, and Donna Hylton.

7: Our Reckoning

1. Ta-Nehisi Coates, "The Case for Reparations, *The Atlantic*, June 2014.

2. Coates, "The Case for Reparations."

3. Fania Davis, "This Country Needs a Truth and Reconciliation Process on Violence Against African Americans—Right Now," *YES!*, July 8, 2016, yesmagazine.org/peace-justice/this-country-needs-a-truth-and-reconciliation-process-on-violence-against-african-americans.

4. Accounting for Violence forum, April 11, 2017, vera.org/events/accounting-for-violence.

5. Personal correspondence, July 2, 2018.

6. "Greensboro Truth and Reconciliation Commission Report: Executive Summary," The Commission, 2006, 2–3, greensborotrc.org/exec_summary.pdf.

7. Maine Wabanaki-State Child Welfare Truth & Reconciliation Commission, www.mainewabanakitrc.org.

8. "The Black Women's Truth and Reconciliation Commission on Sexual Assault: Archival Information," Black Women's Blueprint, 2016, blackwomensblueprint.org/truth-commission.

9. "Boston Busing/Desegregation Project for Truth, Learning, and Change," Union of Minority Neighborhoods, 2011, unionofminority neighborhoods.org/programs-and-initiatives/boston-busingdesegregation -project.

10. Chicago Torture Justice Memorials Project, chicagotorture.org.

11. Davis, "This Country Needs a Truth and Reconciliation Process."

Index of Names

About the Author

Danielle Sered envisioned, launched, and directs Common Justice, based in Brooklyn, New York. Common Justice develops and advances solutions to violence that transform the lives of those harmed and foster racial equity without relying on incarceration. Locally, it operates the first alternative-to-incarceration and victim service program in the United States to focus on violent felonies in the adult courts. Nationally, it leverages the lessons from its direct service to transform the justice system through partnerships, advocacy, and elevating the experience and power of those most impacted. Under her leadership, in 2012 Common Justice received the Award for Innovation in Victim Services from Attorney General Eric Holder and the federal Office for Victims of Crime. She lives in Brooklyn and this is her first book.

Publishing in the Public Interest

Thank you for reading this book published by The New Press. The New Press is a nonprofit, public interest publisher. New Press books and authors play a crucial role in sparking conversations about the key political and social issues of our day.

We hope you enjoyed this book and that you will stay in touch with The New Press. Here are a few ways to stay up to date with our books, events, and the issues we cover:

- Sign up at www.thenewpress.com/subscribe to receive updates on New Press authors and issues and to be notified about local events
- Like us on Facebook: www.facebook.com/newpressbooks
- Follow us on Twitter: www.twitter.com/thenewpress

Please consider buying New Press books for yourself; for friends and family; or to donate to schools, libraries, community centers, prison libraries, and other organizations involved with the issues our authors write about.

The New Press is a 501(c)(3) nonprofit organization. You can also support our work with a tax-deductible gift by visiting www.thenewpress.com/donate.